Nonfederal Housing Programs

How States and Localities Are Responding to Federal Cutbacks in Low-Income Housing

•A15043 342937

by
Michael A. Stegman
and
J. David Holden

Department of City and Regional Planning,
University of North Carolina at Chapel Hill

Revised
June 12, 1987

Prepared under a grant from
ULI–the Urban Land Institute, Washington, D.C.

About ULI–the Urban Land Institute

ULI–the Urban Land Institute is an independent, nonprofit research and educational organization incorporated in 1936 to improve the quality and standards of land use and development.

The Institute is committed to conducting practical research in the various fields of real estate knowledge; identifying and interpreting land use trends in relation to the changing economic, social, and civic needs of the people; and disseminating pertinent information leading to the orderly and more efficient use and development of land.

ULI receives its financial support from membership dues, sales of publications, and contributions for research and panel services.

David E. Stahl

Recommended bibliographic listing:
Michael A. Stegman and J. David Holden. *Nonfederal Housing Programs: How States and Localities Are Responding to Federal Cutbacks in Low-Income Programs.* Washington, D.C.: ULI–the Urban Land Institute, 1987.
ULI Catalog Number: N09

© 1987 by ULI–the Urban Land Institute
1090 Vermont Avenue, N.W.
Washington, D.C. 20005

International Standard Book Number: 0-87420-673-1
Library of Congress Card Catalog Number: 87-51080

Printed in the United States of America

ULI Project Staff

Staff Vice President, Research and Education
J. Thomas Black

Director, Housing and Community Development Research
Diane R. Suchman

Publication and Production Managers
Frank H. Spink, Jr.
Robert L. Helms

Managing Editor
Julie D. Stern

Copy Editor
Ann Lenney

Art Director
M. Elizabeth Van Buskirk

Artists
Helene Y. Redmond
Kim Rusch

Reviewer

Margaret Sowell
Manager
Laventhol & Horwath
Philadelphia, PA

Low-Income Housing Task Force

Nina J. Gruen, Co-chair
Executive Vice President
Gruen Gruen + Associates
San Francisco, CA

M. Leanne Lachman, Co-chair
Managing Director
Schroder Real Estate Associates
New York, NY

James M. DeFrancia
President
Weston Capital Corporation
Sterling, VA

Anthony Downs
Senior Fellow
The Brookings Institution
Washington, DC

David Goss
Executive Director
CLINITEC, Inc.
Cleveland, OH

James D. Klingbeil
Chairman
The Klingbeil Group
Columbus, OH

Jon Q. Reynolds
Partner
Reynolds & Brown
Concord, CA

Donald R. Riehl
President
D. R. Riehl, Inc.
Pacific Grove, CA

Willard G. Rouse, III
Partner
Rouse & Associates
Malvern, PA

Gary M. Ryan
President
Grupe Development Company–
Colorado
Englewood, CO

George Sternlieb
Director, Center for Urban
Policy Research
Rutgers University
New Brunswick, NJ

Contents

Foreword

In 1986, ULI's National Policy Council, led by Leanne Lachman, proposed that ULI give attention to what the council felt was an emerging social crisis in the housing situation for low- and moderate-income families and individuals in the United States. Leanne's plea for support from the ULI Board of Trustees was enthusiastically given, and a task force consisting of representatives from several ULI Councils, including the National Policy Council and the ULI Research Committee, was formed to explore the problem and to develop a program that could best bring ULI's resources and talents to bear on the problem. As first steps in planning the program, the task force, through ULI's research program, commissioned two efforts. The first was a big-picture review of current conditions and trends in the housing situation of low-income households, underlying causes of the problem, general remedies, and specific actions that ULI might take to help alleviate the problem. Anthony Downs, a senior associate at the Brookings Institution and a ULI Fellow and Trustee, undertook this effort and made his report to the task force and trustees in October 1986. Tony concluded that the incidence of housing problems among low- and moderate-income households, in terms of both affordability and physical adequacy, remains widespread and has increased substantially since 1975. He concluded that the most effective strategies for addressing the problems involved the use of federal programs operating on a national basis and deploying a combination of supply-side and demand-side subsidies depending on local conditions. However, given the current national policy climate, Tony suggested that ULI was not likely to influence the federal government at this time and that, therefore, ULI should focus its attention on actions that could be taken at the state and local levels.

Anticipating the need to know what programs state and local governments have been operating or are currently setting up to address low- and moderate-income housing needs, ULI provided a grant to Michael Stegman at the University of North Carolina to survey what state and local governments were doing and to provide a report to ULI on the results of this survey. This document is the published version of that report. Stegman and J. David Holden have successfully compiled an impressive file of information on the various types of programs currently being operated. For the benefit of the reader, they present summaries of various types of programs, as well as liberal doses of information about specific cases. This information should be very useful to those struggling to help improve the housing situations of most low- and moderate-income households. The information is being used by ULI as a footing for additional ULI research and technical assistance efforts related to low-income housing, which, at this writing, are still being formulated.

J. Thomas Black
Staff Vice President,
Research and Education

Introduction and Executive Summary

This monograph is part of ULI–the Urban Land Institute's efforts to explore alternative means of meeting the housing needs of low- and moderate-income Americans in the face of steep reductions in federal housing assistance. It presents the results of a national survey of state and local housing initiatives that are either planned or underway, and describes the nonfederal revenue sources being used to support them.

Chapter Highlights

This book contains eight chapters that, taken together, assess state and local experiences to date and comment on their collective potential to meet urgent low-income housing needs in the absence of a substantial federal presence. Whereas the analysis contained in the body of the monograph is filtered through the eyes of the authors, this is not the case with the material presented in the appendices. There, we present more than 60 program abstracts that were prepared from the hundreds of telephone interviews, mail surveys, and program reviews that were carried out over the course of the project. In addition to program information, each abstract contains the name(s) of the program official(s) from whom the information was obtained, plus the agency's mailing address and/or telephone number, so that the reader can follow up program ideas that have potential for local applications.

Following this introduction and summary of our major findings, Chapter 1 reviews recent changes in national housing conditions and the availability of federal housing funds. In Chapter 2, we discuss the array of new revenue sources that states and localities are tapping to support their indigenous low-income housing activities, while in Chapter 3, we describe planning activities that are now underway in what we refer to as second-tier communities—places that have not yet mounted substantial housing programs of their own but will do so in the next year or so.

Chapter 4 examines a variety of creative leveraging techniques used by housing finance agencies to extend the benefits of their below-market financing to lower-income families; the basic approach used is that of piggybacking state and local subsidies on top of their own tax-exempt bond programs. Given the Tax Reform Act's stricter low-income targeting requirements for use of tax-exempt housing bonds, these programs are likely to become prototypes of the future. Chapter 5 describes state and local "wanna bees," or clones of federal housing assistance programs. These clones involve regulations and eligibility criteria that generally mirror those of their rapidly disappearing federal counterparts.

Chapter 6 assesses the rationale and record, to date, of local inclusionary housing programs. Such programs impose requirements or provide incentives to developers to sell specified fractions of their residential projects at "affordable" prices. Linkage programs, which impose either fees or low- and moderate-income housing production requirements on nonresidential developers to help meet communitywide housing needs, are also examined in this chapter.

Chapter 7 assesses the low-income housing implications of the Tax Reform Act of 1986, while the final chapter describes the rise of public/private partnerships as important vehicles for financing and administering low-income housing developments. To the extent that they can successfully exploit the new tax law, these partnerships will play a prominent role in the future of low-income housing.

Major Findings

During the course of this project, the authors spoke with many state and local housing officials and reviewed more than 100 reports, program regulations, and other materials describing the full range of nonfederal housing programs that are either planned or underway. We have met with difficulties in distilling from those masses of information a set of internally consistent and comprehensive findings. These findings needed, at one and the same time, to do justice to the rich variety of activities we found to exist, and also to give some direction for the channeling of our future energies, so that they can maximize the impacts of limited local housing funds.

Below, we summarize 12 key findings from our survey. (The reader should be aware that the bases for our conclusions, as well as much useful information on creative state and local low-income housing initiatives, are presented in the eight chapters that follow this introduction.) The key findings are as follows:

1) To a greater extent than ever before, housing needs are being recognized as a legitimate area of state and local concern. Thus, the legitimacy of housing's claim to a growing share of locally generated revenues is now more widely accepted than it ever has been.

2) In addition to appropriating more general revenues for housing, states and localities are now searching aggressively for new revenue sources for housing and are succeeding in that search. The array of new revenue sources is extensive and includes new real estate–related taxes, fees on new development, the use of excess housing-finance-agency and other bond reserves, and community loan funds.

3) Many localities (and a few states) that have not previously financed low-income housing are now preparing to proceed. In the course of our survey, we came across reports issued by legislative study commissions, affordable-housing task forces, and other official and quasi-official groups whose job is to educate decision makers and citizens about local housing problems, and to lay the groundwork for appropriate responses. The sheer quantity of these reports shows that both the aggregate volume and the geographic representation of nonfederal housing activities will substantially increase in the years ahead. Moreover, it shows that the diversity of the local programs' approaches will also increase, as jurisdictions with no prior history of locally funded low-income housing begin to implement housing strategies that are tailored to their own political, social, and fiscal situations.

4) While not all states and localities have responded to federal housing cutbacks with locally designed and funded programs

of their own, a surprisingly large number of them have done so.

The scale of these responses is in rough proportion to the local perception of the "crisis" nature of the problem; to the extent to which the federal withdrawal is seen to be permanent; and to the localities' earlier experiences as subsidizers and producers of low-income housing. The most active units of government are thus becoming exporters of new program ideas.

5) As a direct result of tax reform, a smaller amount of tax-exempt capital will be available for financing low-income housing: the new low-income housing tax credit will be less effective than the host of tax preferences it replaces, so that large state and local subsidies will prove necessary to make its use worthwhile.

To the extent that tax reform does stimulate low-income housing activity, rehabilitation will be favored over new construction, and nonprofit and community-based housing organizations will play a more important role in production than at any time since the late 1960s.

6) Stand-alone linkage programs that exact high square-foot payments from downtown developers to support local low-income housing programs are not likely to proliferate. But we will be seeing more comprehensive, fee-based affordable housing programs being adopted locally.

7) Despite great reluctance to do so, some states and localities are finding the problem of excessive housing costs for low-income renters so serious that they must now fund their own housing voucher (rent certificate) programs. These municipalities' reluctance to take over this function is based on the continuing high subsidy costs, on the fact that vouchers do little to increase the permanent supply of affordable housing, and on administrative considerations.

8) An important new kind of housing delivery system has emerged that consists of formally structured partnerships among the corporate, financial, public, and community sectors. In these partnerships, each partner has a specific role to play in planning, financing, building, and operating low-income housing projects.

9) In spite of the above trends, and although the search for new revenues and revenue sources for housing seems to be succeeding in many places, the fact remains that the sum total of all state and local housing activity represents only a small

fraction of the body of federal programs that this activity is trying to replace. The gap might narrow in the future, as more places mount local housing efforts. But without a substantial federal production presence, urgent needs will continue to outstrip available resources by a wide margin.

10) In general, the subsidy term of locally assisted units is shorter than it is under many of the vanishing federal programs. Local programs also have more of a homeownership emphasis than their federal counterparts have had. These two factors are stimulating experimentation in ways to assure the continuing availability of locally subsidized housing to low-income people over the longer term. This experimentation is being reflected in, among other trends, the greater use of limited-equity cooperatives and of community land trusts.

11) Most state- and locally funded housing programs are on too limited a scale to reverse the fortunes of older, deteriorating neighborhoods. For this reason, these programs can complement but can never replace comprehensive neighborhood revitalization programs. An acceleration of neighborhood decline, or just the threat of it, can undermine the viability of an otherwise sound housing project. It may even frighten away equity capital in the first place.

These facts suggest that the greatest challenge to the long-term success of local housing initiatives is the further curtailment of federal community-development and other funds earmarked for the support of neighborhood stabilization activities.

12) Finally, while state and local programs can serve really poor people in limited numbers, readers should understand the difference between cost-effective vehicles for expanding the supply of affordable housing and broader-based efforts to ameliorate and ultimately to solve the intergenerational problems of the permanently poor. By themselves, narrowly structured housing programs will not and cannot have a significant impact on the lives of the underclass that seems to be permanently entrapped in a world apart at the bottom of society. Without a national response to this problem, continued social upheaval will cause housing programs to fail and scarce subsidy dollars to migrate—away from the people and places most in need, toward less distressed areas and toward the "more deserving poor."

The multiple problems of the underclass must become the focus of high-priority national concern. We recognize, however, that whatever the "national response [albeit one of negligence], it will ultimately involve billions of dollars in outlays or losses." (9a)

We now turn to an analysis of national housing conditions and of changing federal housing budgets.

Chapter 1
National Housing Conditions and the Federal Retreat

Long-Term Trends

The Moving Target Problem

The extent to which America's housing problem is seen to be changing for the better or for the worse depends upon how we define the problem, and upon the length of time over which we monitor the changes. One analyst refers to the first issue as the "moving target problem":

> Not only have we constantly changed the criteria for assessing housing inadequacy, but [also we have changed these guidelines] in a direction away from specific intolerable, measurable, and remediable conditions, such as density of occupancy, availability of plumbing facilities, and the like, and toward more subjective, and therefore often insoluble, conditions. The identification of housing problems has been moving steadily toward conditions that defy consistent measurement and that many analysts—or the tenant sufferers themselves—do not find unacceptable, and toward conditions that are more descriptive of the tenants and their behavior than of the housing stock. Obviously, such housing conditions can never be eliminated. (34, p. 6)

The time-frame issue has to do with the fact that, by almost every available measure, the United States has enjoyed a steady improvement in housing quality throughout most of the post–World War II period. Indeed, the incidence of substandard housing declined from 49 percent of the total stock in 1940 to just 6 percent in 1970. (40, p. 69)

Conditions Are Deteriorating

More recently, however, "there are indications that inadequate housing persists and is actually on the rise in parts of the country." We do not think these changes in our housing fortunes are simply another example of the "moving target problem." In our judgment, the changes are real, and a cause for national concern:

- Some 16.4 percent (11.6 million units) of all occupied units in 1974 were structurally inadequate. The number of structurally inadequate units fell slightly from 1974 to 1981. However, this overall decline can be attributed to a decline in structurally inadequate *owner-occupied* units. During the same period, the number of structurally inadequate *renter-occupied* units increased by nearly 200,000. (2, p. 99)
- Between 1974 and 1983, for every 100 inadequate units that were taken off the market, 107 other units slipped into the "inadequate" category because of a lack of maintenance and upkeep. (5, p. 12)
- In 1983, 177,000 more single-parent families and 334,000 more low-income families resided in inadequate housing than in 1974. (5, p. 12)
- Also in 1983, over 330,000 more low-income renters lived in structurally unsound housing than in 1974. (5, p. 1)
- In 1981, 32.2 percent of all black renter households lived in structurally inadequate housing, compared with 17 percent of white renter households. Even among owners, blacks were more than twice as likely as whites to live in inadequate housing and inadequate neighborhoods. (2, p. 123)
- Until 1980, homeownership rates had increased steadily for 35 years. Today, only 63.5 percent of all U.S. households are homeowners, compared with 65.7 percent in 1980. (5, pp. 2, 6)

Furthermore, today, "America's housing problem is one of affordability as well as of inadequacy" (5, p. 1):

- Forty-seven percent of low-income renters must now spend more than half of their incomes for rent, compared with 34 percent in 1974. (5, p. 1)
- In 1983, the median rent burden for households in the lowest income class was 46 percent of their incomes. (5, p. 13)
- The share of households with rent burdens below one-quarter of their incomes dropped from 60 percent in 1974 to 40 percent

in 1983. The share of households with rent burdens above 75 percent of their incomes rose from 8 percent to 13 percent. (5, p. 13)

- In 1985, the after-tax costs of purchasing . . . for the typical homebuyer held at just over 31 percent of his or her household income, compared with an average of about 26 percent in the early part of the 1970s, and of 35 percent in the early part of the 1980s. (5, p. 2)
- In 1978, the typical buyer had to make a downpayment of about one-third of his or her household income. By 1985, the share had risen to 50 percent. (5, p. 2)

The Downward Spiral of Federal Housing Funds

Although the 1970s represented a decade of expansion in federal housing assistance, the 1980s mark a period of severe contraction of the federal role. Thus, for example, subsidized housing constituted 29 percent and 21 percent of all housing starts in 1970 and 1971, respectively, and averaged more than 14 percent of all starts for the decade. (31, p. 7) In contrast, 7 percent of all housing starts were subsidized in 1983, and just 5 percent in 1984; and the percentage continues to decline.

In an absolute sense, since the early 1970s, the number of new assisted housing starts per year has fallen from the 300,000–400,000 mark to that of fewer than 100,000, and when the pipeline has been emptied of earlier funding commitments, the number will inevitably decline even further. This is reflected in the fact that, in inflation-adjusted dollars, the amount of HUD's new spending authority in 1985 was less than one-third as much as it was in 1977. (27, p. 42)

HUD's fiscal-year 1987 budget is no more encouraging. Over the administration's strenuous objections, the Congress has recently approved 14,000 new construction units as part of HUD's total of 65,000 incremental units for FY'87. The remaining assistance is in the form of housing vouchers. To give the reader a sense of how inconsequential the allocation for new units is, we note that if the nation's entire 1987 new-construction budget were to be assigned to the District of Columbia, it would still take two and one-half years (at that annual rate) just to meet the needs of low-income families who are currently on the Washington, D.C., public housing authority's waiting list. (15, p. 8)

In Chapter 2, we will begin to explore local responses to this supply crisis.

Chapter 2
The Search for New Revenues

Earmarked Housing Funds

Although on a smaller scale, the search for new revenues and revenue sources for housing, especially those that can be earmarked and counted on from year to year—as federal housing dollars no longer can be—is as intense in small states and localities as in larger ones. General appropriations are being used to capitalize housing trust funds, to subsidize interest rates, to finance "soft" second-mortgage loans for low-income families, and to provide loans and grants for building and rehabilitating shelters for the homeless (see Table 2.1). This search has also led to:

- *Renewed support in Massachusetts for state-funded low-income public housing.* Under the Massachusetts Housing Act of 1985, $344.4 million in bond revenues is being made available to fund 3,500 units of public housing, as well as to give other housing assistance—including $35 million to help renovate deteriorated federally sponsored public housing projects in localities throughout the state.
- *The pioneering use of taxable housing bonds in Alaska, Louisiana, and Memphis.* This will become a much more common financing technique, now that tax reform is a reality (see Chapter 7).

Table 2.1
Representative State and Local Appropriations for Housing

Place	Year	Amount	Program
Minnesota HFA	1982	$2 million	Interest-rate writedowns for elderly rentals
New York State Housing and Community Renewal	1985	$24.6 million	Housing Trust Fund: Rehabilitations/ conversions, up to $40K per unit
Maryland Department of Community Affairs	1986	$2 million	Low-Income Rental-Housing Production Program: Low interest rates and deferred payments
	1986	$1 million	Rental Allowance Pilot Program: Rent subsidy for Marylanders not eligible for federal program
	1986	$2 million	Nonprofit Housing Rehabilitation Program: Low interest rates and deferred payments to nonprofits, for rehabilitation of housing serving low-income special populations
	1986	$1 million	Care Homes Program: Domiciliary care for disabled adults in private homes
Colorado Division of Housing	1985	$1.45 million	Housing Development Grant Program: Matching financial assistance
	1985	$450,000	Revolving Loan Program: Short-term loans for development costs
California Department of Housing	1980	$7.5 million	Homeownership Assistance Program: Mortgage participation loans
	1986	$2.2 million	Self-help housing
	1986	$2.5 million	Mobile-Home Park Assistance Program

Place	Year	Amount	Program
California Department of Housing (Cont'd.)	1986	$2.5 million	Special-User Rehabilitation Program: Assistance for the elderly, handicapped, and very low-income
	1980	$4–5 million per year	Predevelopment Loan Program
Delaware Department of Community Affairs	1968 1971 1986 1987	$3 million $5 million $2.5 million $3 million	Housing Development Fund: Seed and construction loans to nonprofit and limited-profit housing providers. As of 1986, there were no restrictions on the use of the fund, other than to encourage development of housing for low- and moderate-income families.
Pennsylvania Department of Community Affairs	1986	$3.5 million	Single-Room Occupancy Program
	1986	$10 million	Bridge Housing: Short-term and intensive-care
Pennsylvania Housing Finance Agency	1984 1985 1986	$25.7 million (in each year)	Homeowners' Emergency Mortgage Assistance Program: Assistance to families facing foreclosure for up to 36 months, with assistance to be repaid at 9 percent when beneficiary is able
Washington, D.C.	1985	$5 million	Tenant Assistance Program
New Jersey HEW	1985	$15 million	Affordable Housing Program: Local governments' housing-program assistance

Place	Year	Amount	Program
New Jersey Department of Community Affairs	1985	$2 million	Neighborhood Community Preservation Balanced Housing Program: Loans and grants to municipalities, plus $8 million from transfer-tax proceeds
Raleigh, North Carolina	1986	$1 million	Deferred-payment second-mortgage loans to moderate-income homebuyers ($250,000); developer incentives ($350,000); elderly home repairs ($90,000); and low-income construction ($300,000)

- *The use of general obligation bonds to build low-income housing.* In November 1982, for example, Seattle sold a $48.1-million bond issue at 9.68 percent. The issue was approved by 76 percent of the voters and was earmarked to finance housing construction. Its provisions transferred its proceeds to the Seattle Housing Authority for the purpose of developing the units. Even though the bond's proceeds cover capital costs, rental income must cover the full operating costs, with no subsidy for vacant units.

    (Under the new tax reform act, general obligation bonds can no longer be used to finance housing, as reported in Chapter 7.)
- *The imposition of new taxes and the increasing of old taxation rates.* These moves have included:
  –A 2 percent tax on gross casino revenues in Atlantic City.
  –A 4 percent tax on the initial sale of rental buildings that are being sold for condominium conversions in Montgomery County, Maryland.

    This law also provides the county with the right of first refusal on the sale of rental projects for conversion. It has recently exercised this right in order to buy two small buildings, containing a total of 83 apartments, to prevent displacement. The acquisition, which was financed with revenues from the conversion tax, is expected to generate between a 5 and an 8 percent cash return on the county's investment.

–Taxes related to the transfer and recording of real estate (see Table 2.2). These have included 1) a $3.00 document surcharge on all deed recordings in Delaware, with 95 percent of the revenues earmarked for housing; 2) an increase in Maine's title transfer tax of $2.20 per $1,000, with half the additional revenues going to the state's general fund, and half earmarked to subsidize interest rates on housing bonds; and

Table 2.2
Selected Real Estate Transfer Taxes

Place	Type	Amount on $100,000 Sale*	Earmarked for Housing?	Year Enacted
Howard County, MD	1% of the sale price of all property transferred in county; $2.20/$500 documentation stamp/ deed recordation fee	$1,440	Yes	1970
Dade County, FL	$0.45 per $100 value on deed transfers of *commercial property* only, payable by both buyer and seller	$900	Yes	1983
Maine	Title transfer-tax assessment in the range of $2.20 per $1,000 of evaluation; buyer and seller each pay $2.20	$450+	Yes	1985
Delaware	2% of purchase price; $3 documentary surcharge	$2,000	Yes	1986
Connecticut	0.45% of purchase price	$450	No; general fund	1983
Georgia	$1.00/$1,000 (or 0.10%); and $1.50/$500 mortgage tax	$400	Yes; in-state real estate trust fund, for one year	N.A.
Nantucket and Martha's Vineyard, MA	2% residential	$2,228	No; purchase of recreational and conservation land	1985
New York State	$2.00/$500 transfer tax; mortgage tax of $0.50/$100 of first $10,000 and $0.75/$100 of everything over	$1,125	No; state general fund	1985
New York City	1.5%	$3,025	No; city general funds	N.A.
Washington State	1.07% transfer tax; $2.00/$1,000 documentation stamp/deed recordation fee	$1,270	No (Efforts to *increase* taxes/fees for low-income housing were defeated.)	N.A.

* Includes transfer tax, documentation stamp/deed recordation fee, and mortgage fee.

3) a $0.45/$100 real estate transfer surtax on commercial property sales in Dade and two other Florida counties. The last of these tax levies had half of its revenues earmarked for homeownership and for rental production subsidies.

We should note that real estate transfer taxes are not always earmarked for housing, and that efforts to impose them are not always successful (see Table 2.3). Opposition to real estate–related taxes by the real estate brokerage industry has resulted in the defeat of various recently proposed measures in Ohio, Oregon, Washington State, and Memphis.

–The creation of housing trust funds that are capitalized by dedicated revenues from 1) off-shore oil leases (California);

Table 2.3
Defeats of Transfer Taxes

Place	Proposal	Action Taken	Year
Ohio	To increase transfer tax to 0.25%, only on residential transfers. Ohio has existing transfer tax ($0.10/$100, or 0.10%, up to $100 total cost on a $100,000 sale). Transfer tax was to be increased to assist laid-off steelworkers facing foreclosure.	Introduced in House and Senate, but died when legislature adjourned	1985
Oregon	To introduce transfer tax to establish housing trust fund for low-income families. Rates proposed were in range of $0.15/$100 to $0.50/$100.	Defeated in legislature	1984
Washington State	To increase existing statewide transfer tax from 1.07% to 1.12%, to fund statewide housing trust fund for low-income housing.	Defeated in legislature	1986
Shelby County, TN	To allow counties to impose transfer tax of 0.51% for low-income housing fund. Tennessee transfer tax remains at 0.28%, or $280 on a $100,000 sale.	Brought before Shelby County Board of Commissioners, then dropped before state legislative session	1985

2) in-lieu fees from inclusionary housing programs (San Diego); 3) real estate transfer taxes (Maine, Florida); 4) a housing finance agency's excess reserve funds (Kentucky, Maine); and 5) state and city appropriations (New York).

At least one of such trust funds, in Washington State, still has no revenues or dedicated revenue sources at all (see Table 2.4).

–The enactment of impact fees on new market-rate housing in Cherry Hill, New Jersey. The rate equals 1.5 percent of the median price of new construction in the region, and the proceeds are escrowed for the "sole purpose of aiding in the provision or rehabilitation of modest-income housing."

–The creation of community loan funds for housing in New Hampshire. These funds are capitalized by corporations, individuals, banks, and church groups that are willing to accept a lower rate of return on their investments, in order to assist housing and community development activities.

–The beginning of a state-supported secondary market for UDAG and other community development loans.

The Rhode Island Housing and Mortgage Finance Corporation has purchased a $5.8-million UDAG loan from the city of Providence that bears an effective interest rate of about 6.6 percent. The corporation's purchase provides the city with cash to support additional development. As for the corpora-

Table 2.4
Revenue Sources for Housing Trust Funds

Place	Year	Source
Washington State	1986	"Empty Bucket Law," establishing a trust fund; funding source not yet determined
California	1985	Revenue from tideland oil leases
Maine	1985	Title transfer tax
New York State	1985	$24.6 million from appropriations
North Carolina (legislation pending)	1987	Stripper well litigation (oil overcharge) funds
Florida	1986	$2.7 million from appropriations
San Diego, CA	1984	In-lieu fees for replacement units
Kentucky	1986	$5 million from excess debt-service reserves of Kentucky Housing Corporation
Massachusetts	1985	Excise tax on the withdrawal of reserve funds by savings and loans, converting to federal insurance

tion itself, it is recommitting all future principal and interest payments it receives on the UDAG note to new low-income housing activities in Providence. The revenue stream from this one loan is about $500,000 per year, and it will last for 28 years.

New York City's Bold Initiative

Perhaps the most aggressive local housing response to federal cutbacks has been in New York City, where some 4 percent of the city's current expense budget dollars are now devoted to housing. Although this figure might not seem to be in keeping with the critical nature of the problem in a city whose public housing waiting list exceeds 200,000 families, we found no other city that has committed more of its own local resources to housing than New York has. Included in the city's FY'86 expense budget was $147 million in capital budget funds, which was an increase of more than $100 million over the previous year.

Moreover, housing's priority will continue to increase under the city's new capital improvement program. The 10-year plan calls for $2.1 billion to be spent on housing between fiscal years 1987 and 1996, and of this amount, nearly three-quarters will be targeted to meet low-income needs. Housing will account for 4.6 percent of total capital costs over the period; this is more than a fourfold increase, relative to housing's share of the city's 1984 10-year plan. (10, p. 19)

With federal aid of all kinds to New York having declined from nearly 20 percent in FY'80 to just 12 percent of the city's current expenses budget in FY'87, the mayor's latest budget proposes to make up for some of the federal cuts by raising four different taxes by a total of $220 million a year—$60 million of which would be earmarked for a low-income housing trust fund. (11, p. 10) The earmarked taxes include a 1 percent increase in the city's mortgage recording tax on cooperative apartments, and an increase in the maximum city hotel tax on luxury rooms. The taxes that the mayor does not currently propose to earmark for housing include a transfer tax on the sales of cooperative apartments, and a 25 percent increase in the capital gains tax on the sales of those nonresidential real estate properties that are valued at over $1 million.

Finally, at the state level, the mayor and governor reached an agreement in May 1986 on a major new housing package to provide an additional $1.2 billion in housing funds to the city over the next 10 years. The program goal is to produce 75,000 units of new and rehabilitated housing for low-, moderate-, and middle-income families. If all necessary legislative and other approvals are obtained (which has not yet occurred), all but $250 million of the total will come from previously untapped revenue sources. Plans for the $1.2 billion include the flow of $25 million per year from state appropriations into the state's housing trust fund. The plans also call for the following revenues:

- $400 million from the Battery Park City Authority, to be raised through the sale of bonds that would be paid off from revenues the Authority will receive from its commercial and residential development activities. The bond sale must be authorized by the state legislature.
- $200 million from the Port Authority, to be obtained through increases in payment in lieu of taxes on the World Trade Center.
- $100 million from a Port Authority fund, to be created by rent increases paid by private tenants moving into those offices at the World Trade Center that were previously occupied by state agencies.
- $250 million from a proposed Port Authority Bank for Regional Development. These funds will pay for infrastructure projects that otherwise would have been funded from the city budget, freeing the city budget's resources for housing expenditures. (22b, pp. 93–94)

Chapter 3
Second-Tier Players

U nderstandably, those localities that have never before appropriated general revenues for housing are usually more reluc-
tant than their more experienced counterparts to respond to
the federal retreat with bold housing programs of their own. After
all, in many of these places, low-income housing has never before
been a part of the political agenda, and little or no formal discussion has until lately taken place about the appropriate state or
local role in housing. This is even true in those few states whose
sole ventures into housing are through quasi-independent housing
finance agencies that cannot, on their own, meet the needs of
really poor families. Among other things, this has meant that
there was no politically powerful constituency exerting pressures
on elected officials to respond to local low-income housing problems; the lack of pressure was matched by a lack of housing expertise in legislative and executive chambers. Given these political
realities, and the fact that deep-subsidy housing is both expensive
in the short run and even more costly in recurring obligations, we
can understand why many chief executives and legislative leaders
across the country have initially responded to the federal housing
retreat by appointing "blue-ribbon panels" to study the problem.

While serving their traditional purpose of giving politicians
some breathing space, housing commissions, task forces, and
study committees also serve to familiarize key decision makers

with the nature and extent of local housing problems; to assess the locale's institutional needs and its capacities to address them; and to create a valuable data base upon which informed state and local housing policies can eventually be built. North Carolina is a good example of how the task force approach is working to develop policy responses to the change in the federal housing presence at the state level.

The North Carolina Legislative Study Commission

Not all of the recommendations of the Commission to Study Housing Programs in North Carolina—which was appointed by the governor and by the state general assembly's leadership in 1981—were positively received by the legislature. (38) As a direct result of the commission's work, however, the general assembly took the following actions:

- Appointed standing committees on housing in each legislative chamber, to introduce housing legislation, to review other legislative proposals for their impacts on housing, and, in general, to develop centers of housing expertise in the state legislature.
- Created a permanent housing commission within the office of the governor, to define the goals and responsibilities of state government in meeting the housing needs of North Carolina's citizens.
- Amended a state law to permit local governments to spend property-tax and sales-tax revenues on housing, without a prior vote of the people.
- Appropriated funds for pilot rental-housing construction and homeownership assistance programs, to be administered by the North Carolina Housing Finance Agency (see Chapter 4).

Some of the study commission's recommendations were rejected by the general assembly, including its most controversial one—enactment of a statewide minimum housing code. For the first time, however, the North Carolina League of Municipalities has made a statewide minimum housing code a high-priority legislative proposal. (The proposal is to be made to the 1987 session of the general assembly.) (26, p. 1)

While there are no formal ties between the league and the study commission, it is highly unlikely that the league would be calling for the housing code if not for the commission's efforts.

Local Housing Task Forces: Austin and Raleigh as Cases in Point

In a similar fashion, blue-ribbon panels at the local level can help lay the foundations for well-tailored responses to community housing problems. By documenting the severity of low-income deprivations, by identifying feasible policy alternatives, and by helping to forge a political consensus, local housing task forces can give elected officials the courage to adopt action programs. As the Austin (Texas) City Council Housing Task Force report has indicated, "In recent years, the Austin community has raised its level of consciousness regarding local housing conditions and needs. Public debate now reflects a common interest in providing for affordable housing." (7b, p. 1) That common interest is a necessary prelude to action because the development of locally funded housing programs raises specific issues that local officials have not had to consider, as long as federally funded programs identified those activities that were eligible for funding. In view of the federal retreat, it is now up to the community to define the full range of its local program parameters, including the eligible populations and the income limits of the families to be served. In Austin, the task force proposed programs to benefit the employable homeless, the first-time homebuyer of moderate means, the very-low-income tenant, and the senior citizen.

As shown by the following summary of the Raleigh (North Carolina) Housing Task Force's recommendations—recommendations that were responded to by a city council appropriation of $1 million to begin immediate implementation—local task forces' proposals tend to be hand-tailored to meet well-documented needs, and are highly targeted (33, pp. 1–3):

Raleigh

Low-Income Renters. The city of Raleigh should make an ongoing commitment to support the construction of at least 100 units a year of rental housing for low-income persons.

- The city should appropriate funds to build at least 50 units a year to be developed, operated, and maintained by the housing authority.... If necessary, the city should be prepared to subsidize continuing costs of such units.
- The city should take a leadership role in seeking funding sources for an additional 50 units of low-income rental housing units a year.

City Cost: $2.1 million. (Capital expenses for 50 units, plus escrow reserve fund for continuing operations.)
Sources of Funding: Sales- and property-tax revenues.

Occupants of Substandard Housing. The city of Raleigh should make available loans to encourage the rehabilitation of at least 100 substandard housing units a year. The depth of subsidy necessary to make rehabilitation economically feasible at affordable rents or repayments shall be determined by the community development department on a case-by-case basis. Most of this housing is not owner-occupied. Code enforcement, coupled with such loans, should be used to encourage rehabilitation by landlords.

City Cost: $550,000 to buy down rates from 8 percent to an average of 4 percent for 100 loans.

Source: Remaining Community Development Block Grant (CDBG) funds (approximately $550,000 per year), plus a portion of proceeds from bond financing.

Special Populations. The city of Raleigh should take the initiative in bringing together county and state officials to address the housing needs of special populations, including homeless families and individuals, the chronically mentally ill, the mentally retarded, the developmentally disabled, abused women and children, and ex-offenders. The city should also take a leadership role in formulating a plan that addresses the housing and social-service needs of these populations. The city should do its part in supporting housing for these populations by:

- Increasing public awareness of the need.
- Continuing to provide seed money to private agencies that serve the housing and related social-service needs of these populations.
- Supporting changes to the city code that would:
  –Allow the location of overnight shelters, transitional housing, permanent group homes, and residential hotels on a scattered-site basis throughout the city. Rather than using straight-line distance alone as a spacing requirement, the city should also consider population density, zoning density, and access to supportive services and facilities.
  –Permit more emergency and transitional housing for families.
- Lobbying for increases in county, state, and federal funding to house these populations. The city should request specific assistance from the state in addressing housing needs of persons discharged from state penal and mental institutions located in Raleigh.

First-Time Homebuyers. The city of Raleigh should assist at least 100 families a year who would not otherwise qualify under conventional financing to become first-time homebuyers, through the use of tax-exempt revenue bonds and by offering deferred-interest second-mortgage loans. This would serve to free currently occupied rental units, including assisted units, and to increase the total housing stock. The program should operate on a citywide basis, with preference given to housing in the city's redevelopment and conservation areas.

The educational value of local housing panels cannot be overstated. Even when community consensus has been achieved on desired ends, however, it does not necessarily follow that widespread agreement exists on the most appropriate means to accomplish them. Frequently, special-interest and more broadly representative task forces compete for political support of their preferred program approaches, a byproduct of which contention is a more informed citizenry and elected officials. This is what is happening in Austin, where three separate task forces are promoting their own programs.

Austin

In September 1986, the Austin City Council voted to put $22.5 million into a capital improvements program for housing to finance infrastructure, land banking, public housing improvements, construction of rental housing, and facilities for the homeless, in line with its task force recommendations. But it refused to act on the task force's proposal to rebate impact fees to developers who built affordable housing. This proposal was also rejected by another panel, the mayor's select committee on affordable housing, which found that "rebates or waivers of the capital recovery and other subdivision and building-related fees are not effective means of resolving the affordable housing problem." (7c, p. 7)

The select committee offered a two-pronged program. First, it wanted to eliminate unnecessary land use and environmental regulations, to expedite the development review process, and to institute a housing-affordability fiscal impact assessment requirement of all proposed city laws and regulations, to help ensure the long-term benefits of regulatory reform. Second, it sought to help remedy the current shortage of affordable housing through creation of a city-funded shared-equity and other direct-subsidy programs. These new programs would be financed through a new levy on nonresidential construction at a rate necessary to raise $10 million a year. (7c, p. 5)

In the meantime, a third ad hoc group, the Coalition for Affordable Housing, which comprised commercial developers, bankers, and other business leaders of Austin, retained the firm of Peat Marwick and Mitchell to design an affordable housing strategy that would not rely on linkage fees for funding. (12) In May 1986, Peat Marwick and Mitchell unveiled its proposal to create the Greater Austin Housing Development Corporation (GAHDC), which would use $75 million in state and city bond money, and $6 million in city startup funds to build 2,000 for-sale and rental housing units for Austin families with incomes of $25,000 or less. GAHDC, a nonprofit corporation, would have a 15-member board of directors, to be selected by the business community (eight members) and the city council (seven members). The board would be broadly representative of the "businesses and professions required for the delivery of affordable housing programs, as well as those organizations committed to neighborhood improvements and revitalization." (12, p. 7)

In addition to its production responsibilities, the corporation would provide and encourage essential financing for all forms of housing, construction management, and property management services, and would work with builders, architects, bankers, city officials, social service organizations, neighborhood groups, and others.

By the end of 1986, the people of Austin had yet to decide which way to go. Despite this lack of political consensus, however, few would question that the level of discourse about what is best for the people of Austin is far more informed and sophisticated today than it was a year ago, before the various task forces began their work. Undoubtedly, too, the program and funding approaches that eventually win out in Austin and in other communities that have gone through similar debates will have broader and deeper political support than if they had been mandated by federal regulations and paid for entirely by federal tax dollars.

Wider Implications of Local Task Force Activities

For three reasons, we have taken the time to highlight the work of a few of the many housing task forces whose reports we reviewed. First, their histories suggest that local strategies developed by second-tier communities are likely to be much more tailored to local needs and conditions than are low-income housing programs that are delivered directly from Washington. Should the federal government eventually reassert its leadership in the low-income housing arena, the way that it does so, and the shape that new federal programs take, are both likely to be heavily influenced by the activity now taking place in units of local government that have never before administered programs of their own.

Second, communities like Austin and Raleigh are spending a great deal of time and effort on important institutional issues that were of little consequence, as long as the federal government paid the bills and dictated program structures and regulations. The way in which locally funded housing programs will be administered, however, can now be determined locally. The allocation of housing responsibilities should be among local housing authorities, community development agencies, existing nonprofit development entities, and community-based organizations. And whether new, nongovernmental umbrella organizations should be created to orchestrate multifaceted local housing programs is now an issue of lively concern in many communities for the very first time.

While neither of these two city councils has yet agreed to cede its authority or to delegate its low-income housing decision-making responsibilities to a third party, it is interesting to note that both Austin's business-oriented housing coalition and Raleigh's more broadly representative task force have proposed the creation of a new nonprofit organization to manage locally funded housing programs. Raleigh's alternative to the Greater Austin Housing Development Corporation is a nonprofit corporation whose prestigious board would broadly represent both private and public organizations concerned with housing issues—including the city council, citizens' groups, lenders, homebuilders, and current low- and moderate-income housing providers (33, p. 8).

The third reason for which we have highlighted these two case histories is to emphasize the point that many local governments without a prior history of supporting low-income housing with their own funds are now gearing up for action. This means that, in a year or two, the cumulative amount of nonfederally funded housing activity, measured in terms of the number of programs, as well as the volume of units, will be much greater than it is today. This conclusion is similar to that reached by the Council of State Community Affairs Agencies (COSCAA) in its survey of the recent rise of state housing programs. COSCAA determined that the "number of state-funded housing initiatives has doubled since 1980, and increased by 50 percent during the last two years alone...." (6g, p. 230). We think the same geometric rate of increase will prevail for localities over the next two years.

This is the good news. The bad news is, as we indicated earlier, that without a major, continuing federal production presence, net additions to the nation's permanent stock of low- and moderate-income housing will remain far below the demonstrated levels of urgent need. This fact can be documented for large and small communities alike. While New York's dynamic new $1.2 billion housing program is scheduled to produce 75,000 housing units over the next 10 years (if fully funded), the city's waiting list for public housing already contains more than 200,000 families. Moreover, according to some estimates, the city faces an additional shortage of affordable housing of more than 372,000 units between now and the year 2000, when anticipated household growth and losses from the stock are taken into account. While $1.2 billion is a great deal of money, we should point out that just between 1976 and 1980, the federal Section 8 program produced or aided 93,000 housing units in the New York area at a cost to the federal government of about $518 million a year, and a long-term budget commitment of more than $1 trillion. (1, p. 3)

In less populous metropolitan cities like Raleigh, the absolute numbers are smaller, but the size of the relative resource gap is no different. Should Raleigh's city council finance 50 units of low-income housing a year, as its housing task force has urged it to do, this action would increase the size of Raleigh's public housing inventory by just 3 percent a year. Like that of New York City, Raleigh's public housing waiting list of more than 2,000 families equals the size of its entire occupied inventory. Clearly, local programs alone can do little to close the housing gap.

Chapter 4
Tax-Exempt Add-Ons

A Continued Need for Tax-Exempt Funds

The Council of State Community Affairs Agencies'
(COSCAA's) recently published compendium of state-funded
housing initiatives excluded programs that were financed by tax-
exempt bonds because tax reform is likely to make these programs more difficult to use in the future. (15a, p.1) We agree
with COSCAA that the lower borrowing limits and stricter targeting requirements for the new law adversely affect bond programs,
and we devote an entire chapter of this monograph (Chapter 7) to
the potential effects of tax reform on low-income housing.

We remain convinced, however, that despite the limiting effects of tax reform, for sustained levels of low-income housing
production to be achieved, the continued availability of tax-
exempt financing must be assured—and supplemented by state
and local subsidies, in order to lower development costs and drive
down interest rates below their tax-exempt levels. If it turns out
that the restrictions of the Tax Reform Act prove to be so intrac-
table that higher-cost taxable bonds must substitute for tax-
exempt financing, the resulting higher debt-service requirements
will call for even more generous subsidies to make low-income
projects feasible. For these reasons, unlike COSCAA, we have

decided to include in this monograph tax-exempt add-ons, which are supplements to the tax-exempt financing programs of state housing finance agencies, and which are designed to make housing affordable to low-income families.

HFA Reserves as Sources of Subsidy

The Michigan and California Programs

As we indicated in Chapter 1, in the face of the elimination of the Section 8 production program, several state housing finance agencies have begun to tap their excess reserve funds as a way of subsidizing the rents in projects they finance. Still others are now receiving state appropriations for the same purpose.

The Michigan State Housing Development Authority (MSHDA), for example, uses its reserves to drive down the rents on 8 percent of the units in a selected number of their multifamily projects, in order to make them affordable to families with incomes at 50 percent of the median. Without the subsidy, the minimum income served would be closer to 80 percent of the median. MSHDA also uses reserve funds to write down mortgage interest rates on those of their projects that are located in distressed areas, where market rents are not high enough to cross-subsidize the amount of units (20 percent of the total) that must be set aside under federal law for low-income families in every bond-financed rental project. MSHDA has also used reserves to help finance alternative "intermediate service group homes," in cooperation with the state department of mental health.

The California Housing Finance Authority's so-called 80/20 multifamily pilot program differs from conventional mixed-subsidy bond-financed projects in that its qualifying projects contain no market-rate units at all. Indeed, 80 percent of the units in approved projects must be targeted to low-income households, while the remaining 20 percent are set aside for very-low-income households and individuals. The dual add-on subsidies to the HFA's tax-exempt financing come from 1) the local government's 20 to 30 percent writedown of development costs, and 2) an interest-rate buydown from the HFA reserve funds that reduces project mortgage rates to as little as 5 percent in the first year. Each year, rents are scheduled to increase by an average of 4 to 5 percent, thereby allowing an increase of effective mortgage rates up to the full tax-exempt rate on the agency's fixed-rate 30-year loans. At the time of this writing, CHFA had one pilot 80/20 project under construction and six others in various stages of processing.

Massachusetts's SHARP Program

The Massachusetts State Housing Assistance for Rental Production program (SHARP) was created by the state in 1983 and administered in conjunction with the Massachusetts Housing Finance Agency (MHFA). In its first three years of operation, the program committed funds to 64 developments, with a total of 7,813 units. (24a)

SHARP is a shallow-subsidy loan program designed to stimulate the development of privately sponsored multifamily housing in which at least 25 percent of the units will be occupied by households with incomes below 80 percent of the areawide median. The SHARP add-on to MHFA tax-exempt financing is in the form of an interest-rate writedown to as low a rate as 5 percent, and for a term of up to 15 years.

In the case of the 25 percent of low-income units, maximum rents can be no higher than HUD's published *Section 8 Existing Fair Market Rents,* rather than Section 8's higher new-construction rents. This means that SHARP-assisted housing projects are available to low-income families with Section 8 housing certificates. It is expected that most SHARP projects will become self-sustaining over the 15-year period of assistance, as the state subsidy is treated as a loan, not a grant. "However, the statute allows repayments to be recycled back to a project, when such a plan will clearly benefit low- and moderate-income tenants." (34b, p. 1)

New Jersey's Initiatives

In line with the municipal affirmative affordable housing requirements that have been outgrowths of the Mount Laurel exclusionary zoning litigation in New Jersey, the New Jersey Housing and Mortgage Finance Agency (NJHMFA) has set aside 25 percent of its total mortgage-bond authority for use in conjunction with tax-exempt add-ons. The add-ons come from a $20 million appropriation under the state's Fair Housing Act. Fifteen million dollars of this appropriation is being used for loans and grants, averaging $7,000 a unit, to support local affordable housing programs.

Affordable housing programs that are eligible for add-on financing include:

• Assistance for home purchases and improvements, including interest-rate assistance, down-payment and closing assistance, and direct grants for principal reduction;

- Rental programs, including loans or grants for developments containing low- and moderate-income housing, for moderate rehabilitation of existing rental housing, and for congregate-care and retirement facilities;
- Financial assistance for the conversion of nonresidential space to residences; and
- Other assistance, including grants or loans for infrastructure, or construction loans to be taken out with permanent financing provided by the agency.

Minnesota and North Carolina

Minnesota and North Carolina, with equally creative add-ons, support their low-income projects somewhat differently.

To our knowledge, Minnesota's is the first HFA to finance multifamily rental projects using a graduated-payment mortgage. Reserve funds have been set aside to make up the difference between the below-market graduated rate and the fixed interest rate on the bonds, if future rents do not rise high enough to pay the full debt service.

North Carolina is using a combination of HFA reserves and state appropriations to supplement four tax-exempt programs (35a):

The single-family subsidy program combines a reduced-interest, fixed-rate mortgage loan with a monthly mortgage contribution. The first-mortgage interest rate is based on the lowest rate available on any of the agency's outstanding bond issues. This base interest rate is reduced by up to 4.5 percent, depending on the borrower's income.

The maximum allowable home prices also vary according to income:

Borrower's Annual Income	Maximum Home Value	Reduction in Tax-Exempt Interest Rate
up to $14,000	$40,000	4.5%
14,001 – 16,000	45,000	3.5
16,001 – 18,000	50,000	2.5
18,001 – 20,000	55,000	1.5

In addition, borrowers receive up to $115 a month, to make mortgage payments even more affordable. The subsidy payment decreases, and the interest rate increases, as the borrower's income rises. Upon sale of the property, the HFA recaptures the subsidy from the home's appreciated value. However, no more than 30 percent of the appreciated value may be recaptured.

The elderly rent subsidy program offers 1 percent permanent financing under the Farmers' Home Administration's Section 515 program. It also confers a subsidy of up to $100 per month per apartment, to provide affordable housing for low-income senior citizens. This pilot program will subsidize 60 percent of the units in selected projects located in rural counties with median incomes of $20,000 or less. The low-income units will be reserved for occupants earning 50 percent or less of the area median income, ranging from $6,500 to $12,200 a year. The subsidy is renewable after five years.

The home-improvement loan subsidy program provides rehabilitation loans to owner/occupants. The agency's regular home improvement program provided loans at tax-exempt rates that participating cities subsidized until they bore as low a rate as 1 percent, by using their own Community Development Block Grant funds. The new program uses HFA funds to lower borrower interest rates to 3 percent. Local governments still have the option to subsidize the loans further.

Program participants average 57 years of age, with an average annual income of $14,000, and have lived in their houses for an average of about 20 years.

The loans, which are limited to a maximum of $45,000, are typically used to repair roofs and foundations, to upgrade electrical and plumbing systems, to make homes more energy-efficient, and to add new rooms. Loan terms are for five, 10, and 15 years.

The multifamily rental subsidy program subsidizes rents in projects in smaller communities and rural areas where tax-exempt financing alone requires higher rents than many low-income families can afford. The HFA subsidy is up to $100 per unit for the full term of the mortgage—usually 40 years. The pilot effort in 1985 supported 40 units in five projects in nonmetropolitan counties. The state general assembly appropriated $2 million of support.

Projects in metropolitan areas will be considered for agency support in the program's second round. However, local governments in these areas may be asked to help fund a portion of their higher development costs, in order to make the program work in these higher-cost areas. The subsidy maintains rent (including utilities) at 30 percent of a household's monthly income.

Chapter 5
State and Local "Wanna Bees"

As we indicated in the introduction to this monograph, "wanna bees" are state- or locally funded housing programs whose basic designs, delivery systems, and regulations have been heavily influenced by the shape of federal programs that have been either eliminated or severely curtailed over the past six years.

Some "wanna bees," like Massachusetts's low-rent public housing program, which is now being revived, have long traditions and predate the federal retreat. These programs were originally intended to supplement, rather than to replace, their federal counterparts, and they have the same administrative structures as do their counterparts—that is, they are operated by local housing authorities. Other examples of wanna bees that were intended to supplement rather than to replace federal programs are Massachusetts's moderate rehabilitation and rent certificate programs and its Community Development Action Grant (CDAG) program, which is a UDAG look-alike that helps to finance necessary site improvements in distressed areas, and thus makes housing and economic projects feasible.

A second category of wanna bees will eventually replace federal programs that are threatened with extinction by Congress. For reasons of economy and efficiency, and because these clones of federal housing programs have the benefit of shorter learning curves for those who must administer them, their regulations tend to resemble the programs that they will ultimately replace. An example of this kind of wanna bee is Kentucky's homeownership assistance program, a Section 235 look-alike. In the course of our survey, we identified five different kinds of wanna bees that fall within this category:

1) Long-term, below–market-rate rehabilitation loan programs for owner/occupants and investors in small rental properties (Section 312 loan wanna bees);
2) Homeowner below-market interest-rate subsidy programs for acquisition of houses by lower- and moderate-income families (Section 235 wanna bees);
3) Long-term rental assistance programs to support new rental construction for low-income families (Section 8 new-construction wanna bees);
4) Front-end grant (and other kinds of one-time assistance) programs for new construction and for substantial rehabilitation of rental housing (HoDAG wanna bees); and
5) Housing-voucher and rental assistance programs for low-income families (Section 8 existing-housing wanna bees).

Direct Rehabilitation Loans

One of the most long-lived federal housing assistance efforts is the Section 312 rehabilitation loan program. Enacted as Section 312 of the Housing Act of 1964, the program was designed to encourage "localities and property owners to upgrade and preserve existing neighborhoods and to rehabilitate private properties." (35, p. 1-1) As it was then and continues to be today, Section 312 "operates as a cooperative venture between the federal government, which furnishes the loan funds, and localities, which process loans." (35, p. 1-1)

In the program's early years, Section 312 loans had a 3 percent interest rate and were limited to lower-income owner/occupants in urban renewal areas. Today, however, Section 312 loans are also available to multifamily investors and cooperatives, and interest rates now depend upon the property type and the income of the borrower. Homeowners whose incomes do not exceed 80 percent of the area median and who own one- to four-family units are still eligible for the 3 percent interest rate. So are housing cooperatives in which all units are occupied by cooperative members and in which 80 percent of the residents have incomes not exceeding 80 percent of the median. All others, including corporations, partnerships, absentee owners, and borrowers whose incomes exceed 80 percent of the median, pay a higher rate based on the yield of U.S. government securities of a term comparable to that of the Section 312 loan. Although Congress stopped appropriating new monies for the program several years ago, borrowers' repayments form a revolving loan fund from which new loans, albeit in lower numbers than before, continue to be made.

Local experience with the Section 312 programs is so extensive that it is understandable that several states and localities should have used it as a model for their own rehabilitation programs. Delaware's housing rehabilitation loan program (HRLP), which is one of several state initiatives, is typical of these. Created in 1985, the HRLP provides 3 percent direct loans, up to a maximum of $15,000 for up to 10 years, to rehabilitate owner-occupied and investor-owned properties. Loans, which are administered locally, are limited to 75 percent of the actual rehabilitation cost and require the execution of rent regulatory agreements in the case of investor-owned residential properties.

While most state-administered rehabilitation loan programs are run by housing finance agencies using the proceeds of tax-exempt bonds, Delaware's program has been capitalized by a $2 million loan from the state's housing development fund (HDF). The HDF was created by the state in 1968 with an initial appropriation of $8 million. Through 1986, the HDF had accrued $600,000 in interest income, which was supplemented by a state appropriation of $2.5 million in 1986, bringing the total fund balance to more than $11 million. Also in 1986, a document surcharge of $3.00 on all deed recordation filings was established, with 95 percent of the revenues from this new real estate transfer levy being earmarked for the HDF. This assures a continuing flow of funds into the HDF to help support the housing rehabilitation loan program, as well as Delaware's other housing initiatives.

Homeowner Subsidies

Several states administer clones of the federal Section 235 homeownership assistance program, which, when enacted in 1968, provided interest subsidies to eligible borrowers that reduced effective mortgage interest rates to 1 percent. Today, interest rates under the Section 235 program are a higher 4 percent, but few new loans are now being made because of a lack of congressional appropriations.

As we stated earlier, Kentucky's homeownership program resembles Section 235 in concept. Using surplus agency funds, the Kentucky Housing Corporation capitalized the Kentucky Housing Trust in 1985. The trust subsidizes interest rates on the corporation's tax-exempt mortgage loans down to a 1 percent interest rate (see Table 5.1). Eligible families must have incomes below $15,000, and loans can be for either purchase or rehabilitation. In 1986, the corporation transferred $15 million of excess debt-service reserves into the trust fund to continue the program.

In contrast to Kentucky's homeownership program, North Carolina's Section 235 wanna bee, which was discussed in the previous chapter, is funded by state appropriations rather than by excess reserves. Hawaii's program was privately financed by the development community. The so-called "Hula Mae" program, which operated from 1982 to 1984, was a type of builder mortgage buydown program. By charging developers six points for tax-exempt financing during a period when conventional interest rates were very high, the Hawaii Housing Authority was able to capitalize an interest-bearing account from which subsidies were fully paid out over a four-year period. The subsidy was highest in the first year and was phased out over the next three years, with the borrower paying full mortgage costs from the fifth year onward. Although the Hula Mae program was discontinued when con-

Table 5.1
Selected Homeowner Subsidies

Administrator	Form	Source of Funds	Recipients
North Carolina Housing Finance Agency	Combines a reduced-rate mortgage loan with a monthly mortgage contribution. Interest rate may be reduced to as little as 4.5 percent. The interest rate increases, and the subsidy amount decreases, as the borrower's income rises. Upon sale of	Appropriations	Low-income, first-time home-buyers

Administrator	Form	Source of Funds	Recipients
North Carolina Housing Finance Agency (Cont'd.)	home, the subsidy is recaptured from home's appreciated value.		
Kentucky Housing Corporation	Writes down mortgage interest rates to as little as 1 percent, depending on a family's income.	Excess from debt-service reserve funds	Borrowers of single-family insured loans, considered on a case-by-case basis
North Carolina Housing Finance Agency	Makes rehabilitation loans to owner/occupants for renovation. Writes down interest rates to 3 percent. Local governments can further subsidize.	Agency funds	Statewide
Minnesota Housing Finance Agency	Provides down-payment and monthly-payment assistance, in the form of a no-interest second-mortgage loan with gradual payment increases.	Appropriations	Low-income, first-time home-buyers
Hawaii's Hula Mae Program	Makes monthly subsidy to qualified borrowers' debt-to-income and housing expenses–to-income ratios. Phased out over four years.	One discount point on sales prices, collected from developers.	Low-income, first-time home-buyers.

ventional interest rates fell, the concept of a buydown type of short-term subsidy, financed either privately or publicly, remains a feasible concept.

The Alaska Housing Finance Corporation's homeownership assistance program (HOAP) combines a subsidy that drives effective interest rates for first-time homebuyers down to 6 percent, with a growing-equity mortgage (GEM) that reduces agency borrowing costs by shortening the maturation periods of their securities. HOAP provides income-eligible borrowers with a subsidy sufficient to reduce monthly payments for mortgage principal, interest, taxes, and insurance (PITI), up to a maximum of 28 percent of income or of a 6 percent effective interest rate—whichever is less. Under this GEM-type program, fixed-rate loans require monthly payments to be increased by 5 percent a year for five years, with the full amount of all increased mortgage payments being used to retire the principal. This type of mortgage permits borrowers to increase their equity rapidly, while reducing their total borrowing costs, as well as the necessary subsidies. Under this arrangement, a loan with a 30-year amortization schedule can be fully paid off in 16 to 18 years.

In August 1986, the Rhode Island Housing and Mortgage Corporation approved regulations for a new homeownership assistance program. Using state appropriations, instead of developer charges such as those levied by Hawaii's Hula Mae program, the agency will subsidize an 8 to 8.5 percent, tax-exempt mortgage interest rate down to a 6 percent rate in the first year, to a 7 percent rate in the next two years, and to an 8 percent rate for the remainder of the loan term. The temporary subsidy is premised on the assumption that homebuyer incomes will rise high enough over the four-year period of assistance to permit full housing costs to be affordable at a payment ratio of no more than 28 percent of income.

Section 8 New-Construction Look-Alikes

Few states and even fewer localities have used the long-term deep-subsidy approach to stimulating new low-income rental production that is found in the Section 8 new-construction program. Based upon the approved rent for an eligible unit and upon a subsidy term of up to 30 years, the total of the Section 8 new-construction subsidies for a single unit can easily exceed $110,000, and can even run much higher than that in high-cost locations. This is why most state and local rental stimulus programs adopt the more cost-effective one-time subsidy approach in their new construction and substantial rehabilitation programs. The latter was first introduced in HUD's Urban Development Action Grant (UDAG) program for economic development projects, and was then institutionalized for housing in HUD's Housing Development Action Grant (HoDAG) program in 1983.

Not all low-income rental construction programs, however, are UDAG and HoDAG wanna bees. (These two types we will examine more closely in the following section.) Some are modeled after the continuing-subsidy approach of Section 8, with certain cost-containing modifications. The simplest means of limiting costs, of course, is to reduce the subsidy term, and this is what New York State did. Building on the Farmers' Home Administration's (FmHA's) Section 515 interest credit program—which provides 1 percent mortgage loans to housing sponsors—the state has appropriated funds to provide Section 8–type rental assistance payments to selected projects for renewable five-year terms. Rent subsidies, equal to the difference between project-approved rents and 30 percent of a tenant's income, permit this moderate-income program to serve low-income families, too, although only for a very limited time, unless the legislature renews its subsidy commitment. While it is possible that low-income occupancy could be phased out as part of the normal turnover process without causing much displacement, this consequence is not a likely one. Serious hardship and political fallout would accompany the state's decision to discontinue rental assistance. Hence, the short-term contract approach to cost containment is probably not a very effective means of limiting long-term subsidy costs.

Hawaii's Section 8 look-alike operates quite differently from New York's. The long-term rental subsidy comes from interest earned by a state-capitalized revolving fund. The law requires that the principal of the revolving fund must be preserved, and, to prevent overcommitment of the fund, that sufficient principal for each assisted project must be set aside in a separate account. Rather than offering renewable five-year subsidy commitments, which do not provide lenders sufficient security to warrant their making long-term project loans, Hawaii's program provides that subsidies' durations "shall not be less than 10 years, nor in excess of the period for which the authority has invested the principal amount of the revolving fund (committed to the eligible project) at a known rate of return, to fund rental assistance payments for the eligible project." (20a, p. 22) For nonprofit sponsors, the maximum subsidy term is extended to 25 years, as long as the escrowed principal is sufficient to fund the long-term subsidies with certainty. As do most other rental assistance programs, Hawaii's program bases a tenant's rent on 30 percent of his or her household income.

UDAG/HoDAG Wanna Bees

We define HoDAG wanna bees as state and local housing development programs that provide project-specific capital grants or other kinds of front-end construction cost writedowns such as would be required to make a project financially feasible. Using the vernacular popularized in the UDAG program, HoDAG-type assistance must generally meet the "but-for" test: but for the HoDAG, the project would not go forward. As illustrated below, with reference to Pennsylvania's housing assistance grants program's regulations, UDAG/HoDAG look-alikes also tend to include in their project selection criteria such factors as extent of community or neighborhood distress, leveraging ratios, and expected neighborhood impacts of the proposed project (32a, p. 3):

> Guidelines for the housing and development assistance program will give high-priority consideration to community conservation and economic development projects that:
> • Focus on the neediest areas and individuals within a given community;
> • Maximize leveraging of other public and private funds, e.g., local revenues, other federal or state funds, private banks, loan pools, or other private gifts, donations, or contributions;
> • Restore downtown commercial centers;
> • Restore housing and neighborhood residential areas;
> • Benefit unemployed or underemployed residents by creating or retaining jobs;
> • Expand business opportunities and activities in a given community;
> • Include substantial community/local-government and local-agency commitment to the proposed project; and
> • Attract broad community support, as evidenced by the involvement of citizens during the planning process, and by support from elected officials, business leaders, and civic groups.

Many states and localities have adopted HoDAG look-alikes as their primary production vehicles, even though their upfront subsidies make these look-alikes expensive in the short run. Principalities adopt these programs because they are more cost-effective over the longer term than are programs that deliver continuing project-based subsidies. They also provide more flexibility in defining the optimal form and amount of the required subsidy on a project-by-project basis.

Maryland's new rental production program is a good example of a HoDAG wanna bee. The $9 million earmarked for the new program will provide no- or low-interest deferred-payment loans that will subsidize rental units occupied by families with incomes no higher than 60 percent of the state median. (6g, p. 238). Available on a first-come, first-served basis, funds can be used to help finance new construction, acquisition, or substantial rehabilitation, and will be repaid when projects have been sold or refinanced, or when they have reached a stage at which they no longer serve an income-eligible population. When used to provide mortgage assistance—as in the case of Hawaii's rental production program—capital funds will be escrowed in interest-bearing accounts, the earnings from which will subsidize mortgage payments. At the end of the assistance period, which will be at least 15 years, loan repayments, released principal funds, and other paybacks will form a revolving fund from which new projects will be supported. As a condition of loan approval, Maryland's program requires the state or locality in which a project is located to help defray its development costs.

Local Housing Vouchers

In the first chapter of this monograph, we indicated how serious the housing affordability problem has become. Nationally, the median rent/income ratio for low-income renters in 1983 was 0.46, and nearly half of these renters spent more than 50 percent of their income on housing. Both figures are probably even higher today. There is no community anywhere that is struggling to define for itself an appropriate housing role that can ignore the affordability issue. The report of Raleigh's blue-ribbon housing task force illustrates this point:

> The most serious . . . housing problem in Raleigh involves the city's low-income renters—over 17,000 low-income households (35 percent of all renters) pay excessive proportions (greater than 30 percent) of their incomes for rent. All of these families make less than $15,000 per year, and almost one-third have incomes under $5,000. Paying excessive rents (in some cases for substandard housing) means that these low-income families also lack adequate resources for food, medicine, child care, clothing, and other necessities. One group is particularly hard-hit: female-headed households account for 59 percent of all excessive-rent payers in Raleigh. The elderly constitute 14 percent, and black households make up 33 percent of the 17,000 families paying excessive rents.

These low-income families need housing that rents for less than $300 per month, including utilities. Yet the average gross rent for two-bedroom units in Raleigh in 1985 was $539—this average Raleigh rent was three times what a person living on minimum wages or on social security payments could afford, and more than seven times the rent affordable by an AFDC mother with two children. (33, p. 4)

Faced with the certain knowledge that the federal government will do little to lessen the housing expense burdens shouldered by growing numbers of their lower-income residents, many communities, like Raleigh, have begun to formally assess the wisdom and feasibility of creating locally funded rent certificates or housing vouchers. Local reluctance to do this is based on cost-effectiveness and on administrative considerations. With respect to cost, average subsidy requirements for each housing voucher in a community like Raleigh would be about $3,000 a year, and if just 350 families (2 percent of all income-eligibles) were awarded vouchers during the first year, direct subsidy costs would consume the entire $1 million that Raleigh's city council appropriated for housing in 1986, without adding a single unit of standard housing to the permanent stock of affordable units.

The effectiveness issue concerns this last point. It has long been known, for example, that a large portion of all Section 8 rent certificates has been awarded to families who did not have to move to qualify for assistance because their present housing accommodations met the program's quality standards. Conversely, a large portion of households awarded Section 8 certificates whose present housing did not meet program standards were forced to drop out of the program because they were unable to find another place to live that was in good physical condition and that had a rent within the Section 8 limits.

Similar problems are now plaguing HUD's new housing voucher program, which the administration proposes to make the centerpiece of its low-income housing policy. As of November 1986, 40 percent of the 12,000 voucher recipients in the national demonstration have had to return their vouchers unused, even after they had won extensions of the 60-day search period, because they were unable to find suitable housing. (24, p. 1)

Raleigh's city council responded to its task force's assessment of the affordability crisis with a variation on the voucher theme that would involve leasing individual units in privately owned multifamily developments that are scattered throughout the city. These units would then be sublet to low-income families at very low rents. The task force unanimously opposed the council, arguing that:

- Voucher systems are a "band-aid" approach and are at best only a temporary solution. Ownership is a permanent solution.
- Although vacancy rates for high-priced apartments have jumped dramatically as the market has been overbuilt, vacancy rates for low-priced apartments have changed little, if at all.
- According to the lessons of past experience, apartment owners who may be interested in vouchers while vacancy rates are high will be unwilling to commit themselves to long-term lease arrangements.
- Voucher systems are highly susceptible to fraud. This is particularly true in an unstable market, in which it is hard to determine the real value of a rental property.
- Voucher systems that embody controls with which to determine rents, to review eligibility, or to ensure code compliance quickly become bureaucratic nightmares that are difficult and costly to administer with accuracy.

After much public debate, the council and the task force agreed that the community's long-term interests would better be served if the $300,000 initially set aside the council for housing vouchers was instead used to acquire housing units on the open market. These units would then become permanent additions to the city's stock of low-income housing.

Unlike Raleigh, which rejected the concept, at least two states and one locality are moving forward with their own voucher-type programs. Because many states and localities should be seeking to learn more about the fate of these programs over the longer term, we summarize the key features of Pennsylvania's, Maryland's, and the District of Columbia's voucher programs.

Maryland's and Pennsylvania's programs provide temporary, stop-gap rental assistance to families and individuals "in crisis." In Pennsylvania's case, "crisis" is defined as the imminent danger of becoming homeless, and payments for up to four months (or a total of no more than $750—whichever is less) are available to pay a security deposit, rent, or utilities, in order to keep a family from losing its place of residence. In Maryland, recipients of emergency rental assistance must either be 1) homeless or lacking in sufficient resources to secure permanent housing, and able to maintain independent living quarters; or 2) experiencing a critical housing need—including one caused by impending eviction, by court order to vacate, by property condemnation, or by other events beyond the recipients' control. Assistance is not available to households experiencing eviction because of behavioral problems or because of other circumstances within their control. Rental allowances in Maryland vary with household size, rather than with either the income or the actual rent paid by the recipients. The allowances range from a low of $100 a month for a two-person household in the western part of the state, to a high of $250 a month for a family of six or more persons in the Baltimore/Washington area. (25a, Attachment 2)

To qualify for aid in Maryland, families must have incomes below certain thresholds, which range from a low of $6,741 a year for a single-person household (regardless of location) to a high of $15,638 for a household containing eight or more persons (in the Washington area). (25a, Attachment 2) While rental assistance is only available on a temporary basis, program regulations are more liberal and flexible in Maryland than in Pennsylvania. Although households in Maryland can receive no more than six consecutive monthly housing-allowance payments, extensions may be granted for additional three-month periods "if it is determined that undue hardship would result. . . ." (25a, p. 3)

Because of the crisis orientation of these two state housing-allowance programs, applicable housing-quality standards are less stringent than those associated with either Section 8 or the District of Columbia's tenant assistance payments (TAP) program, which we will discuss shortly. Under Maryland's program, for example, recipients living in housing with shared kitchens and bathrooms qualify for aid, as do those in boarding houses, other SRO arrangements, group homes, transitional housing, or mobile homes. Even motel and hotel rooms and housing units without access to kitchen facilities may be permitted, if no other cost-effective housing is available. (25a, p. 4) From the standpoint of physical condition, however, all housing must either conform to the local housing code or to Maryland's state livability code, whichever is applicable.

In contrast to the Maryland and Pennsylvania emergency allowance programs, which are funded at $1 million and $750,000 respectively, the District of Columbia's $20 million voucher program is a true derivative of Section 8. (37a) Unlike the temporary, flat grants that are paid directly to recipients under the two state programs, TAP payments in Washington, D.C., are made directly to participating landlords and are equal to the difference between an approved dwelling rent and 30 percent of a tenant's income (25 percent, if a tenant is elderly or handicapped). Dwelling rents that earn approvals, which are based on the cost of standard housing in the District, vary by number of bedrooms and range from $350 a month for an efficiency unit, through $530 for a two-bedroom unit, and up to $969 for a six-bedroom unit.

Applicants are certified for income eligibility and, once approved, are placed on a waiting list, which grew to more than 10,000 households within a few months of the program's startup in mid-1986. Due to such high demand, recipients of rent certificates are selected from the waiting list by lottery. Certificate holders have 60 days in which to find suitable housing that meets D.C.'s housing code and that has a rent at or below the maximum approved rent. To avoid undue competition for scarce apartments, the D.C. Department of Housing and Community Development (DHCD), which administers the program, issues no more than 200 rent certificates at any one time. Despite this precaution, however, many recipients still find it very difficult to find qualifying units.

As of August 1986, only 25 landlords had signed up to participate in the TAP program, which simply fails to offer attractive incentives to suppliers in a tight housing market. (19a, p. 1) Perhaps the most serious limitation is the fact that landlords are guaranteed no more than one year's housing-allowance payments because appropriations are for one year only. Why commit an apartment to a family who may not be able to afford to stay beyond 12 months, and raise the specter of an eviction to reclaim the unit? The dilemma, of course, is that longer-term subsidy commitments would probably make more housing available to allowance recipients but would, at the same time, incur much higher costs. (However, this would not be true in Washington, D.C., or similar tight housing markets.)

Chapter 6
Inclusionary Housing Programs

As we noted earlier, a large and growing number of localities require (or provide incentives to) developers to sell or rent specified fractions of their residential projects at affordable prices. We include linkage programs, which impose fees or low- and moderate-income production requirements on nonresidential developers, as part of this expanding web of locally initiated inclusionary regulations. We have made a national survey of locally funded low-income housing initiatives, seen the elimination of important real estate tax preferences by the Tax Reform Act of 1986, and noted the surplus of new, unoccupied office space in major urban centers. Accordingly, we have concluded that stand-alone linkage programs that exact high square-foot payments from downtown developers are unlikely to be widely adopted in the immediate future. As federal cutbacks deepen, however, more communities may be forced to adopt comprehensive fee-based or production-driven housing programs that more modestly assess all types of new development.

This chapter has four main sections, each of which describes a major aspect of inclusionary housing activity. The first section tells of the evolution of inclusionary zoning programs, from the earliest mandatory local ordinances, which were first adopted by many California communities during the early 1970s, to the more flexible incentive-based programs that are now being adopted by localities in Florida and elsewhere.

In the second main section, we define linkage programs, which, like their zoning counterparts, fall normally within two subcategories. Under mandatory formula-based programs, the developers' fees and their low-income housing production obligations are known with certainty at the earliest stages of project formulation. This is also true for certain voluntary linkage programs, in which, less formally, density bonuses and other incentives are available to development firms that choose to meet locally specified affordable housing requirements. (It is not true, however, for other so-called "voluntary" programs, in which linkage obligations are negotiated during the development review process.) A third subcategory of linkage obligations is discussed in the third subsection of our examination of linkage programs. It is similar to the levying of impact fees on new residential and nonresidential developments to help finance affordable housing.

The third main section of this chapter covers the new generation of comprehensive inclusionary programs that is emerging under recent state laws that have been spurred by the New Jersey Supreme Court's landmark Mount Laurel cases. In these cases, the court ruled that communities have a constitutional obligation to provide affordable housing opportunities and thus to meet their fair-share housing needs. Hence the multifaceted affordable housing program, such as the one in Princeton, New Jersey, which combines inclusionary zoning elements with production incentives and linkage requirements, and provides for an active public development role. While these Princeton-type programs may require explicit state-level enabling legislation—in contrast to their more traditional inclusionary zoning and linkage counterparts, which are grounded in a community's authority to regulate land use—these multifaceted approaches could well represent the next generation of affordable housing programs.

In the fourth and final main section of this chapter, we concern ourselves with extrapolations as to the future of the inclusionary concept.

Inclusionary Zoning

General Definition

The objective of inclusionary zoning programs is "to establish a permanent housing stock that is affordable to low- and moderate-income households and acceptable to the surrounding community, through requirements that are fair to the developer and allow a reasonable profit." (8, p. 1) As we have indicated above, the legal basis for inclusionary zoning is generally the same as that for other land use regulations that localities promulgate under the police power to protect the general health, safety, and welfare of their citizens. This is why, for example, the preamble to the model inclusionary zoning ordinance written by the California Department of Housing and Community Development (DHCD) contains the following finding:

> The housing shortage for persons of low and moderate income is detrimental to the public health, safety, and welfare, since low- and moderate-income households are forced to live in unsafe, unsanitary, overcrowded housing, and/or housing that they cannot afford. Thus, in the name of the public interest, inclusionary programs promote the development of community housing that would not otherwise be built. (8, p. 2)

Whether based on mandatory construction requirements or on development incentives such as density bonuses and expedited regulatory review procedures, all inclusionary programs contain the following elements:

- inclusionary requirements;
- income-eligibility criteria for defining affordability;
- provisions for in-lieu fees;
- pricing criteria for affordable units;
- restrictions on the resale and re-rental of affordable units; and
- miscellaneous provisions regarding on-site versus off-site construction requirements, transfer of excess affordable housing credits, and the like.

Mandatory Inclusionary Programs

Density Bonuses. In general, mandatory inclusionary zoning programs that do not grant density bonuses or provide other forms of financial assistance to developers either contain lower set-aside requirements than those that do and/or set more generous income limits for those eligible for assistance. Thus, for example, when Orange County, California's mandatory inclusionary program was first enacted (it has subsequently become voluntary), it required that 10 percent of all dwellings in subdivisions containing 30 or more units be made available to families whose incomes were equal to 80 percent or less of the county median (see Table 6.1). Density bonuses were only made available to developers who voluntarily agreed to provide more than the minimum 10 percent set-aside. Now that the program is voluntary and provides for density bonuses and other types of development

Table 6.1
Inclusionary Housing Programs

Place	Date	Type	Requirements
Santa Monica, CA	Late 1970's, case-by-case; 1986, formalized.	Mandatory	All residential development of three or more units must have 25% "inclusionary" units. "Low income" is no more than 120% of county median.
Orange County, CA	1979, Affordable Housing Program; 1983, Housing Opportunities Program.	Mandatory (phased out); now voluntary	Mandatory: Developers of 30 or more units that provide 10% low-income (80% or less of county median). Voluntary: 25% or more of new residential or rental to be affordable to households earning 120% or less of county median, with 10% to be low-income, 10% moderate-income group I, and 5% moderate-income group II. Projects signed off before 1983 must include a minimum of 25% affordable (between 80 and 120% of county median) in *all* new housing.
Arlington County, VA	1973, 10% bonus; 1981, increased to 15%.	Incentive	To acquire bonus, developer must provide low-income units. Developers must also provide for low-income housing in site-plan negotiation process.
Monroe County, FL	1986	Incentive	To earn bonuses, developers must fulfill housing need stated, e.g., low-income, employee, or affordable single-family.
Lee County, FL	1986 (No contracts yet)	Incentive	Developer can exceed standard density range for a particular land use category if low-income units are provided, or if cash is contributed to a low- and moderate-income housing fund.

Coverage	In-Lieu Fee	Density Bonus or Other Incentive(s)
Residential	$2.25 per sq. ft. for the first 15,000 sq. ft. of net rentable sq. footage; and $5.00 per sq. ft. for the remainder of the net rentable sq. footage.	–
Residential	Allowable to dedicate land or to write it down in an amount equal to value of excess credit from another project. (Deals with the transfer of vested affordable-unit credits.)	Developers voluntarily agreeing to provide more than 10% low-income units on a project would receive density bonuses and incentives.
Multifamily	None on record, but county "passive" approach would probably consider it.	Bonus of 15%, or additional height of up to six stories.
Multifamily, single-family, and employee housing (bonuses to employer who provides employee housing)	No	Tied into transfer of development rights program.
Multifamily and single-family	Yes	Bonus of 100%, 75%, or 50% to be received by developer, depending on number of criteria fulfilled.

(Table 6.1: Cont'd)

Place	Date	Type	Requirements
Sanibel, FL	1984	Incentive	Density limitations are relaxed for developers who agree to provide low-income units.
Princeton, NJ	1984	Mandatory	Subdivision and site-plan approval is contingent on compliance with affordable housing set-asides—at least 22% of the units in each development; noninclusionary residential is subject to development fee.
Cherry Hill, NJ	Adopted in 1973; amended in 1984 and 1986.	Mandatory	Set-aside of 20% of the total units (one-half for-sale, one-half rental), with noninclusionary residential subject to development fee.
Boulder, CO	1983	Mandatory	Set-aside of 10% of units within city limits; 15% of units in areas annexed.

assistance from the county, a much higher, 25 percent threshold must be met in order to trigger the benefits.

Similarly, while Boulder, Colorado's mandatory program contains no development incentives to minimize the financial impacts of its inclusionary housing program, its affordable housing requirements are relatively modest (either 10 percent or 15 percent of all units, depending upon when the project site was annexed). (7f) Also, Boulder's income limits are set quite high—between 80 percent and 120 percent of the city's median income.

In those ordinances that provide them, the magnitude of the density bonuses varies substantially. California's DHCD model ordinance provides that "any development that includes inclusionary units shall be entitled to a density bonus at least equal to the percentage of inclusionary units, or to other development incentives of equivalent financial values, if the density bonus is infeasible." (8, p. 7) In contrast, Lee County, Florida's inclusionary ordinance, which was enacted in January 1986, contains a more modest, variable density bonus for those developers who voluntarily set aside 10 percent of the proposed residential units for low-income families. The bonus ranges from four to eight dwell-

Coverage	In-Lieu Fee	Density Bonus or Other Incentive(s)
	Yes	Case-by-case consideration of projects.
Residential market zone; high-density residential zone	No	Built into zoning for inclusionary developments.
Multifamily	No	
Residential	No	Available for providing affordable units above the requirement.

ing units per acre, depending upon the existing land use classification of the project site, and upon how many of seven site-specific priority criteria the project meets.*

* The actual density bonus to which a developer is entitled in Lee County is determined by the degree to which he meets the following criteria, namely, that:

1) the project is located in a state-approved enterprise zone;
2) fifty percent or more of the bonus density units are set aside for low-income families:
3) at least 10 percent of the bonus units contain three bedrooms (for construction option only);
4) the project site has direct access to two or more public collectors or arterial streets;
5) the site has access to public water and sewer facilities;
6) the project is compatible with the density and intensity of surrounding land uses; and that
7) no part of the development site exhibits resource protection area or transitional zone area criteria.

The construction option must meet all seven criteria to earn the full density bonus. Developments opting for the in-lieu fee option must meet all criteria, except numbers 2 and 3, to be eligible for the maximum density bonus. (22a, pp. 8–9)

In-Lieu Fees. Inclusionary housing programs also vary significantly in their treatment of so-called in-lieu fees. These are cash contributions to a municipal housing fund that substitute for the developer's direct construction of low-income housing as part of an approved residential project. Boulder, for example, makes no provisions for in-lieu fees; all residential developments containing 10 or more units must set aside at least 10 percent of the units for moderate-income households. California's model code, on the other hand, does provide for in-lieu fees, but only for small residential developments wherein the city determines that the provision of inclusionary units will constitute an extreme hardship because of high development costs.

In still other cases, inclusionary zoning ordinances are structured to make in-lieu fees the preferred way for developers to meet their low- and moderate-income housing obligations. San Diego's affordable housing program sets total in-lieu fees at the greater of either a $10,000 payment for each required affordable unit, or a payment of 2 percent of the gross selling price of the entire project. For instance, for a 100-unit subdivision with house prices averaging $150,000, a 20 percent low-income set-aside requirement translates to a total in-lieu fee of $300,000 or of $3,000 per house.

Lee County's incentive program also provides for an in-lieu fee, the amount of which depends upon the number of dwelling units by which the developer desires to exceed the standard density range, up to the prescribed maximum. The in-lieu fee for each bonus unit is $6,000 for houses with a selling price of less than $100,000, and 10 percent of the selling price for houses with a price of more than $100,000. To assure payment of the in-lieu fee, "the building permit shall not be issued until the required contribution is paid in full, and, once it is made, no refunds are granted, even if the development in question fails to occur for any reason." (22a, p. 15) Thus, in Lee County, density bonuses for which in-lieu fees are paid run with the development order and not with the land.

Income Limits. As we indicated earlier, mandatory inclusionary zoning programs that contain no development incentives generally require smaller set-asides and are aimed at serving moderate- rather than low-income families via a lessening of their ordinances' financial burdens on developers. Thus, Boulder's affordable housing program serves moderate-income families whose incomes are between 80 percent and 120 percent of the city's median. Maximum sale prices of affordable units, which are adjusted as frequently as twice a year, are based on current mortgage terms. Specifically, these maximums reflect the maximum amount of money that a moderate-income household can afford to pay for a house and still qualify for a bank loan (assuming a 10 percent or 20 percent downpayment and current market interest rates). Permissible rental ranges for affordable apartments are based upon the amount of money a household earning the city's median income can pay without spending more than 28 percent of its gross income on rent.

Lee County's sale prices and rent limits are determined by the developer, provided that the monthly rent or mortgage payment shall not exceed 30 percent of the gross monthly incomes of the lessors or buyers, who must have incomes below 80 percent of the county median.

Resale Restrictions. In general, resale restrictions apply to affordable dwelling units produced under *all* inclusionary housing programs. In Lee County, resale restrictions apply for a period of 10 years from the issuance of the certificate of occupancy (C of O); they are enforced through a deed restriction prohibiting the transfer of an affordable unit to any other person than a low-income person who has never before owned a home. The income of the new buyer must meet the ordinance's low- or moderate-income limit, as specified at the time of sale. Thus, the resale prices of affordable housing units are set according to future income levels and mortgage terms.

Affordable rental units must remain affordable for a period of 10 years from the date when the permanent C of O was issued. However, in the case of affordable rental housing, developers must annually certify the continued income-eligibility of their low- or moderate-income tenants. Should the income of a low-income tenant increase above the levels established for continued occupancy, the developer is responsible for designating another unit in his project as a low- or moderate-income unit, in order to maintain the required level of affordable occupancy. It is administrative responsibilities like these that make paying an in-lieu fee a preferred alternative to meeting the costs of an inclusionary housing requirement.

Boulder's program also includes a 10-year resale restriction. The maximum resale price is determined according to the length of the initial ownership, the annual growth in household incomes in Boulder, and the value of the improvements made by the first owner. If, after six months of trying, a developer is unable to sell an affordable house because of the resale restrictions, he may petition the administering agency for the removal of those restrictions.

Affordable Housing Credits. Inclusionary ordinances also vary in their treatment of affordable housing credits, which are earned by dedicating a larger-than-required fraction of a housing development to low- or moderate-income families. Many ordinances, including Lee County's, do not permit developers to bank unused density credits for later use. Boulder prohibits the transfer of excess density credits to other developers, while allowing the developer who has earned them to transfer them to one or more of his other projects within five years of the date when they were initially earned. The law also limits the number of credits that can be banked to 25 housing units in any five-year period.

Orange County, California's original inclusionary zoning program provided that a developer who chose to build more than the required percentage of affordable units in a subdivision could sell his excess credits to another developer at whatever price the market would bear. The buyer of the credits would be able to use them to earn himself density bonuses for meeting affordable housing requirements, without actually having to build any affordable housing. Of course, the sale of excess density credits must result in neither a greater net dwelling density in a community, nor any fewer affordable housing units than would be built in the absence of such a provision. However, Orange County's transfers of credits do provide financial incentives for some developers to specialize in the development of affordable housing projects.

The Types of Linkage Programs

Linkage programs are designed to mitigate the adverse impacts of large-scale real estate projects by requiring either that developers directly provide affordable housing, job training, or related community services, or that they pay in-lieu fees as a condition for obtaining development approval. Thus, like their zoning counterparts, most linkage programs derive their legal authority from a community's power to regulate land use in order to promote the public interest and protect the general welfare.

Linkage programs are of essentially four types. They are either of a mandatory or of a "voluntary" nature, and they either impose just housing requirements on the developer or specify that a broader array of exaction requirements be met. Although the nation's two best-known linkage programs (in San Francisco and Boston) began as mandatory housing programs, both have recently been expanded to include mandatory in-lieu payments to help finance nonhousing facilities and services.

Mandatory Linkage Programs

As the preamble to San Francisco's Office Affordable Housing Production Program (OAHPP), originally called the Office of Housing Production Program (OHPP), states, "Large-scale office developments in the city and county of San Francisco have attracted and continue to attract additional employees to the city, and there is a causal connection between such developments and the need for additional housing in the city, particularly housing affordable to households of low and moderate income." (9, p. 251) By asserting that a rational nexus exists between new office developments and the rising demand for affordable housing, communities like San Francisco, Boston, Santa Monica, Palo Alto, and others, are successfully using the development approval process to trigger housing mitigation measures through linkage programs (see Tables 6.2–6.4). In San Francisco, linkage require-

Table 6.2
Sample Linkage Programs

Place	Date Enacted	Contributor
San Francisco	1980—Guidelines 1985—Ordinance	Downtown developer of new or substantially rehabilitated office buildings of over 50,000 square feet.
Boston	1983, 1986	Downtown and neighborhood development of office, hotel, retail, and institutional uses over 100,000 square feet.
	1986	Parcel-to-parcel linkage—same developer requirements as above. Program links the disposition of publicly owned downtown parcels with publicly owned parcels in the neighborhoods.
Santa Monica	1981, 1986	Office development/new construction over 15,000 square feet, or additions of 10,000 square feet.
Jersey City	1985	Any developer
Cambridge, MA	1985	Any developer
Seattle	1984	Developers of downtown office buildings
Miami	1983	Nonresidential developers
Hartford	1986	Any developer

Table 6.3
A Closer Look at the Sample Linkage Programs

Place	Type	Requirements	Results
San Francisco	Mandatory	Construction as rehabilitation, either directly, or in joint venture with a housing developer; or in-lieu fee contribution of $5.34 per net additional gross square foot, paid within three years.	Housing units in the amount of 4,975 have been assisted; 3,093 of these were new-construction projects. Twenty-seven million dollars in private contributions to housing have been generated.
Boston	Mandatory	Construction of units by developer or by contribution. Downtown: fee of $6.00 per square foot, paid over seven years; Neighborhood: $5.00 per square foot, over 12 years, to housing trust fund.	More than $35 million in housing contributions has been committed.
	Mandatory	Same as above	None to date
Santa Monica	Mandatory	In-lieu fees of $2.25 per square foot for first 15,000 square feet of net rentable square footage, and $5.00 per square foot for remainder. On-site or off-site development of units equal to in-lieu payment.	$300,000 has been committed, with another $100,000 in the pipeline.

Place	Type	Requirements	Results
Jersey City	Negotiated	Developers of retail and commercial projects are asked either to directly build or rehabilitate units, to participate in financing or sponsoring of affordable housing, or to contribute to a housing fund.	Currently, 250 units are under construction, and another 1,150 units are committed.
Cambridge, MA	Negotiated (Case-by-case)	Developers are asked to make contributions to the city's linkage fund, or to provide affordable units.	An amount of $700,000 has been contributed from two projects, and three units were provided from a 30-unit project. –
Seattle	Incentive for floor-to-area ratio (FAR) increases	Developers can exceed FAR limits by providing public amenities or housing under housing bonus or TDR programs.* FAR increases are earned by cash contributions or by actual construction of housing. The bonus values are $10.00 and $15.30 per square foot, depending on zone. Bonus ratios range from 3.0 to 7.6 (bonus square foot to housing square foot), depending on the income level served.	

Place	Type	Requirements	Results
Miami	Incentive for FAR increases	Fee of $4.00 or $6.67 per square foot of added space, or developer construction of 0.15 square feet of residential space per square foot of added non-residential.	Contribution of $200,000
Hartford	Mandatory for any publicly assisted projects in the city; incentive for FAR increases in the downtown district	Publicly assisted projects are required to meet construction employment criteria for Hartford residents, minorities, and female trades-workers. FAR bonuses are in return for special amenities, housing, employment requirements, or contribution of $5.00 per square foot of bonus area.	None to date

* Transfer-of-development-rights programs.

ments have been incorporated into the development-permit approval process, while in Boston, linkage payments are required as a condition for receiving approval of any deviation from the zoning map or text.

Since linkage programs require the establishment of a cause-and-effect relationship between new development and increased housing needs, exaction requirements or in-lieu fees should be set according to empirically based evidence of that relationship. Thus, for example, the initial version of San Francisco's linkage program based its housing requirements on the following empirical relationships, namely, that:

• forty percent of new office workers would seek housing in the city if it were available;
• a typical worker occupies 250 square feet of office space; and that

Table 6.4
Formulas for Linkage

Place	Formula
San Francisco	(Net Additional Gross Square Feet) × (0.000386) = Housing Requirement (Net Additional Gross Square Feet) × ($5.34) = In-Lieu Contribution
Santa Monica	(15,000 × $2.25) + (Sq. Ft. over 15,000 × $5.00) = In-Lieu Contribution
Seattle	(Per-Sq.-Ft. Bonus Value) × (Sq. Ft. of Bonus Floor Area) = Cash Value of Bonus Area ($10 or $15.30 per Sq. Ft.)
Miami	(Additional Sq. Ft. of Nonresidential) × (0.15) = Gross Sq. Ft. of Affordable Housing Required
Jersey City	$\dfrac{\text{Sq. Ft. of Office Space} - 100,000}{250} \times \dfrac{(0.30 \times 0.42)}{1.09}$ = Number of Affordable Units Required 250 = Square Feet/New Employee 0.30 = Percent of Workforce in Commercial Employment 0.42 = Percent of City Residents Employed in City 1.09 = Number of Adults per Household Employed Full-Time
Princeton, NJ	$\left(\dfrac{\text{Gross Floor Area (GFA)}}{\text{GFA per Job Created}} \times 0.775 \times 0.219 \times 0.25\right)$ × $20,000 = Affordable Housing Contribution 250 = GFA per Job (Office) 0.775 = Households per Employee 0.220 = Percent of Job-Linked Lower-Income Households 0.250 = Nonresidential Developer Obligation

- the average residential unit contains 1.8 employed adults. (34a, p. 40)

San Francisco first adopted the Office of Housing Production Program (OHPP) as a policy in 1981. The OHPP provided linkage guidelines for new commercial projects exceeding 50,000 square feet and located in the central business district (CBD). Developers could satisfy their housing requirements in one or more of three ways: 1) by directly constructing units or restoring them; 2) by contracting with a housing developer and providing financial aid; or 3) by paying an in-lieu fee of $6,000 per unit to the city's home mortgage assistance trust fund. Criticisms arose of the effectiveness of the OHPP, pinpointing its lack of clear-cut evidence that downtown development exacerbates housing problems, and indicating that relatively little housing that has been produced under the program has been affordable to low-income families. In response, San Francisco enacted legislation in August 1985 that fine-tuned the program.

Under the new OAHPP, downtown office developers still have three ways of meeting their linkage housing obligations. Now, they can either 1) construct housing directly or participate in a joint venture to help finance it, at a rate of 0.386 units of new housing for every 1,000 square feet of office development (9, p. 252)*; 2) pay an in-lieu fee of $5.34 for each square foot of new office space**; or 3) meet their housing requirement through a mix of direct construction and payment. If a developer chooses the third option, the in-lieu fee for each housing unit that is not constructed is set at $13,834.20. Finally, 62 percent of all units produced by a developer must be reserved for households with incomes less than 120 percent of the regional median. Since 1981, San Francisco's linkage program has generated commitments for nearly 3,800 housing units—2,700 of which are low- and moderate-income units (71 percent), and 1,100 of which are market-rate units (29 percent). (21a, p. 102)

Boston's mandatory linkage program, as originally created in 1983 and as revised in January 1986, differs from San Francisco's in at least six ways. (2c) First, Boston's exemption level is higher than San Francisco's. The first 100,000 square feet of all assessable projects, and all projects *under* that size in Boston are exempt from linkage requirements.

Second, Boston's linkage program is broader in coverage than San Francisco's, which is limited to new office buildings.*** Boston imposes linkage requirements on all large-scale commercial real estate developments, including retail businesses and

---

   * The parameters for the direct-production option are "based on a report commissioned by the city that concluded that the impact of downtown development on the city's housing market would be mitigated if 0.386 units of new housing were built for every 1,000 square feet of office space. The report was prepared by Recht Hausrath & Associates and entitled *Summary of Economic Basis for an Office Housing Production Program* (July 18, 1984). (41, p. 3)

  ** San Francisco's affordable linkage ordinance states that studies determined "that the cost of providing affordable housing to persons attracted to large office developments is $9.47–$10.47 per square foot. However, in recognition of the numerous assumptions that were made, and hence of the potential inexactness of the final calculation, the city has selected the conservative figure of $5.34 per square foot as the cost."

*** San Francisco's program exempts all retail businesses, federal and state government office buildings, and office developments built on San Francisco Redevelopment Authority land.

institutional, educational, and hotel projects, as well as office buildings.

Third, Boston dispenses with the direct-production option of meeting linkage requirements, levying instead a fee of $5.00 per square foot for every square foot of new space above 100,000 square feet.

Fourth, Boston permits developers of downtown projects to make their payments over a seven-year period, beginning with the issuance of a building permit. (Projects in neighborhoods have 12 years.) In contrast, San Francisco requires that all linkage requirements be met before a final certificate of occupancy will be issued.

Fifth, Boston's linkage program contains a housing set-aside for the specific neighborhood that a new development affects. Ten percent of the payments made on behalf of any given downtown project, and 20 percent of the payments made on behalf of an assessable project built outside of the downtown area are targeted to those neighborhoods that the projects impinge on most seriously.

Sixth—although San Francisco's linkage program has been expanded recently to require payments to support child-care facilities, transit improvements, and the arts—Boston is the first city in the United States to incorporate a fee for job training into its zoning regulations and linkage program. Boston's job-training linkage requirement is $1.00 per square foot over 100,000 square feet of new or substantially rehabilitated commercial space. (41, p. 4)* In contrast to the housing linkage fee, the job training fee is collected in two annual installments, beginning with the issuance of the building permit.

In a continuing effort to connect the booming vitality of its downtown economy with the needs of its neighborhoods, Boston has recently added a new wrinkle to its linkage program. The city's new land disposition policy, referred to as parcel-to-parcel linkage, connects the disposition of prime, publicly owned downtown sites to less valuable neighborhood-surplus land parcels. By requiring developers who wish to acquire the development rights to prime sites to formulate a strong and feasible redevelopment plan for one of the city's long-neglected neighborhood sites, in tandem with neighborhood interests, the city hopes to "create

---

* The job-training linkage fee is based on the finding that Boston residents are losing Boston jobs to suburbanites. In 1950, for example, Boston residents held 54 percent of all Boston jobs; in 1970, 37 percent; and in 1985, just 31 percent.

opportunities for those who have been excluded from the development economy to become equity partners, owners of major community development." (32b, p. 5)

In addition to mandatory formula-based programs, there are voluntary incentive-based linkage programs, as well as less formal ones in which developers' obligations are negotiated as part of the development approval process. Miami's linkage program is a good example of an incentive-based program, while those in Hartford, Jersey City, and Honolulu are typical of negotiated programs.

Less Formal Linkage Programs

Miami's incentive-based linkage program is the outgrowth of a negotiated agreement between the city and the development community, concerning the housing-market impacts of office development on neighborhoods adjacent to its expanding central business district (CBD). Miami's linkage ordinance provides developers with a density bonus in the form of a higher maximum permissible floor/area ratio (FAR) for office buildings constructed in two "special-interest" districts, in exchange for the direct provision of low- and moderate-income housing, or in exchange for payment of an in-lieu fee. The ordinance provides developers with a choice of building housing or contributing to the city's housing trust fund, as follows: (25b, pp. 15–26)

SPI-5 District. The floor/area ratio may be increased for any permitted use, up to a total increase in FAR of 1.0, provided that for every one square foot of FAR increase, there shall be either;

- A nonrefundable developer contribution of $4.00 to the city of Miami's affordable housing fund; or
- Developer-sponsored construction of 0.15 gross square feet of affordable housing, defined as sales housing with a retail sales price not in excess of 90 percent of the gross median new-housing sales price in Dade County, or rental rates (project average) not in excess of 30 percent of the gross median monthly income in Dade County.

SPI-7 District. For residential uses, the floor/area ratio shall be increased according to either of the following alternatives. (However, in no case shall the increase in nonresidential floor area exceed 2.75 times the gross land area.) These are the two alternatives:

- For every one square foot of residential floor area provided on-site, the maximum nonresidential floor area shall be increased by one square foot. Such residential floor area shall be constructed concurrently with any uses receiving this bonus.

- For every $6.67 contributed to an affordable housing fund established and administered by the city of Miami, an increase of one square foot of nonresidential floor area shall be permitted. All funds so contributed shall be expended solely within the SPI-7 district.

Although they are somewhat more flexible than other programs, negotiated linkage programs are in fact not much more voluntary than are mandatory ones. This is also true for negotiated programs that are in ordinance form, as well as for those that, though lacking the force of law, are incorporated into the operating policies of those agencies responsible for the development review process.

Jersey City's negotiated program provides developers of large commercial projects with three ways in which to meet linkage requirements. They may build or rehabilitate low- and moderate-income housing themselves, preferably on-site; they may participate in the financing or sponsorship of affordable housing elsewhere in Jersey City; or they may make payments to a housing development trust fund. As with housing requirements in Boston, San Francisco, and elsewhere, housing requirements in the linkage program of Jersey City are based on the incremental housing demand that new office space generates, according to these assumptions: (41, p. 4)

- Each 250 square feet of rental space generates one new employee;
- Thirty percent of Jersey City's workforce is employed in commercial and office occupations;
- Forty-two percent of Jersey City's residents are employed in Jersey City; and
- The average household contains 1.09 working adults.

The above assumptions translate into a housing need of one affordable unit for each 2,200 square feet of office space in excess of 100,000 square feet.*

In contrast to those of some other linkage programs, Jersey City's negotiations process is geared toward making the housing construction option more attractive to developers than the option

---

* Using the above assumptions, the housing requirement for a 200,000-square-foot office building is 46 units—which translates to a ratio of one housing unit for each 2,173 square feet of new office space in excess of 100,000 square feet (22a):

$$\frac{200,000-100,000}{250} \times \frac{(0.30)(0.42)}{1.09} = 46 \text{ housing units}$$

of paying the in-lieu fee. Not only is the city willing to reduce the housing unit requirement for those developers who are willing to build affordable housing, but it also facilitates production by waiving certain development fees, making available vacant city-owned land and buildings; and arranging tax-exempt financing from the New Jersey Housing and Mortgage Finance Agency; funds for these loans have been set aside by the state, in accordance with the Mount Laurel rulings.

Hartford's experience with the linkage concept began in 1983. In June 1986—after three years of community discussion, task force reports, and legal opinions on its legality, and in the absence of explicit state authority to do so—the Hartford City Council defeated a linkage ordinance similar to San Francisco's. That ordinance would have imposed an in-lieu fee of $1.90 on every square foot of new office space built in the city. While defeating that ordinance, the council did enact an ordinance creating a linkage trust fund for the purpose of providing funds for job training, housing, and economic-development assistance.

The linkage ordinance also established employment requirements for "publicly assisted projects," a term that is broadly defined as projects receiving tax abatements or Industrial Development Bonds (IDBs), using public land, and the like. All such projects are required to meet minimum construction employment criteria for resident Hartford tradesworkers (40 percent), minority tradesworkers (25 percent), and female tradesworkers (6.9 percent). Failure to meet these construction labor requirements will cause all public assistance to the project to be terminated, and require the developer to pay $10,000 for each job below the minimum to which he committed. (32c, p. 7)

Like Miami's ordinance, Hartford's linkage ordinance provides for bonus floor space for certain proposed uses, in return for the construction of housing, pedestrian-centered retail uses, transient parking, and cultural, entertainment, and daycare facilities. Floor area bonuses are also provided, in exchange for developer-instituted job training and employment programs for Hartford residents. Employment-related bonus floor area agreements require that Hartford residents be employed in 25 percent of the total permanent jobs, and that each job above this amount is worth an additional 625 square feet of bonus floor area, up to a maximum FAR of 6.0.

In lieu of meeting the employment requirements or providing an eligible bonus use, developers may contribute $5.00 per square foot to the linkage trust fund for each square foot of bonus area.

Honolulu's negotiated linkage program closely resembles the broad-based impact or capital-recovery fee systems that have been implemented in many rapidly growing communities to help finance their expanding infrastructure needs. For the past several years, through the rezoning mechanism, the city and county of Honolulu have been negotiating affordable housing agreements with developers that have required 10 percent of the residential units in a development to be set aside for households with incomes of less than 80 percent of the area median. Approximately 1,000 units of affordable housing have been produced in Honolulu under this system.

Because negotiated linkage agreements triggered by rezonings treat similar projects differently (depending upon whether a rezoning is necessary) and different projects similarly (as long as they require rezoning, they are hit with a linkage obligation), the lack of fairness in this system has raised serious controversy. To bring more order, predictability, and consistency to the practice of negotiated linkage agreements, Honolulu has introduced the concept of community benefit assessments (CBAs) to its land development regulations. (32d, p. 7) Linked to all rezonings of land for more intensive uses, the CBA is based on the rational-nexus concept, namely, that new development above and beyond that permitted by current zoning uses imposes additional capital costs upon the community, and that the developer should pay for these. While the rezoning of land to a higher use will permit development to take place that will expand the tax base beyond the rate that would otherwise occur, the negotiated CBA is intended to compensate the community for the lag between the time when the additional tax revenues from the additional growth are realized and the time when the upfront capital costs that new development requires are incurred.

The applicable community benefit assessment is determined by a formula that includes such factors as the land area to be developed, the difference in densities between the new and former zoning classes, a location factor, and a cost factor, which is adjusted annually according to changes in the Honolulu consumer price index. The CBA sets the developer's maximum financial obligation to the community under the linkage program. This is how the program has added predictability and certainty to the system.

Negotiations still play a major role, however, in that a developer can significantly reduce his financial obligations through the direct provision of various facilities to the community in lieu of paying the full CBA. Each affordable housing unit, for example, reduces a CBA by $10,000, and by an additional $5,000 if the developer will keep the unit affordable for 20 years instead of 10 years. Other credits against the CBA can be earned by providing oversized infrastructure, child care facilities, police and fire stations needed to serve the new developments, and so forth.

Linkage Payments as Impact Fees: Cherry Hill, New Jersey

Under state enabling legislation spurred by the New Jersey Supreme Court's landmark Mount Laurel decisions, several New Jersey communities have combined inclusionary zoning and mandatory linkage programs into comprehensive affordable housing programs. Cherry Hill's ordinance, which was enacted in July 1986, is characteristic of these comprehensive programs. For residential projects requiring major subdivision approvals, developers must pay a housing impact fee equal to 1.5 percent of the square footage of the project, multiplied by the median price per square foot for new housing in the Northeast region as published annually by the U.S. Bureau of the Census. (7a, p. 1)

For nonresidential projects, Cherry Hill's housing impact fee is the greater of 3 percent of construction cost (as stated on the construction permit application) or $1.00 per square foot of building area. Whereas residential developers must pay their impact fees before the issuance of a building permit, nonresidential developers can pay their fees in equal installments beginning with the issuance of a building permit.

To encourage the construction of affordable housing in Cherry Hill, the impact-fee ordinance exempts 1) any housing unit that is part of an inclusionary housing development that already requires a set-aside for modest-priced housing, or 2) any unit of detached housing of less than 1,500 square feet in size that is sold for a price not exceeding the median square-foot price for housing in the Northeast region. Similar exemptions apply to nonresidential projects that are part of mixed-use developments that already contain a set-aside of modest-priced housing.

Housing impact fees are placed in an escrow account, to be used at the township's discretion for the "sole purpose of aiding in the provision or rehabilitation of modest-income housing." (7a, p. 2)

Princeton's Affordable Housing Program

In addition to helping assure that developments that create additional affordable housing demand will share in the burden of expanding the supply, Princeton, New Jersey's affordable housing ordinance has broader objectives:

[to] provide housing opportunities for lower-income families, in order to meet the existing and anticipated housing needs of such persons; to maintain a socioeconomic mix in the community; to provide a range of housing types dispersed throughout the community in a suitable living environment; to satisfy the community's obligation to provide a fair share of the region's housing needs; and . . . to provide for housing opportunities for those who work in Princeton and who provide the community with essential services but who cannot currently afford to live in the community. (32e, Section 10B—p. 332)

Its broader social purposes are reflected in the ordinance's more comprehensive nature, which combines inclusionary zoning, impact fees, and linkage requirements while providing a more active, entrepreneurial development role for the township itself. To accomplish these goals, Princeton's affordable housing ordinance, which was enacted in November 1984, created two new higher-density zoning districts to encourage the development of affordable housing. Next, it instituted a set of fees for developers whose projects are not located in either of these new use districts, and created two new entities to set operating policies and to administer the program.

The Princeton ordinance created a residential market program district (RM) in the township zoning code. The RM district provides for medium-density (for Princeton) residential uses, to be developed at 3.25 units per acre. In the RM district, subdivision and site-plan approvals are conditional on the developer complying with affordable housing set-aside requirements. At least 22 percent of the units in each RM development must be sold or rented at prices qualifying the units as lower-income ones—which means they must be affordable to families with incomes not exceeding 80 percent of the area median. The set-aside requirement is justified on the basis that RM densities are higher than those permitted in other zoning districts, which are generally no higher than two units per acre.

The ordinance also created an even higher-density zone (RH) which would permit residential densities up to 12 units per acre. The RH zone is an overlay zone that permits land to be used more intensively only if the township is the developer or co-developer of the site, and only if at least half of the site is being developed for affordable housing. The combination of the density bonus with the strong demand for market-rate (high-price) housing in Princeton allows profits from the market-rate portion of an RH development to help underwrite or cross-subsidize the lower-income housing portion of the project.

Earlier, we referred to Princeton's affordable housing program as more comprehensive than most others. An element of its broader base is its requirement that developers of all residential projects outside of RM or RH zones pay a housing impact fee based on the square footage of the housing they build. In addition, most nonresidential developers must also pay an impact, or formula-based linkage, fee.

For residential development, the impact fee ranges from a low of $0.25 per square foot for housing units containing less than 1,000 square feet, to a high of $749.75 plus $0.75 per square foot for each square foot over 1,999 for larger houses. This progressive rate structure means a fee of $250 for a 1,000-square-foot house, and a fee of $1,125 for a 2,500-square-foot unit.

The housing impact fee for nonresidential developers is determined by a now-familiar type of formula—which takes into account the square footage of the planned improvements; the gross floor area per job created for different nonresidential uses; the number of employed persons per household; the share of the housing demand created by new development for which non-residential developers should pay; and the unit cost of low-income housing.*

Princeton's affordable housing ordinance also sets up two new entities to administer the program: 1) the Princeton Township Housing Board is the policy-making body that ordains the operating rules for the program; and 2) the Princeton Township Housing Fund, whose members are appointed by the housing board, is a separate corporate entity that is the entrepreneurial arm of the program. The housing fund acts as developer or co-developer of mixed affordable/market-rate housing developments

---

* The linkage formula is:

$$\frac{GFA}{GFA/J} \times 0.775 \times 0.22 \times 0.25 \times \$20,000$$

where: 1) GFA/J = gross floor area per job created, according to use:

Office, including banks, savings and loans, etc.	250
Research, laboratory, and education, other than part(s) of a nonprofit organization	500
Retail, commercial, hotel/motel, light industry	600
Warehouse/storage, parking garages	1,000
Nonprofit institutions	5,000

2) 0.775 = percentage of households per jobholder;
3) 0.22 = percentage of job-linked lower-income households;
4) 0.25 = nonresidential developer obligations; and
5) $20,000 = average cost of creating a low-income housing unit.

Under this formula, the linkage fee for a 100,000-square-foot office complex is:

$$\frac{100,000}{250} \times 0.775 \times 0.22 \times 0.25 \times \$20,000 = \$341,000,\ \text{or }\$3.41\text{ per square foot.}$$

(32e, Section 10B—p. 340)

in high-density RH zones. Since its inception, the housing fund has codeveloped one 280-unit residential project that contains 140 units of affordable housing. So far, six tracts of land have been zoned RH.

Among the operating policies that are set by Princeton's housing board are those relating: to the definition of low and moderate income*; to the rental and resale restrictions that will maintain the affordable nature of housing over the longer term; to the conditions under which developers who build in RM zones may satisfy some or all of their affordable housing obligations off-site; and to the share of affordable housing units that must be designed for and marketed to families, rather than to elderly households.

The Future of the Inclusionary Concept

In a recent assessment of the likely future of linkage programs, Dennis Keating argues that it is not likely that linkage programs will be adopted by most central cities because "most cities lack the characteristics of the cities that have adopted linkage policies." (22, p. 134) Among those characteristics are:

- Significant and enduring downtown development booms;
- Civic leaders who perceive that such booms cause or exacerbate problems related to the supply of low-income housing;
- State-imposed limitations on ad valorem taxes that restrict the ability of cities with downtown development booms to raise revenues from new development; and
- The political support of progressive political slates, and of candidates backed by neighborhood organizations that oppose prevailing downtown development policies.

To be added to Keating's list of reasons why linkage policies might not be widely exportable to other cities is the tandem team of tax reform, coupled with the unprecedented national boom in office development that has been underway since the mid-1970s and that now seems to have largely run its course. By eliminating significant tax preferences for real estate development, tax reform means that in the future, linkage payments will have to come out of cash flow, and thus will be more likely than in the past to become significant factors in the financial feasibility of nonresidential developments. This means that organized resistance to linkage within the development community will intensify.

---

*Low = 0 to 50 percent of the area median; moderate = 50 to 80 percent of the area median.

The waning of the office construction boom presents an even more compelling reason why the popularity of linkage policies might have crested. A recent study by MIT's David Birch indicates that, of all primary office space in the United States, more than one-third—about 1.3 billion square feet—has been built since 1975. (18, p. 7) With the national office vacancy rate currently at 16 percent, giving credence to Birch's finding that "one of five office buildings constructed in the last decade was not needed," it is unlikely that office development booms will characterize downtown and suburban real estate markets over the next 10 years to the same extent as they did over the past 10 years. According to Birch, the combination of excess office space with the slowdown in new job growth means that the nation will need only about half as much new office space between now and 1995 than was built from 1975 to 1985.

The glut of unused office space will not only discourage cities without linkage programs from adopting them, but also significantly reduce the revenue potential of linkage programs that are already in place. This latter probability is reflected in Birch's estimate that over the next 10 years, for example, Boston will need only 60 percent, and San Francisco only 38 percent, as much new office space as was built in their respective cities over the last 10 years. The ratio of office space required in the 10 years between 1985 and 1995 to that built between 1975 and 1985 in most other major cities is no more favorable to linkage: 0.41 in Miami/Fort Lauderdale; 0.38 in Austin; 0.44 in Dallas/Fort Worth; 0.33 in San Diego; and 0.22 in Houston. (18, p. 7) According to Birch, only two of the nation's 20 largest cities—New York and Washington, D.C.—will have a need for more new office space over the next decade than was built over the past decade.

Future downtown development conditions might indeed militate against the adoption of stand-alone linkage programs in major centers currently without them. But with the continued reliance on linkage revenues to finance affordable housing programs in communities that already have them, it would be a mistake to conclude that impact fee–type programs for affordable housing will fade from the scene. Quite the contrary. In our judgment, the changing state of downtown real estate markets suggests that local affordable-housing programs are likely to become more comprehensive in nature, to spread the financial burden more broadly. This means expanding these programs' financial bases to include assessments and housing production requirements made of all forms of development, as has been done in Princeton.

Chapter 7
The Potential Effects of Tax Reform on Low-Income Housing

As we have implied throughout this monograph, the Tax Reform Act of 1986 is certain to have profound effects on the real estate sector. According to Michael Lea—"Freddie Mac" 's chief economist—although the net effect of tax reform will be to increase housing affordability over the longer term, the short-run effects will not be as positive because:

> the combination of lower marginal tax rates with increases in the standard deduction and with reductions in nonhousing interest deductions will reduce the value of tax breaks for individual homeowners. Abstracting from other changes, homeownership costs will rise for all but the lowest-income groups, with upper-income households experiencing sizable increases. In the short run, this may depress housing demand and property values, and could result in a modest first-year reduction in single-family housing starts. (19, p. 2)

The combination of lower marginal rates, lengthened depreciable lives for real estate assets, the repeal of accelerated depreciation, and the elimination of favored capital-gains tax rates is also expected to curtail short-term investment in new rental housing (see Table 7.1). According to the National Apartment Association, for example, "Rents would have to be 22 percent higher than current levels to compensate investors for lost tax benefits in order to justify new apartment construction." (6i, p. 318) The

National Association of Home Builders (NAHB) suggests that because of tax reform, "rents may rise by 15 to 20 percent more than would normally be expected to occur over the next five years." (6i, p. 318)

Table 7.1
Highlights of The Tax Reform Act of 1986*

	Previous	New Law
Capital Gains	Maximum effective rate of 20%.	Taxed as ordinary income; maximum rate of 28%.
Depreciation	Nonresidential: 19 years; 175% declining balance.	Straight line; 31.5 years.
	Residential: 19 years; 175% declining balance.	Straight line; 27.5 years.
	Low-income housing: 15 years; 200% declining balance.	Straight line; 27.5 years.
Construction-Period Interest and Taxes for Low-Income Housing	Expensed fully during construction period.	Included in depreciable base.
Expensing of Rehabilitation Costs (167(k))	Option of amortizing rehabilitation costs over five years.	Repealed.
Historic Properties/ Older Buildings Tax Credit	Credit for historic properties, 25%. Buildings older than 30 years, 15%. Buildings older than 40 years, 10%.	Tax credit for historic properties, 20%. Credit for buildings built before 1935, 10%.
Passive Losses	Deductible against other income, as well as against investment income.	Cannot be deducted from other income. Investors earning under $100,000 can use up to $25,000 in passive losses from rental activities in which they materially participate, to offset other income. Has been phased out for incomes between $100,000 and $150,000.

	Previous	New Law
Low-Income Housing Tax Credit	None.	Ten-year credit on expenditures for new construction and rehabilitation for each qualifying low-income unit with a present value equal to 70% of the qualifying expenditures. Size of the annual credit is fixed at the time the project is placed in service. For 1987, the annual credit is 9% per year for 10 years. Credit is reduced to a total present value of 30% of the qualifying expenditures (4% per year for 10 years if placed in service in 1987) for projects financed by tax-exempt bonds or low-interest federal loans. This lower tax credit also applies to acquisition of existing low-income housing.

Credits can be applied against taxes due on up to $25,000 of other income; deduction phased out as income of investor increases from $200,000 to $250,000. Volume limitation for credit of $1.25 per capita in each state; projects involving tax-exempt bonds do not apply against volume cap. Qualifying projects must reserve 20% of units for persons below 50% of median income, or 40% for persons below 60% of median income, adjusted for family size.

	Previous	**New Law**
Individual Rates	Fourteen rate brackets, from 11% to 50%.	In 1987, five brackets from 11% to 38.5%. In 1988, two brackets of 15% (up to $29,750) and 28%. Lower rate and personal exemption phased out for incomes above $71,900 on joint returns, producing effective top rate of 33%.
Corporate Rates	Maximum rate of 46%.	Maximum rate of 34%.
Alternative Minimum Tax (amount)	Amount of 15% for corporations and 20% for individuals, with certain tax preferences included as income in calculating amount.	Strengthened AMT of 21% for individuals and corporations with expanded list of tax preferences included as income. Interest on IDBs included as a tax preference for first time.

TAX-EXEMPT BONDS

Governmental Public-Purpose	Tax-exempt if no more than 25% of proceeds is used in trade or business, and if repayment is secured by trade or business.	Tax-exempt if no more than 10% of proceeds or $15 million is used in trade or business, and if repayment is secured by trade or business.
Volume Cap	Separate volume caps for single-family housing and most IDBs; no volume cap for TIF and multifamily housing.	Single- and multifamily housing, TIF, student loans, and most IDBs under a single-state volume cap of the greater of $75 per capita or $250 million. Cap declines to $50 per capita or $150 million in 1988.
Multifamily Housing	Tax-exempt IDB; targeted to low- and moderate-income; no volume cap.	Tax-exempt IDB; tighter targeting (20% units for persons below 50% median, or 40% for persons below 60%); subject to single-state volume cap.

(Table 7.1: Cont'd.)

	Previous	New Law
Single-Family Housing	Tax-exempt IDB; purchase price limits; separate volume cap; sunset December 31, 1986.	Tax-exempt IDB; tightened purchase price limits of 90% of average; purchase income limits of 115% of median income; subject to single-state volume cap; sunset extended to December 31, 1988.
Tax Increment Financing	Tax-exempt public-purpose government bonds; no volume cap.	Tax-exempt IDB, if redevelopment area meets certain requirements; limitations on eligible uses; subject to single-state volume cap.

* See text for details.

Above-average rent increases will certainly be necessary to compensate for lost tax preferences, although local market conditions may not permit suppliers to recoup their lost tax preferences all at once. Thus, we can expect after-tax returns on rental investments to decline as a result of tax reform, as will new starts, until market conditions stabilize at higher rent levels. NAHB, for example, predicts that "new construction of multifamily rental housing will drop 250,000 to 300,000 units in the first year after the bill's passage," while the National Multihousing Council's equally pessimistic forecast is for "rental production to fall to one-third to one-half of the 1985 level of 656,000 units." (6i, p. 318)

Some analysts expect further curtailment in the rental housing supply because the elimination of preferential treatment of capital gains could encourage the conversion of existing apartment buildings into condominiums. This could well happen because owners will now be able to convert directly, rather than having to sell properties to an intermediary. With the value of real estate as a tax shelter diminished, market prices for rental housing should decline, although "the impact should be minimal on profitable existing properties, which should even increase in value as rents rise." (6i, p. 318)

Despite short-term problems, however, economists generally agree that tax reform will benefit housing over the longer term:

Because rents may increase more than the after-tax costs of homeownership, for moderate- and middle-income households, homeownership rates may rise. Falling interest rates—a byproduct of tax reform—will also increase the affordability of owning a home.

The increase in rents may also ultimately improve the cash flow on existing properties. Thus, in most areas, soundly underwritten properties generating a positive before-tax cash flow will be better off. . . . (19, p. 2)

Even though the long-term impacts of tax reform on rental housing may generally turn out to be less negative than many industry experts anticipate, or may even be positive, the same cannot be said of the private production of low- and moderate-income housing, which is sure to slow down. This is because the new bill eliminates virtually all tax preferences for low-income housing (including a shorter depreciable life, a more accelerated depreciation schedule, more liberal recapture rules, and a more rapid amortization of rehabilitation costs). Until now, these preferences have permitted wealthy investors to write off substantial "losses" against other income. New passive-loss limitations also make infeasible the deep tax-shelter housing investments that have been the "bread and butter" of the low-income housing syndication industry.

Housing advocates have successfully lobbied the Congress for a new low-income housing tax credit that is better targeted than the host of tax preferences it replaces. But without a substantial financial commitment of state and local governments toward the subsidization of privately sponsored projects, investors might not find the new tax credit very attractive. This is partly because of targeting and other conditions attached to the use of the credits, which were themselves advocated by the low-income housing community. It is also partly because tax reform will make it more difficult in the future to finance low-income housing with tax-exempt bonds. Thus, in a kind of pincer movement that may not have been wholly intended by Congress, the Tax Reform Act hits low-income housing on both the debt and equity sides. For this reason, future levels of production are much less certain, and the cost of raising capital for low-income housing is higher than it was in the past.

We discuss the tax reform law's specific treatment of low-income housing in the next section, and follow that up with an analysis of the relevant changes in the tax code's treatment of tax-exempt housing bonds. We conclude with an assessment of how we expect tax reform to affect the low-income housing activities of state and local governments, and include a discussion of why the corporate sector is well positioned to pick up some of the slack left by wealthy individuals who can no longer take advantage of deep tax-shelter syndication opportunities.

The Low-Income Housing Provisions of the New Law

The Passive Loss Rules

Prior to tax reform, the law placed no limitations on the ability of a taxpayer to use deductions from one business activity to offset income from other activities. Under the new law, passive (or tax) losses from housing and other investments are deductible only against passive income from the same activities, and not against a taxpayer's nonpassive income from salaries, wages, dividends, and interest:

> Losses and credits disallowed are carried forward and treated as deductions and credits from passive trade or business activities in the next year. Any remaining losses are allowed in full when the taxpayer disposes of his entire interest in the activity.* (6)

A taxpayer with an adjusted income of $100,000 or less, however, can offset up to $25,000 of nonpassive income with passive losses from rental real estate activities in which he or she actively participates. The $25,000 allowance is phased out between $100,000 and $150,000 of adjusted gross income. Under the new law, however, a limited partnership is defined as a passive business activity in which the taxpayer does not actively participate, so that a limited partner's share of the partnership's tax losses are not deductible from other income. This is not entirely true in the case of the new low-income tax credit, which we discuss below.

The Low-Income Housing Tax Credit

Previous law provided tax incentives for low-income housing, in the form of accelerated depreciation rates, shorter useful lives, five-year amortization of rehabilitation expenses, and a full write-off of construction-period interest and taxes during the construction period. The Tax Reform Act replaces these incentives with a new, highly targeted tax credit, for dwelling units with rents that remain affordable to low-income families for at least 15 years, that can take the following values:

● Nine percent each year for 10 years on expenditures for new construction or rehabilitation of each qualifying low-income unit. This credit rate is equivalent to a credit with a present value of 70 percent. Rehabilitation or construction expenditures

---

* Unless otherwise noted, substantive details of the Act are quoted from Brownstein, Zeidman, and Schower (6).

must exceed $2,000 a unit within a 24-month period to qualify for this credit.

- Four percent each year for 10 years for expenditures for new low-income housing construction and rehabilitation financed with tax-exempt bonds or similar federal subsidies. The 4 percent credit rate is equivalent to a credit with a present value of 30 percent.*
- Four percent each year for 10 years on the cost of acquiring existing low-income housing units, including minor rehabilitation projects costing up to $2,000 a unit. A project must have last been placed in service at least 10 years before, in order to qualify for this credit.**

There is no rehabilitation requirement associated with the acquisition tax credit, nor does a qualifying low-income unit have to change hands for the owner to be eligible for the 9 percent rehabilitation tax credit. The rehabilitation tax credit may also be taken on a building that qualifies for the acquisition credit. Finally, the tax credit for the rehabilitation of historic properties may also be taken on a building that qualifies for the low-income acquisition and rehabilitation tax credits as well. In the case of historic preservation, the 20 percent tax credit is taken in the current tax year, while the low-income housing tax credit is applied to the remaining 80 percent of eligible costs and taken at a rate of 9 percent a year. Because more than one tax credit cannot be taken against the same investment outlay, and because some credits must be taken against taxes due on passive income, while others can be used to partially offset taxes due on ordinary income, piggybacking of tax credits under the new law will be a very tricky business.

How the receipt of federal subsidies affects the size of eligible tax credits is also quite complicated. In general, the 9 percent tax credit cannot be used when federal subsidies, in the form of below-market interest-rate loans or grants, are involved in the construction or rehabilitation of a low-income housing project. Such projects would qualify for the 4 percent tax credit. However, the law offers owners of a property receiving a federal subsidy the "option of treating the subsidy amount as if it were a

---

* For buildings placed in service after 1987, the percentages applied to the tax credits will be adjusted by the treasury department to reflect the present values, that is, 70 and 30 percent of the values current at the time the building was placed in service.
** The federal government can waive the 10-year rule in the case of distressed federally-assisted housing projects.

federal grant, and deducting the amount of the subsidy from the qualified losses or costs against which the amount of the [9 percent] credit is calculated." (20, p. 6)

In contrast to most of its predecessors, the new low-income housing tax credit is highly targeted, in that it applies on a unit-by-unit basis and not to an entire property. According to the National Low-Income Housing Coalition, which fought hard for this cost-effective low-income housing subsidy:

> this is a major and fundamental difference from depreciation programs in [past] law, which applied to the entire property once a minimum targeting threshold had been reached. The tax credits provide a major incentive to include *more* low-income units in a property, since each additional unit offers investors an additional subsidy. Properties that exceed thresholds generate credits for investors on all the units occupied by eligible tenants. (23, p. 2)

Significantly, the new law treats low-income housing tax credits as if they were derived from property in which the owner actively participated, which means that up to $25,000 in deductions—or what the conference committee's report refers to as credit-equivalent losses—can be applied against taxes due on income from nonpassive activities.[*]

This translates into a maximum tax shelter to the investor in any one year of just $7,000 ($25,000 × 0.28), which is far less than what was available under the old law. Even the Low-Income Housing Coalition agrees that:

> this restriction limits the value of the credit substantially, since investors will probably be willing to invest only to the extent that the investment generates a credit within this limit. Credits that cannot be taken are not a particularly valuable commodity to anyone. (23, p. 2)

On the positive side, the income phase-out range for the use of low-income tax credits has been increased to between $200,000 and $250,000. Unused credits for any taxable year may be carried back three years and carried forward 15 years, and, in contrast to the provisions of the historic preservation tax credit, the basis of a low-income project for depreciation purposes is not reduced by the amount of the tax credit.

Credit Authority. For the first time ever, the aggregate amount of new, low-income housing tax credits that investors

---

[*] A credit equivalent is the amount of tax savings that the full $25,000 in deductions would be worth to an individual investor after taxes. For example, at a 28 percent rate, the maximum credit that could be taken in any one year would be worth $7,000 ($25,000 × 0.28).

across the country and within each state may take each year is fixed by law. The limit is equal to $1.25 per resident, or to more than $283 million at current population levels (see Table 7.2), and 10 percent of each state's total tax credits must be set aside for use by nonprofit organizations. (23, p. 3) Under the law, a tax credit is not considered used until the project to which it applies is placed in service. Individual state allocations vary from less than $600,000 in the least populous states of Alaska and Wyoming, to more than 40 times as much in California, whose allocation is more than $29.5 million. Qualifying units financed through tax-exempt bonds may also receive low-income housing tax credits, and these credits do not count against a state's per-capita tax credit limit.

Table 7.2
State-by-State Allocations of Low-Income Housing Tax Credits

State	Allocation	State	Allocation
Alabama	$4,867,360	Montana	$983,363
Alaska	502,314	Nebraska	1,962,281
Arizona	3,397,769	Nevada	1,000,616
Arkansas	2,858,044	New Hampshire	1,150,763
California	29,584,878	New Jersey	9,206,029
Colorado	3,612,455	New Mexico	1,628,618
Connecticut	3,884,470	New York	21,947,590
Delaware	742,923	North Carolina	7,352,208
District of Columbia	797,916	North Dakota	814,896
Florida	12,182,905	Ohio	13,497,038
Georgia	6,828,881	Oklahoma	3,781,613
Hawaii	1,205,864	Oregon	3,291,381
Idaho	1,179,919	Pennsylvania	14,829,869
Illinois	14,283,148	Rhode Island	1,183,943
Indiana	6,862,780	South Carolina	3,902,275
Iowa	3,642,260	South Dakota	863,460
Kansas	2,954,599	Tennessee	5,738,900
Kentucky	4,575,971	Texas	17,786,489
Louisiana	5,257,375	Utah	1,826,296
Maine	1,405,825	Vermont	639,320
Maryland	5,271,219	Virginia	6,683,523
Massachusetts	7,171,296	Washington	5,165,195
Michigan	11,577,598	West Virginia	2,437,055
Minnesota	5,094,963	Wisconsin	5,882,209
Mississippi	3,150,798	Wyoming	586,946
Missouri	6,145,858	United States	28,182,256

Source: Low-Income Housing Information Service, *Low-Income Housing Round-Up*, Number 105, September 1986; p. 3.

Allocation of the credit within each state is at the state's discretion, and the law permits the states to allocate less than the maximum allowable credit percentages to any given project. Presumably, this is to avoid giving windfall gains to the owner of a particularly attractive project that does not require the maximum possible tax credit in order to generate competitive returns.

Another interesting aspect of the credit allocation picture is the fact that states are not permitted to carry forward unallocated tax credits into the next year; nor can they reclaim surplus credits allocated to projects that could not fully use them.

In short, how well a state manages its tax credit authority could become a significant determinant of the amount of new low-income housing production that the low-income housing tax credit will stimulate.

Set-Asides for Nonprofits. The creation of the new tax credit, and that of the special set-aside for nonprofits, are especially interesting for three reasons. First, these actions indicate that, on the one hand, Congress was intent on using tax reform to eliminate wasteful real-estate tax preferences used by the for-profit sector to produce projects that could not stand alone on their own financial merits; on the other hand, these actions confirm the legitimacy of the use of the tax code to stimulate low-income housing.

Second, the set-aside reflects a renewed confidence on the part of Congress in the ability of the nonprofit sector to take a leadership role in low-income housing through the remainder of the decade—and perhaps into the 1990s.

Third, since nonprofit organizations have no economic use for tax credits, the set-aside reflects a congressional intent to foster the creation of community-based housing partnerships between nonprofits and for-profit producers, through the syndication of tax benefits. In this regard, we should note that while tax reform has severely limited the value of tax credits to wealthy individuals, the credits should be quite attractive to the corporate sector. This is because, with the repeal of the investment tax credit, despite lower marginal rates, tax reform is expected to increase corporate taxes by $120 billion over the next five years. Because corporations are exempt from the newly imposed passive-loss restrictions that apply to individuals, corporations that have been heavy past users of investment tax credits, and others with high tax exposure, should find the low-income tax credit quite appealing. (6m, pp. 500–501) Thus, to the extent that syndication survives tax reform, it will be because wealthy corporations have replaced wealthy individuals as equity participants in low-income housing deals.

The above conclusion assumes, of course, that an appropriate vehicle can be created to attract corporate capital into low-income housing. In the next chapter, which deals with public/private partnerships, we describe an exciting equity syndication model that has been used in Chicago under the old tax laws to raise equity capital from corporations. This model could become the prototype vehicle for syndicating the new tax credit.

Defining Low-Income Housing

Low-income housing is eligible for the new tax credit if at least 20 percent of the units in a project are occupied by individuals having incomes not exceeding 50 percent of the area's median income, adjusted for family size—or if at least 40 percent of the units (25 percent in New York City) are occupied by individuals with incomes not exceeding 60 percent of the median, also adjusted for family size.*

Nationally, the 50-percent-of-median limit translates to a maximum income of around $13,750 for a family of four, while the 60 percent limit is $16,500. To be eligible for the tax credit, the maximum rents (net of tenant-supplied utilities) charged for low-income units may not exceed 30 percent of the tenants' qualifying incomes. Using the above incomes, this means that the maximum qualifying rents for a two-bedroom unit for a family of four would be around $344 a month and $412 a month, respectively. Since maximum qualifying incomes are lower for smaller families and higher for larger ones, maximum qualifying rents would vary in a similar fashion for smaller and larger units.

The law also permits an owner to elect a stricter set-aside requirement. Under this alternative, at least 15 percent of the low-income units would need to be occupied by tenants with incomes no greater than 40 percent of the area's median income. In exchange for serving poorer individuals than required by the general low-income targeting requirements, projects using the alternative set-aside enjoy more flexibility in handling income increases for those tenants initially qualifying as low-income tenants.**

---

*The owner must irrevocably elect which of the alternative set-aside requirements will be met, at the time when the building is placed in service.

**Under the special rule, a low-income tenant will continue to qualify as such, as long as the tenant's income does not exceed 170 percent of the qualifying income. If the project ceases to comply with the set-aside requirement because of increases in existing tenant incomes, no penalties are imposed—as long as all available low-income units are rented to tenants having incomes of 40 percent or less of the area median income until the project is again in compliance.

Not only are the new low-income set-aside requirements more restrictive than those of the previous law in that they require adjustments for family size. They are also more restrictive in that the set-aside must be for at least 15 years (five years longer than under the old law, and five years longer than the term of the tax credit). Moreover, for the first time, the determination of whether a tenant qualifies as a low-income tenant must be made on a continuous basis; this imposes on developers additional income certification responsibilities that could deter them from investing in low-income housing in the first place. If the administrative burden is not a deterrent, the prospect of a recapture of the tax credit for violating the continuous-eligibility rule could be.[*]

The Future of Tax-Exempt Financing

Congress has taken two significant actions with respect to tax-exempt bonds that promise to wield significant impacts on the use and availability of below-market-rate capital to finance housing in the future. The first action set a maximum limit on each state's issuance of certain types of tax-exempt bonds, including housing bonds, and the second imposed the same targeting requirements on their use as applied to the low-income tax credit. We discuss each of these issues more fully below.

The Volume Ceiling

The Tax Reform Act continues the tax-exempt status of state and local bonds to finance traditional governmental facilities and operations, and places no ceiling on the volume of such bonds that state and local governments may issue each year. On the other hand, private activity bonds, while maintaining their tax-exempt status, are placed under severe volume caps. Unfortunately for low-income rental housing, mortgage revenue bonds (MRBs), which are used extensively to finance single-family housing for first-time homebuyers, are also classified under the new law as private activity bonds and will thus compete with rental

---

[*]The penalty for noncompliance is recapture of the tax credit (plus accrued interest) at the following rates:
- 1/3 for violations after year one and before end of year 11;
- 4/15 for violations after year 11 and before end of year 12;
- 3/15 for violations after year 12 and before end of year 13;
- 2/15 for violations after year 13 and before end of year 14; and
- 1/15 for violations after year 14 and before end of year 15.

bonds for the limited tax-exempt dollars. The volume cap on all private activity bonds—which include, in addition to MRBs, multifamily rental housing bonds, small-issue industrial development bonds (IDBs) for economic development projects, tax increment (redevelopment) bonds, and student loan bonds—is the greater of $75 per state resident or $250 million. In 1988, the volume cap will be scaled down by another one-third, to the greater of $50 per capita or $150 million.

To appreciate the significance of these new, lower bond ceilings, we should note that under prior law, multifamily housing bonds were under no volume cap, while applicable limits for mortgage revenue bonds alone in many states exceeded the new state ceilings on *all* private activity bonds.* As a result of these restrictions, most states face reductions of 50 percent or more in bond activity. In some states, bond-financed activity will have to decline by more than 75 percent to meet the new volume limits. (28c, p. 1)

How the Bond Ceiling Will Hurt Housing. By slapping stiff state-by-state restrictions on the overall volume of private activity bonds, and by providing no mandated set-asides for housing, Congress has all but assured that tough political battles will be waged over state allocation formulas. This is already evident from a review of the executive orders issued by governors who have already determined how bond volumes will be allocated in their respective states. By mid-November 1986, the chief executives of at least 15 states had determined how well housing would fare in head-to-head competition with economic development projects. A sample of the results suggests that housing has fared adequately, but not as well as it has in the past. (6o, p. 582)

- *California.* $710 million (37 percent) of $1.9 billion in private bond volume to housing:
  –$300 million to state department of veterans' affairs;
  –$100 million to California Housing Finance Agency;
  –$10 million to University of California for faculty housing;
  –$113 million for single-family housing bonds to be issued by localities; and
  –$165 million for multifamily housing bonds to be issued by localities.

---

*State mortgage revenue bond ceilings are, for the present, the greater of $200 million or 9 percent of the average annual mortgage volume for single-family houses in a given state over the previous three years.

- *Massachusetts.* $159 million (36 percent) of $436 million for housing, of which the Massachusetts HFA receives $150 million.
- *Maryland.* $164 million (50 percent) of $328 million for housing, of which $83 million goes to the state's community development administration, and $81 million goes to localities.
- *Connecticut.* $75 million (30 percent) of $250 million for housing, of which $65 million goes to the HFA and the Connecticut Housing Authority, and $10 million goes to localities.

Given low-income rental housing's apparent loss of competitive standing, we find it worth noting that housing bonds issued on behalf of nonprofit corporations having tax-exempt status under Section 501(c)(3) of the Internal Revenue Code are not subject to the new private-activity bond ceilings. This is another reason why nonprofits are certain to play a larger role in the nation's future low-income housing picture than they have played at any time since the late 1960s.

Before nonprofits are able to assume this part, however, a lengthy shakeout period may be necessary. Also possibly necessary is legislation enacting certain technical corrections that may be needed to make the production of low-income housing feasible under the Tax Reform Act. It is unclear, for example, whether Congress intended that projects financed by housing bonds issued on behalf of nonprofits should be eligible for tax credits. If this was the intention, then the formation of a limited partnership to syndicate the tax credits could conflict with the law's requirement that the tax-exempt bonds be issued on behalf of the nonprofit, in order not to count the bonds against the state's volume ceiling. (20, p. 30)

No More General Obligation Housing Bonds. The tax law's treatment of housing as a private activity will also cause additional harm to states and localities that, as a result of declining federal assistance, now use capital budget funds for housing. In Chapter 2, we cited Seattle's innovative use of GO bonds to finance senior citizens' housing. New York City has also been using GO bonds in its participation loan program, which combines private market-rate dollars with 1 percent city mortgages, to produce below-market-rate rehabilitation loans. GO bonds have also been used to rehabilitate city-owned, tax-foreclosed (in rem) housing.

Not only does the classification of housing as a private activity call into question whether New York's capital budget housing programs must all come under the states' private-activity bond ceiling. But also, if these programs must come under this ceiling, then it follows that most city bond–financed projects not owned by the city must meet the tax law's strict low-income targeting requirements. This fact alone will cause many otherwise viable new-development and rehabilitation projects to become financially infeasible, without the injection of substantial new state or local subsidies. This will happen because, up to now, most GO bond–financed projects have had no federal targeting requirements, and, to produce viable rehabilitation projects, locally determined income limits have been set substantially higher than have those contained in the new tax law.

Low-Income Targeting Requirements

Those targeting provisions of the Tax Reform Act that apply to the use and issuance of tax-exempt bonds could also depress future rates of low-income housing production. Low-income targeting requirements identical to those that apply to the use of the new tax credit are far more restrictive than those they will supersede.* Moreover, the determination of whether a tenant qualifies as having low income will now have to be made on a continuing basis. Failure to maintain the continuing eligibility of the original qualifying low-income tenants who remain in occupancy over an extended period of time can have seriously adverse financial consequences:

> If a project is not in compliance with the low-income set-aside requirement, each unit in the project that becomes vacant must be rented to a tenant satisfying the low- or moderate-income requirement before any comparable-sized or smaller units can be rented to tenants having higher incomes, until the project is again in compliance. (5, p. 30)

The Challenges of Tax Reform: Walking Through a Project

Although a congressional staffer close to the tax reform process has hailed the low-income tax credit as "the most generous tax credit in history," and although the banner headline of a recent low-income housing newsletter hailed the tax bill as "a victory for low-income concerns," the post–tax reform future of the low-

---

*Under previous regulations, at least 20 percent of all units in a bond-financed project had to be reserved for individuals whose incomes did not exceed 80 percent of the area median, and income limits were not adjusted for family size.

income housing sector remains very much in doubt. While the bill was in the conference committee, housing advocates won some major victories—gaining a tax credit, a stiffer set of low-income targeting requirements, a restriction on the rents that can be charged to low-income tenants, and a 15-year use restriction on all low-income units receiving tax benefits—these provisions do not necessarily form the framework for a healthy development program. Nor do they automatically give rise to the new kinds of institutional arrangements that will be needed in order to deliver low-income housing on a volume basis. As a matter of fact, the limitations attached to the use of the tax credit, and the restrictions placed on tax-exempt financing, could offset the positive impacts of these two low-income incentives.

Given the tax credit's newness, and the various ways in which it may be used, saying anything definitive about its long-term effects is difficult at this point. By referring to a hypothetical project, however, we can illustrate why the tax credit alone may not prove attractive enough to potential equity investors to make volume production likely—either through syndication or otherwise. The example assumes a 100 percent low-income project using the "60-percent-of-median" definition of low income. The reason is that in mixed-income projects, any significant credit to investors would require such a skewed rent schedule that sufficient cash flow to run the property would not be available. (29, p. 104)

Working the Numbers. The economics of a 100-unit, market-rate elderly housing project are depicted in the first part of Table 7.3. Total development costs are $5,500,000, or $55,000 a unit. Market rents average $550 a month, and at prevailing interest rates (9.5 percent), the project's net operating income can support a mortgage loan of close to $4 million. The developer's equity investment comes to just over $1.5 million, and the before-tax cash flow of $44,700 produces a 3 percent cash-on-cash return. This increases to just over 6 percent on an after-tax basis.

The picture is even less bright when the same project is developed as low-income housing. Although the developer can now take advantage of a $450,000 low-income housing tax credit each year for 10 years (9 percent of $5 million), he must reduce his rents to a level affordable by low-income elderly individuals. In this case, this level will mean a maximum of $306 a month (30 percent of the maximum qualifying income of $12,247). (These rents are 44 percent lower than market-rate rents.) Because $306 is the maximum rent that can be charged to qualifying low-income individuals who are at the highest end of the low-income ceiling, then, in order to create a qualifying income range, low-

Table 7.3
Effects of Tax Credit on Elderly Housing Development without Low-Income Tax Credit
(A 100-Unit Building)

Hard and Soft Construction Costs	$5,000,000
Land Cost	500,000
Total Development Cost	$5,500,000

Rents Achievable in Marketplace	$550 per unit per month

Total Potential Rent	$660,000
Occupancy Rate	95%
Effective Rental Income	$627,000
Operating Expenses	180,000
Cash Available for Debt Service (9.5%, 30-year)	447,000
Supportable Mortgage (90% Net Operating Income/Mortgage Constant)	$3,987,017

Total Development Costs	$5,500,000	Net Operating Income	$447,000
Mortgage	3,987,017	Debt Service	402,300
Developer's Equity	$1,512,983	Net Cash Flow	$44,700

Rate of Return on Investment: 3.0%

A. With Low-Income Tax Credit for 100% of the Units

Allowable Income Level for Single-Occupant Housing	$ 12,237
Maximum Rent (including utilities)	30%
Maximum Yearly Rent	$ 3,671
Maximum Monthly Rent	$ 306

(Use $275 monthly rent to create a qualifying "window.")

Total Potential Rent	$ 330,000
Occupancy Rate	98%
Effective Rental Income	$ 323,400
Operating Expenses	180,000
Net Operating Income	143,400
Supportable Mortgage	$1,279,056

Total Development Costs	$5,500,000	Net Operating Income	$143,400
Mortgage	1,279,056	Debt Service	129,060
Developer's Equity	$4,220,944	Net Cash Flow after Debt	$ 14,340
Present Value of Credit at 10%	$2,765,055		

Rate of Return on Developer's Equity after Present Value of Tax Credit: 1.0%

Total Development Costs	$5,500,000	Net Operating Income	$143,400
Mortgage	1,279,056	Debt Service	129,060
Developer's Equity	$4,220,944	Net Cash Flow after Debt	$ 14,340
		(plus 9% credit per year)	450,000
		Total Yearly Cash Flow	$464,340

Rate of Return on Investment: 11.0%

(Table 7.3: Cont'd.)

B. With Sale of Tax Credits

Selling Price of Tax Credits		
($450,000/year for 10 years)	$2,250,000	
Cost of Sale (22%)	495,000	
Net from Sale of Credit	$1,755,000	

Total Development Costs	$5,500,000	Net Operating Income	$143,400
Mortgage	1,279,056	Debt Service	129,060
Developer's Equity	$4,220,944	Net Cash Flow	$ 14,340
Sale of Credit	1,775,000		
Developer's Equity after Sale of Credit	$2,465,944		

Rate of Return on Investment: 0.6%

C. With Tax-Exempt Financing, Assuming Sale of (4%) Tax Credit

Selling Price of Credit	$1,000,000	
Cost of Sale (22%)	220,000	
Net from Sale of Credit	$ 780,000	

Total Development Cost	$5,500,000	Net Operating Income	$413,400
Mortgage	1,538,155	Debt Service	129,060
Developer's Equity	$3,961,845	Net Cash Flow after Debt	$ 14,340
Sale of Credit	780,000		
Developer's Equity after Sale of Credit	$3,181,845		

Rate of Return on Investment: 0.5%

Source: Distributed at National Housing and Rehabilitation Association's fall meeting, Washington, D.C., September 23, 1986.

income rents must be set at $275 a month. The lower apartment rents are able to support a project mortgage of some $1.3 million, which is only about one-third as much as could be supported with market-rate rents.

Because of the level of the rents, the developer's equity contribution has to increase to make up for the lower mortgage amount, with the tandem of positive cash flow from operations and the annual low-income tax credit providing the bulk of project returns.

Table 7.3 measures project returns in two different ways: first, by discounting the tax credit and deducting its present value from the initial equity requirements; and second, by treating the tax credit as an addition to the annual after-tax cash flow. Unfortunately, in both cases, investment returns are too low to make the project attractive: 1 percent a year in the former case, and 11 percent in the latter. These inferior investment returns result despite the fact that our example assumes that the developer is able to use the full $450,000 tax credit each year. In reality, this will only be true if the developer has sufficient passive income from passive activities against which he can apply his full credit-equivalent losses, or if the developer is a corporate investor.

The economics of project ownership are equally dismal under a scenario in which the tax credit is sold (that is, the project is syndicated). And the picture is no brighter if the project is financed with tax-exempt bonds. This is because, at the same time that lower tax-exempt interest rates permit the rents to support a higher mortgage and lower equity requirements, the applicable tax credit is reduced by more than one-half—from 9 percent to 4 percent of development cost.

This illustration demonstrates that under the most straightforward, uncomplicated conditions, the tax credit alone does not produce competitive investment returns. When we consider the uncertainties caused by inadvertent violations of the low-income targeting rules—which include possible recapture of the tax credit or, in the case of a mixed-subsidy project, a requirement to rent market-rate units to low-income tenants at reduced rents—the unattractiveness of the tax credit increases. Evidently, without state or local financial participation in the project to boost cash flows or to reduce equity requirements, big-time developers will likely steer clear of low-income housing. They will leave to the public and to the community the labor-intensive job of piecing together sufficient resources to make projects work on a one-at-a-time basis.

In a newly published guide to the low-income housing tax credit, Joseph Guggenheim analyzes a much wider range of project possibilities, and concludes that the low-income housing picture is much brighter than is suggested by our example. (20) Guggenheim's analysis included four different development/rehabilitation cost scenarios, which ranged from a low of $20,000 to a high of $55,000 a unit, and four area median incomes, which ranged from a low of $23,000 to a high of $36,500 a year. According to Guggenheim:

Of the 56 different scenarios examined in this analysis, roughly one-third were feasible without additional financial aid; one-third were feasible if additional financial aid were available; and slightly more than one-third were not feasible. Of those feasible with financial aid, about one-half required aid under $5,000 per unit, and the other half required aid of between $5,000 and $10,000 a unit. (20, p. 62)

The most favorable market conditions occur when incomes are high and construction costs are low. Conversely, tax-credit projects will need the greatest amount of additional financial aid where incomes are low-to-moderate and construction costs are very high. Such is the case, for instance, in New York City, where the maximum qualifying rent for a two-bedroom low-income unit is around $408, including utilities. This is about $1,000 a month less than the economic rent based on full development costs.

Substantial additional financial assistance will also prove necessary to make tax-credit projects work in rural areas—not because development costs are so high, but because incomes are so low. For this reason, the continued availability of the U.S. Farmers' Home Administration's financing programs is critical to the effective use of the tax credit in rural areas.

Chapter 8
Public/Private Partnerships to Promote Low-Income Housing

S ince the federal retreat began more than six years ago, the
most significant and potentially far-reaching low-income
housing innovation at the local level has been the rise and
institutionalization of public/private partnerships to help finance
and package low-income housing projects. (29, pp. 5–10, 33–39)
In their least structured form, these partnerships may differ little
from those corporate or foundation-sponsored grant programs
that make it possible for a community-based organization to secure an option on a site or a building, to complete a feasibility
study, to collateralize a loan, or otherwise to provide the missing
piece to make a project work (see Table 8.1). In their more
highly developed state, they bring together the corporate, public,
philanthropic, and community sectors into highly sophisticated delivery systems potentially capable of financing and packaging high
volumes of low- and moderate-income housing.

Although we do not deal directly in this chapter with either
of these two types, as such, we should note that many of the
public/private partnerships we surveyed, and all of those partnerships whose programs we discuss in detail, were assisted in some
fundamental way, either by the Local Initiative Support Corporation (LISC) or by the Enterprise Foundation. LISC, a national
nonprofit corporation created in 1979 by the Ford Foundation

Table 8.1
Representative Corporate/Community Loan Funds

Sponsor(s)	Location	Program	Support
Chemical Bank	New York City	Assistance to community-based housing organizations, through recoverable grants to finance upfront development costs, and through grants for general support of well-managed organizations.	$250,000 in recoverable grants; $210,000 for general support.
Aetna Life & Casualty, National Training Information Center	Bronx and Brooklyn, NY; Philadelphia; Cleveland; and Chicago (two)	National Urban Neighborhood Investment Program, 1982. Provides technical and financial assistance to neighborhood organizations.	Grants of $425,000; mortgage financing commitment of $15 million; technical assistance.
Honeywell	Minneapolis	Neighborhood Improvement and Owner Assistance Programs, 1971. Renovates the housing and the neighborhoods surrounding company headquarters.	$1 million for rehabilitation, new construction, and cost sharing.
New Hampshire Community Loan Fund	New Hampshire	Intermediary between community groups and local lenders, 1983. Loans for housing and community development.	$600,000 in loans from corporations and individuals.
Boatmen's National Bank of St. Louis	St. Louis	Boatmen's Community Reinvestment Program. Loans for purchase and rehabilitation; neighborhood grants and banking services.	$50 million loan commitment; grants of $100,000 annually to neighborhood organizations.
South Shore Bank	Chicago	Through its subsidiary, The Neighborhood Institute, bank is launching a block-wide revitalization program called Adopt-a-Block, aimed at promoting home-ownership, employment, and other opportunities to residents of the 7000 block of South Merrill Avenue on Chicago's South Side.	Section 312 loans; gap financing from city; sweat equity; and LISC.

with major insurance and banking companies, assists "local nonprofit organizations to draw new public and private/public resources into their efforts to revitalize communities and neighborhoods" via the following means (29, pp. 5–6):

• Technical assistance in designing, funding, and operating their projects, and in managing their own staff work and finances;

- Design of investments 1) to leverage other investments by local corporations and financial institutions, and 2) to enhance their commitment to community-based undertakings;
- Help in securing loans and grants from government, with emphasis on arrangements and purposes that would have demonstration value for both the funders and the recipients; and
- Core support grants to be matched dollar-for-dollar with new money from local corporate sources. Such grants, not exceeding $50,000 a year for two years, but usually considerably smaller, would be used to cover staff and operating costs and to seed new projects.

The Enterprise Foundation, launched in 1982 by developer James Rouse, is a national nonprofit organization founded "to help the poor help themselves to decent, livable housing, and out of poverty and dependence into self-sufficiency." (29, p. 9) It operates primarily through the creation and strengthening of a national network of nonprofit neighborhood groups, and through the provision for them of access to capital and expertise. Through its own fundraising efforts, through the profits from its for-profit commercial development entity, the Enterprise Development Company, and with equity capital generated by the Enterprise Social Investment Corporation (a subsidiary of Enterprise Development), this trio has raised more than $20 million to support its work. As of June 1986, Enterprise's network included 63 neighborhood groups in 25 cities that had collectively sponsored the rehabilitation and development of 3,400 low- and moderate-income housing units. Among Enterprise's most far-reaching public/private partnerships, whose progress bears close monitoring, is the one it has recently formed in Chattanooga, Tennessee, to carry out a 10-year program to make all housing in that city livable over a 10-year period. (8a)

The Inner City Ventures Fund

The Inner City Ventures Fund (ICVF), administered by the National Trust for Historic Preservation, is another, albeit more specialized and institutionalized, bilateral nationwide partnership that requires its community-based grantees to negotiate on their own for all project-specific public and private assistance they may need. (30a) It has supported the rehabilitation of more than 1,100 housing units in historic structures across the country, for the benefit of low- and moderate-income families. Although most successful ICVF housing projects have all the characteristics of tripartite partnerships among the public, private, and community sectors, each partner's role and responsibility in an ICVF project is not predetermined, as it is in the more formally structured public/private partnerships we will discuss later in this chapter.

To date, the ICVF, which was formed by an initial $400,000 grant from the National Park Service, by $100,000 from the National Trust, and by other foundation grants, has funded 38 historic rehabilitation projects in 26 cities. The funding comes in the form of competitive grants, low-interest loans, and technical assistance to neighborhood-based nonprofit organizations. ICVF awards range in amounts between $40,000 and $100,000, and generally come one-half as a grant and one-half as a loan. The loans, which are typically used for construction financing, have a maximum term of five years, during which time all residential units in rehabilitated buildings must be reserved for low-income families. Through its matching funds and leveraging requirements, ICVF hopes to promote the formation of project-specific public/private partnerships, while it is strenghtening the capacity of the grantee to develop future housing projects on its own.

To be eligible for an ICVF grant, an organization must:

- be community-based;
- demonstrate significant neighborhood involvement;
- be an incorporated nonprofit organization; and
- demonstrate the capacity to manage, staff, and finance the project in question.

Projects eligible for ICVF funding must involve:

- Rehabilitation for continued or adaptive use of buildings of historic significance;
- A neighborhood revitalization focus directly benefiting minority and low- and moderate-income households;
- The capacity to increase the sponsoring organization's financial and staff capacities to undertake future real estate development;
- The realization of the project within a reasonable length of time;
- A location in a neighborhood threatened by or undergoing displacement of low- and moderate-income residents; and
- A location in a historic district listed in the National Register or designated as a historic district by an appropriate local or state government body that has been authorized by the National Park Service to make such designations. The project buildings should at least contribute to the importance of the district.

Less well known than these national partnerships and than those partnerships dealt with at length in this chapter are two other kinds of public/private partnerships. On the one hand are project-based partnerships between the corporate and community sectors that rely upon the proven track records of experienced neighborhood-based organizations to bring the 'public partner' into the fold around a particular deal. While they can be quite effective, and while success in one project can lead to additional collaborations in the future, these public/private partnerships have little permanence and do not constitute formal housing-delivery systems. We highlight the activities of two of these entities. On the other hand are program-based public/private partnerships— entities that include the public, corporate, and community sectors as full participants, and that have the permanence and access to all necessary capital and noncapital resources to deliver relatively large volumes of low-income housing. We examine two of these organizations, the Boston and Chicago Housing Partnerships, in some detail.

Project-Based Corporate/ Community Partnerships

The public sector is only an indirect partner, albeit an important participant, in most housing projects supported by corporate/community partnerships. Characteristic of these bilateral partnerships is their nonpermanent nature. Once a project is completed or turns out to be infeasible, these partnerships dissolve and re-form around new project possibilities. Two examples of project-based partnerships are 1) Chemical Bank's recently announced housing opportunities program in New York City; and 2) Citibank's support of a major housing development project in the South Bronx, also in New York City.

Chemical Bank Housing Opportunities
Chemical Bank of New York City created its housing opportunities program to support the housing development activities of community-based organizations with proven track records. (8b, p. 28) In 1986, Chemical Bank committed a total of $510,000 in assistance to community groups for a recoverable grant program and for general operating support to well-managed community organizations. The recoverable-grants portion of the program— for which $250,000 has been set aside—aims to finance upfront costs, in order to determine the feasibility of those individual

community-sponsored development projects that use city-owned, tax-foreclosed, and other marginal buildings in need of substantial rehabilitation. Successful community-based grantees whose projects go on to secure construction and permanent financing repay their grants without interest, but those grantees whose projects do not make it, do not have to repay their grants.

As implied above, it would be a rare project that did not require substantial city assistance to make it go. Yet, many project-based partnerships, like that of Chemical Bank, leave to their experienced, community-based grantees the responsibility of securing the necessary city support to make their projects work. Indeed, a primary criterion used by Chemical Bank in allocating its partnership dollars is a high probability that the community group/applicant will be able to negotiate successfully for the public assistance that its project requires. The Citibank project that we discuss in the next section further exemplifies a bilateral partnership between a major lender and an experienced, community-based housing development firm that could bring to the partnership all of the necessary city commitments required to put a highly ambitious project together.

Citibank and Banana Kelly

In March 1986, the Banana Kelly Community Improvement Association successfully completed the substantial rehabilitation of 10 buildings in a South Bronx neighborhood that had seen virtually no private housing investment in a decade or more. (6c, p. 901) This major project was made possible by a combination of financial commitments to Banana Kelly by Citibank; by its community-development lending subsidiary; by LISC; and by the city of New York.

LISC provided Banana Kelly with a $250,000 recoverable grant (which has already been repaid) to acquire 10 buildings from eight individual owners for $25,000 each. Citibank Community Development Corporation provided a market-rate construction loan, and permanent financing was jointly provided by the city and Citibank—the former providing $1.1 million for 15 years at 1 percent interest, and the latter, $1.6 million at market-rate interest. A $500,000 equity interest in the project was sold to a single limited partner, which acquired the tax project's shelter benefits from Banana Kelly, and which agreed to pay the money in a lump sum at closing.

Program-Based Public/Private Partnerships

The Boston and Chicago Partnerships are prototypes of a new kind of local institution, which orchestrates the activities of all the key actors in the development process who are needed to make high-volume delivery of low-income housing possible without large federal subsidies. Besides their more formalized and permanent structures, what is especially unusual about these entities is their broad charters, which generally entail:

- Organizing and managing complex programs that can salvage declining and abandoned housing, and convert it into decent affordable housing for low- and moderate-income families;
- Mobilizing funding and other resources of the community and government agencies for neighborhood-based organizations, so that the public and private sectors can attack housing problems jointly; and
- Providing technical assistance to community-based sponsors of low- and moderate-income housing for the purpose of enhancing their capacities to develop and manage housing.

Two Such Partnerships Compared

The Boston and Chicago Partnerships bear striking similarities to each other (see Table 8.2). Both were formed as outgrowths of proposals made by blue-ribbon panels that included major business interests: in the case of Chicago, the panel was the Housing Abandonment Task Force, and in the case of Boston, the Goals for Boston Committee. Both partnerships link their respective cities with major financial institutions, with the corporate and foundation sectors, and with the community-based sponsors that will develop the projects that the partnerships make possible. The equal-partner status of neighborhood groups is underscored in Boston, where the partnership's goal is to turn over ownership of its projects to their community-based producers at the end of 15 years because:

> Community-based ownership of such properties ensures that the process of rehabilitation is undertaken with a long-term commitment to maintaining the property as a community resource. (2b, p. 1)

Both partnerships also have ambitious development agendas. Boston's first project involves the rehabilitation of 701 apartments in 69 buildings in 10 neighborhoods, at an average development cost of $51,000 a unit. This initial effort will be followed up by an even more challenging task of rehabilitating 1,100 units of HUD-foreclosed, federally assisted housing that currently lies largely

Table 8.2
Summary of Key Features of the Boston and Chicago Housing Partnerships

	Boston	Chicago
YEAR FORMED	1983	1985
PARTNERS	• City of Boston; • Local lenders; • Major insurance companies; • Investment bankers; and • Neighborhood-based housing organizations	• City of Chicago; • Chicago Equity Fund; • Community Equity Assistance Corporation (CEAC); • Major lenders; • LISC; and • Neighborhood-based housing organizations
PURPOSES	To secure funding commitments to make projects financially viable; To provide seed money to community sponsors for upfront development costs; To work with the city to expedite the tax-foreclosure process, the needed property transfers, and the possible abatement of former water and sewer fees; and To oversee the development planning and rehabilitation of the property, and to help arrange for sound, long-term property management.	To generate predictable financing to replace the diminishing federal support; To streamline the financial packaging and brokering processes in order to help not-for-profit housing developers to package their projects and build their technical skills; and To develop a blueprint that formalizes the roles and responsibilities of the myriad of housing actors.
CURRENT PROGRAM	To rehabilitate 701 apartments in 69 buildings in 10 neighborhoods; then, to rehabilitate 1,100 HUD-foreclosed, assisted units.	To rehabilitate 957 apartments in 25 projects—520 now underway.
Average development cost per unit	$51,000	$50,000
Project developers	Neighborhood-based organizations	Neighborhood-based organizations
SOURCES OF CAPITAL	Letters-of-credit securing construction loans	
City/state agencies	$223 million (HFA)	$8.1 million (city)
Grants	$4.5 million	–
Equity	$8.8 million	$6.4 million
Permanent lenders	–	$11.4 million
Total development cost of first project	$35.6 million	$25.9 million
SOURCES OF EQUITY FUNDS	Syndication through two-tier partnership structure	Syndication through two-tier partnership structure
Equity raised so far through syndication	$8.8 million	$11.6 million

vacant, in a city with a desperate shortage of affordable rental housing. The Chicago Partnership's initial project, which began in 1985 and is expected to take two years to complete, involves the substantial rehabilitation of 521 apartments in 12 projects, at an average development cost of $50,000 a unit.

Finally, both partnerships have proven their abilities to raise debt financing from a variety of public and private sources, and equity capital through the syndication of tax-shelter benefits using an innovative two-tier partnership structure, which we will describe in detail in the following section.

The Anatomy of the Chicago Housing Partnership

The Chicago Partnership has six types of partners, whose roles in the development process are illustrated in Figure 8.1 and discussed below:

- the Community Equity Assistance Corporation (CEAC);
- the Chicago Equity Fund;
- major private lenders;
- the city of Chicago's department of housing;
- the Local Initiative Support Corporation (LISC); and
- neighborhood-based housing development organizations.

The Community Equity Assistance Corporation. Projects originate with neighborhood-based organizations that are aided in their packaging efforts by a newly formed technical assistance unit called the Community Equity Assistance Corporation (CEAC). (7d, p. 3) CEAC, a subsidiary of LISC, is designed to be a one-stop center at which not-for-profit housing developers can get help putting together workable financial plans for their projects. According to the Chicago Partnership's promotional materials, "the not-for-profit walks into CEAC with an idea and some raw numbers, and walks out with a prospectus for the equity fund."

More specifically, CEAC provides community-based housing sponsors with the following services:

- Budget preparation. Assists in preparing a feasible development budget and in reviewing development cost estimates.
- Development financing. Recommends and helps obtain project financing from public and private sources.
- Equity financing. Recommends financial structure for attracting equity investors. Recommends possible partnership structure to facilitate equity investment. Prepares financial forecasts and assumptions for the community development corporation (CDC).

Figure 8.1
The Anatomy of a Chicago Housing Partnership Program

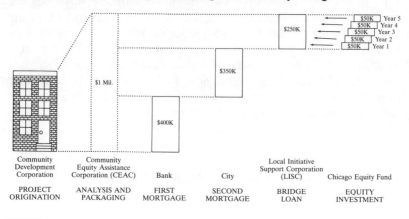

Community Development Corporation	Community Equity Assistance Corporation (CEAC)	Bank	City	Local Initiative Support Corporation (LISC)	Chicago Equity Fund
PROJECT ORIGINATION	ANALYSIS AND PACKAGING	FIRST MORTGAGE	SECOND MORTGAGE	BRIDGE LOAN	EQUITY INVESTMENT

- Project proposals. Prepares project proposals with narrative and financial data for presentation to potential equity investors.
- Development team. Assists in identifying general contractors, architects, and attorneys.
- Partnership accounting. Makes recommendations regarding special accounting procedures required by the partnership's structure.

As the project underwriter, CEAC charges a fee for services of between 1 and 2 percent of the total development costs. This fee is not payable until CEAC has successfully negotiated the sale of the project's equity.

The Chicago Equity Fund. The Chicago Equity Fund (CEF) is a unique legal entity that was created specifically as a member of the Chicago Housing Partnership. CEF is a nonprofit organization that provides the opportunity for corporations to participate in equity financing of housing rehabilitation projects. In return for their equity investments, corporations receive substantial tax benefits, cash flow distributions, potential appreciations in value, and positive community relations. The chance to earn competitive returns while contributing to community revitalization makes the CEF an attractive investment for Chicago corporations.

The CEF is the managing partner for the series of partnerships to be formed annually by Chicago's major corporations, each as a general partner. As the managing partner, CEF forms the partnerships and retains tax and legal support, both for analyzing the feasibility of prospective deals and for managing and administering the investments. An initial capital grant for CEF's first three years of operation was provided by Chicago United and by major corporations. By 1988, CEF is expected to be self-supported by investment and management fees based on the capital raised, and by the maintenance of a modest ownership interest (0.1 percent) in the partnerships it manages each year.

Beginning in 1985 and continuing in each year thereafter, the CEF, as the managing partner, forms a two-tiered partnership by offering units of general partnership interests to qualified corporate investors. The general partnership will then use the capital proceeds of the offering to acquire a 99 percent, sole limited-partnership interest in qualified, low-income multifamily housing rehabilitation projects in various city neighborhoods. The partnership's objectives in acquiring project investments are to:

- preserve and protect the partnership's capital and earning power;
- provide growth of capital through appreciation of the partnership's properties;
- increase the partnership's equity through reduction of mortgage debt secured by the properties;
- provide diversity of investment and diversity of risk by investing in a number of different neighborhood projects;
- provide tax deductions eligible to be passed through to the investors' income taxes; and
- provide cash distributions to the investors that will be partially sheltered from income taxes.

Eligible corporations may invest in units of the partnership by executing a subscription agreement to purchase these units. After the acceptance of the subscription agreement, and after the donation of an initial capital contribution, the investor executes a promissory note, to be due and payable in installments in accordance with capital calls of the managing partner. The managing partner contributes $100 in cash as its initial capital contribution to the partnership. The investors each provide an initial capital contribution per unit purchased, and in the future, will contribute to the partnership the balance, up to a maximum of $100,000 per unit. It is anticipated that each project investment will require the partnership to invest funds over a pay-in period of five to seven years. The managing partner will make capital calls on investors from time to time, in accordance with the aggregate pay-in requirements of all the project's investments. After the closings on the sales of each of the units, the partnership agreement is executed.

The partnership agreement contains detailed provisions for the allocation of net profits, net losses, low-income housing tax credits, and cash flow for each taxable year. The investors will receive 99.9 percent of all such items allocated to the partnership, and the managing partner, 0.1 percent. Each investor receives allocations based on the proportion of units purchased by that investor, relative to the total number of units purchased. Net proceeds from a sale or a refinancing are divided equally between the general partner and the limited partner. As limited partners, the corporations are expected to receive a minimum 15 percent annual return on their investments, based on tax benefits, distributions from cash flow, and sales proceeds.

Project investments are selected by the CEF after the formation of the partnership. The offering is consequently a "blind pool" offering. Project investments are subject to the fund's general qualifications; that is, they are restricted to:

- properties located within the city of Chicago;
- census tracts in which the median family income does not exceed 80 percent of that of the Chicago SMSA;
- projects that provide apartments for low-income tenants at affordable rents;
- investments that are expected to consist of a 99 percent limited-partnership interest, representing the entire limited rehabilitation project; and
- projects that can be sold, resyndicated, or otherwise liquidated approximately nine to 12 years after rehabilitation.

For a rehabilitation project to qualify as a project investment, its limited partnership must involve a general partner (or partners) falling into one of the following categories: a recognized nonprofit neighborhood organization; a recognized nonprofit organization with a for-profit developer as co-general partner; or a for-profit developer sponsored by a recognized nonprofit neighborhood organization.

As the managing partner, CEF is governed, and all its investment decisions are made, by a board of directors elected by the investors in the partnership. The community development corporations (CDCs) submit their CEAC-enhanced project proposals to CEF, offering a 99 percent limited partnership share. After receiving a project investment proposal, CEF meets with the nonprofit or developer proposing the project, and visits the property. Then, CEF drafts recommendations to the board of directors for action on the proposal. The board may approve or reject project investments, or grant approvals subject to contingencies. For the

1985 and 1986 partnerships, all of the projects submitted to the board were approved, with varying degrees of contingencies. This record attests to the efforts of CEAC in developing attractive and feasible investment packages. Before closing a project, the CEF requires several items from the sponsoring CDC, from CEAC, and from the various tax and legal counsels. The closing checklist is shown in Table 8.3.

In addition to the general requirements discussed above, the partnership agreement calls for each project investment to meet certain criteria before the CEF can be authorized to acquire the investment on behalf of the partnership. These criteria include, but are not limited to, the following standards:

- An upper limit pertains to each individual project-investment amount.

Table 8.3
Chicago Equity Fund: Project Investment Closing Checklist

PRECLOSING

1) Project Investment Proposal. Describes in detail the business plan for the project, including acquisition, financing, rehabilitation, leasing, and management. Also includes:
   - Schedule identifying the directors and officers of the project sponsor and of the general partner;
   - Current financial statements of the project sponsor and general partner;
   - Background descriptions of the project general contractor, architect, and property manager; and
   - A summary breakdown of the nature and scope of the rehabilitation.
2) Supplemental Materials.
   - Project appraisal. Appraisal submitted to the lender.
   - Project insurance. Certificate of insurance showing acceptable builder's risk, casualty, and liability coverage.
   - Project title report. Title insurance or commitment.
   - Project use restriction. Covenant restricting use of project to low-income rental housing.
   - Final projection for project investment.

CLOSING
1) Project Partnership Agreement.
2) CEF Partnership Interim Note.
3) CEF Partnership Note.
4) CEF Partnership Financing Statement.
5) Project Revolving Note.
6) Project Guaranty Agreement. Pledge, guaranty, and escrow agreement.
7) Project Management Contract.
8) Project Tax Opinion.
9) Project Tax Shelter Registration.
10) Project Investment Closing Letter.

- The CEF's board of directors must interview and approve all personnel participating in project management.
- The CEF's board must review and approve the financial projections for the project, including its ratio of tax deductions to capital contributions, its cash flow after lease-up, and the net proceeds of its sale.
- The CEF's legal and tax counsel must review and approve the partnership agreement.
- Each project's partnership agreement must require the project's general partner to investigate and report to the partnership with respect to the sale of the project.
- Each project's partnership agreement must forbid both discretionary capital calls and the admission of additional partners.
- Each project's partnership agreement must give the partnership the right to replace the project's general partner for the occurrence of: operating deficits, loan defaults not cured within reasonable time, substantial mismanagement, or failure to comply with the obligations of the partnership agreement.

Except for certain limited rights to replace project management, the partnership will not have control over the management of project partnerships, or of the projects operated by them. In fact, most of the projects are managed by the CDCs or their affiliates. The CEF closely monitors projects through a monthly reporting system: the project management must provide monthly financial and management reports on the project's status. Of course, the success of project investments depends to a large extent on the quality of project management. Thus, as a performance incentive, the CEF sets development and management fees that are payable as conditions for project completion and lease-up. These fees are escrowed to secure guarantees for cost overruns and operating deficits. Also, the partnership agreement between the general partner and the CEF covers the responsibilities and liabilities of the general partner, including:

- a construction-completion guaranty covering cost overruns, construction defects, and deficits during construction;
- an operating-deficits guaranty;
- project reserve funds for overruns and deficits;
- project insurance (title, casualty, liability) that meets CEF's standards;
- annual financial statements to advise partners on their investments, for federal income-tax reporting purposes;

- records and certification for the numbers and sizes of units; their occupancy by qualified tenants; the income levels of the tenants; and the set-aside for low-income tenants.

The CEF's goal when it began in 1985 was to raise $10 million of capital over three years. That goal will be exceeded in the first two years. Thirteen of Chicago's most prominent corporations joined the first CEF partnership in mid-1985. Each of these partners invested an average of $500,000, for a total of $6.4 million. The 1985 partnership invested this equity in 12 projects in several Chicago neighborhoods (see Figure 8.2). The 1986 partnership raised $5.2 million from 15 corporations, this amount to be invested in 13 projects. Eight corporations have invested in both partnerships. These repeat investors, as well as the new investors, demonstrate that the CEF remains attractive to the original investors while it expands its resource base. The CEF has established a $5 million goal for the 1987 partnership. This is expected to be the annual goal for each subsequent partnership.

The equity invested by the CEF provides from 20 to 30 percent of a project's costs. In 1985, the equity investments in individual projects ranged from $145,000 to $785,000, while in 1986, these equity investments ranged from $179,000 to $1.3 million.

The Roles of the Other Partners. Permanent financing for the Chicago Partnership's projects comes partly from private lenders that provide first-mortgage loans at somewhat reduced interest rates, and partly from the city, which, as the public partner, provides "soft seconds." LISC's role is to provide gap financing, which takes the form of short-term bridge loans that cover the difference between the total equity funds committed by a limited partner, and that partner's initial equity contribution. A bridge loan is retired over a five-year period, as additional limited-partner equity installment payments are made.

The most distinctive characteristic of partnership projects, as compared with their 100 percent federally subsidized counterparts of an all-but-bygone era, is twofold: 1) the complexity of the former's financing arrangements, due principally to the fact that rents are only high enough to support a 40 percent first mortgage or even less, if a mortgage is written at market rates; and 2) the greater equity commitments that their projects demand. Because partnership projects require proportionally greater equity contributions than do deep-subsidy federal projects, preservation of capital will rival the after-tax rate of return as an important investment criterion for potential corporate investors in the equity fund—as in other, similarly structured, entities that have been formed to attract corporate capital into low-income housing. This

Figure 8.2:
The Chicago Equity Fund 1985 Partnership

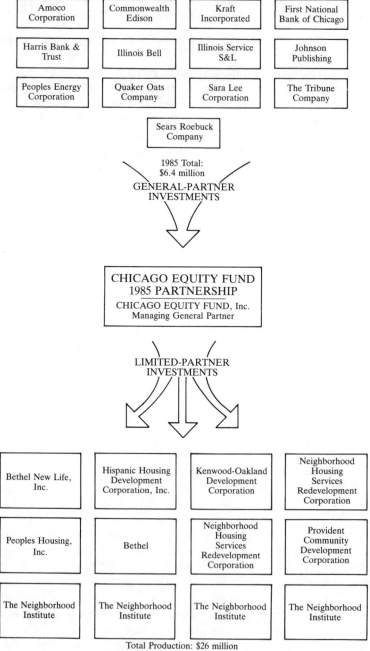

Amoco Corporation

Commonwealth Edison

Kraft Incorporated

First National Bank of Chicago

Harris Bank & Trust

Illinois Bell

Illinois Service S&L

Johnson Publishing

Peoples Energy Corporation

Quaker Oats Company

Sara Lee Corporation

The Tribune Company

Sears Roebuck Company

1985 Total: $6.4 million

GENERAL-PARTNER INVESTMENTS

CHICAGO EQUITY FUND 1985 PARTNERSHIP

CHICAGO EQUITY FUND, Inc. Managing General Partner

LIMITED-PARTNER INVESTMENTS

Bethel New Life, Inc.

Hispanic Housing Development Corporation, Inc.

Kenwood-Oakland Development Corporation

Neighborhood Housing Services Redevelopment Corporation

Peoples Housing, Inc.

Bethel

Neighborhood Housing Services Redevelopment Corporation

Provident Community Development Corporation

The Neighborhood Institute

The Neighborhood Institute

The Neighborhood Institute

The Neighborhood Institute

Total Production: $26 million
(521 units of low-income rental housing)

suggests a growing role for cities as insurers or guarantors of equity capital.

Walking Through One of Chicago's Actual Tax Credit Projects

The Chicago Housing Partnership is one of the first corporate investment entities in the nation to close a low-income, top-credit deal. Using the information on the provisions of the new tax laws contained in Chapter 7, one might "walk through" an actual project to see how the various provisions actually apply.

The 20-unit project located at 5700 West Washington is sponsored by a nonprofit development corporation active since 1981 in the Austin neighborhood (in the west of Chicago). The CDC has successfully developed and currently manages two buildings, with a total of 32 units. The nonprofit corporation formed a for-profit affiliate as the general partner for the project. The for-profit subsidiary is used to limit the direct liability to the nonprofit sponsor. The CEF's 1986 partnership purchased a 99 percent limited partnership interest in 5700 West Washington for the total purchase price of $178,955, to be paid in six installments. The CEF's 1986 partnership will be entitled to 99 percent of the partnership's ordinary profits and losses, as of its proceeds at sale.

The summary of 5700 West Washington's funding sources and uses (Table 8.4) itemizes the total project costs, as well as the financing provided by each of the partners. The private first mortgage is for 29 percent of project costs; the second mortgage, from the city, for 49 percent; and the equity investment is for 22 percent. The specific line items that make up the project costs are further detailed in the development summary (Table 8.5). Since the equity investment is to be paid in six installments, interim equity financing has been needed. The equity (or bridge) loan of $86,675 is being provided by LISC, at 8 percent for five years. The amount of the equity loan has been based on the net cash needed to close (Table 8.6), and this loan is to be retired as the remaining equity contributions are made.

When the project is finally placed in service, use of the tax credit requires selection of the tenant income standard to be used for the duration of the project. Because it is anticipated that all of the units will be occupied by low-income families, the applicable income limit is 60 percent of the area median, adjusted for household size. The qualifying incomes and allowable rents, in-

Table 8.4
5700 West Washington:
Funding Sources and Uses Summary
(20 Units)

SOURCES	
First Mortgage/First National Bank of Chicago (8% for 30 years, adjustable every three years by a maximum per year of two points, a maximum over the life of the loan of five points)	$244,000
Second Mortgage/Chicago Department of Housing (0% for 30 years, the principal being deferred until sale or refinancing)	410,000
Total General-Partner Capital Contribution	100
Total Limited-Partner Capital Contribution (1987–1992)	178,955*
Total Sources of Funds	$833,055
USES	
Acquisition	$115,000
Basic Construction	546,238
Other	171,817
Total Uses of Funds	$833,055

*Interim equity financing of $86,675, repayable to the Local Initiatives Support Corporation (LISC) from the limited-partner capital contribution, at 8 percent for five years.

cluding utilities, are detailed in Table 8.7. The actual rents in the rent schedule are less than the allowable rents because of adjustments for tenant-paid utilities and for market conditions. Given the low-income requirements of tax credit projects, the available rental income is projected to cover the full operating costs, as well as a limited permanent mortgage. Table 8.8 gives a 15-year pro forma analysis of projected cash flow from operations.

The amount of permanent debt that can be supported is determined by capitalizing 90 percent of the net operating income for the first year. This yields a first mortgage of $244,000. As indicated in Chapter 7 of this book, the available tax benefits under the new law are insufficient to attract equity investment for the balance of the project costs. Equity capital must be supplemented by funds from the city, to be secured by a second mortgage.

After operating expenses and debt service payments, a replacement reserve payment equal to 0.003 percent of the total project costs, or $2,700, is required by the partnership. Of the remaining cash flow, 50 percent is allocated to the city. This allocation, which takes the place of any interest payments on the city's deferred second mortgage, is paid after partnership management fees, and then only when available. The unpaid balance accrues and is paid to the city as soon as sufficient cash flow becomes

Table 8.5
5700 West Washington:
Development Summary

USES OF FUNDS	Budget	Non-depreciable	Depreciable	Amortized
Acquisition/Building	$115,000	$11,500 (land)	$103,500	
Basic Construction	473,238		473,238	
Construction Contingency	45,000		45,000	
Architect				
Design	21,000		21,000	
Supervision	7,000		7,000	
Carrying Cost	6,826		6,826	
Construction Interest	5,994		5,994	
Financing Costs/Fees	150		150	
Title/Recording	1,200		1,200	
Surveys/Appraisals	1,400		1,400	
Inspection Services	3,500		3,500	
Relocation Costs	3,500		3,500	
Financial Consulting	14,000		7,000	$ 3,500
Real Estate Taxes (development period)	10,000		10,000	
Insurance (development period)	12,000		12,000	
Legal	19,000	2,000	8,000	4,000
Accounting	1,000			
Marketing				
Developer Fees	61,000		61,000	
Organization Costs/Fees	5,000			5,000
Partnership Management	5,000			
Equity-Loan Interest	21,380			
Equity-Loan Fee	867			867
Total Uses of Funds	$833,055	$13,500	$770,308	$13,367

SOURCES OF FUNDS	
First Mortgage	$244,000
Second Mortgage	410,000
General-Partner Capital	100
Limited-Partner Capital	178,955
Total Sources of Funds	$833,055

available. The partnership management fees are set at $2,500 per year, plus 25 percent of the excess cash available. Any remaining cash flow will be distributed between the partners, according to their respective ownership shares.

The returns on the equity investment by the CEF, the sole limited partner, are based almost exclusively on the tax benefits from the project (see Table 8.9). The amount and the schedule of equity payments are both based on a benefit/pay-in ratio of 1.3 during the pay-in period. Investors receive $1.30 in benefits for each $1.00 invested. Estimated tax benefits for each year of the pay-in period are divided by 1.3 in order to calculate the required

Table 8.6
5700 West Washington:
Net Cash Needed to Close

TOTAL DEVELOPMENT COSTS	$833,055
LESS: ADJUSTMENTS	
Developer Fees	61,000
Organization Costs/Fees	5,000
Partnership Management Fee	5,000
Equity-Loan Interest	21,380
LESS: MORTGAGES	654,000
NET CASH NEEDED	$ 86,675

Table 8.7
5700 West Washington:
Affordability, Rents, and Occupancy

AREA MEDIAN INCOME: $34,600

INCOME TARGETING: 60% of area median income

SCHEDULE OF MAXIMUM RENTS

	Income	Maximum Rent (including utilities)
One-Person Household	$14,532	$363
Two-Person Household	16,608	415
Three-Person Household	18,684	467
Four-Person Household	20,760	519

SCHEDULE OF ACTUAL RENTS

	Number of Units	Actual Rent	Monthly Rental Proceeds
One-Bedroom	1	$300	$ 300
One-Bedroom	6	350	2,100
Two-Bedroom	6	375	2,250
Three-Bedroom	4	400	1,600
Three-Bedroom	3	450	1,350
Totals	20		$7,600

SCHEDULE OF OCCUPANCY: 50% by 1/88; 75% by 2/88; 100% by 3/88.

equity contribution for that year. This is known as "pricing the equity." The CEF's administrative expenses are also included in these returns, so that the actual returns realized by the investors are somewhat less than the 30 percent return used to price the equity.

While depreciation and amortization of organizational costs and fees contribute to the tax benefits, the major portion of the benefits is provided by the tax credit. The investment summary (Table 8.10) shows the relationship between the capital contributions and the flow of project benefits. Using a "hurdle rate" of 15 percent to discount the net benefits produces a net present value of $69,471.

As Table 8.11 shows, the available low-income housing tax credit can be maximized by an allocation of that part of the city's share of project costs that comes from federal loans and grants to the acquisition costs, and by a deduction of any remaining federal subsidies from eligible rehabilitation costs.* When computed this way, the available tax credit is $37,603 per year for 10 years.**

Although investor returns are not contingent upon the proceeds from a sale of the property, it is important to consider the tax implications of a sale. Because of the limited income potential of one of the properties, its realistic sale price would either be the amount of the remaining mortgage principal, or the original cost. These two scenarios, in year 10 and year 16 of the project, are shown in Table 8.12.

Any change in ownership of a building within the 15-year compliance period, however, will trigger a recapture of some portion of the tax credit (unless the original owner posts a bond with the U.S. Treasury Department, and the project is expected to stay in compliance for the remainder of the period). This recapture will equal the difference between the amount of credit earned and the amount of credit claimed. A sale in year 10, for in-

---

* This is because the "higher 9 percent (70 percent present value)" tax credit for new construction or rehabilitation is not available if federal subsidies are used to pay for the new construction or rehabilitation. Only the 4 percent credit is available in this situation. There is one exception to this rule, however. The owners of a property receiving a federal subsidy may treat the subsidy amount as if it were a federal grant, and deduct the subsidy amount from the qualified bases or costs against which the amount of the credit is calculated (20, pp. 5–6)

** This is $3,418 per year higher than the annual tax credit contained in Table 8.10. The basis for this discrepancy is in the treatment of the federal subsidy.

Table 8.8
5700 West Washington:
Analysis of Projected Cash Flow from Operations

ANNUAL INCREASES: Rents 5%; expenses 5%

INCOME	1987	1988	1989	1990	1991	1992	1993	1994
Gross Rental Income		$ 85,500	$ 95,760	$100,548	$105,575	$110,854	$116,397	$122,217
Less: Vacancy (5%)		4,275	4,788	5,027	5,279	5,543	5,820	6,111
Effective Gross Income		$ 81,225	$ 90,972	$ 95,521	$100,297	$105,311	$110,577	$116,106
EXPENSES								
Property Management								
(6% of effective gross)		$ 4,874	$ 5,458	$ 5,731	$ 6,018	$ 6,319	$ 6,635	$ 6,966
Utilities		22,000	23,100	24,255	25,468	26,741	28,078	29,482
Repairs/Maintenance		7,500	15,000	15,750	16,538	17,364	18,233	19,144
Real Estate Taxes		10,000	10,500	11,025	11,576	12,155	12,763	13,401
Insurance		8,000	8,400	8,820	9,261	9,724	10,210	10,721
Scavenger/Exterminating		1,500	1,575	1,654	1,736	1,823	1,914	2,010
Other		500	525	551	579	608	638	670
Total Expenses		$ 54,374	$ 64,558	$ 67,786	$ 71,176	$ 74,734	$ 78,471	$ 82,394
Net Operating Income		$ 26,852	$ 26,414	$ 27,734	$ 29,121	$ 30,577	$ 32,106	$ 33,711
DEBT SERVICE								
First Mortgage: $244,000								
at 8% for 30 years								
Principal		$ 2,038	$ 2,207	$ 2,391	$ 2,589	$ 2,804	$ 3,037	$ 3,289
Interest		19,446	19,277	19,094	18,896	18,681	18,448	18,196
Debt Coverage								
Ratio: 1.25								
Total Debt Service								
Payments		$ 21,484	$ 21,484	$ 21,485	$ 21,485	$ 21,485	$ 21,485	$ 21,485
REPLACEMENT								
RESERVES		2,700	2,700	2,700	2,700	2,700	2,700	2,700
OPERATING CASH								
FLOW		$2,668	$2,230	$3,549	$4,936	$6,392	$7,921	$9,526
Less: DOH* Interest								
(50% of cash flow)		1,334	1,115	1,775	2,468	3,196	3,961	4,763
Less: Partnership								
Management Fees		2,500	2,500	2,500	2,500	2,674	2,865	3,066
CASH FLOW								
AVAILABLE FOR								
DISTRIBUTION								
(accrued)		$−1,116	$−1,385	$−725	$−32	$522	$1,036	$1,697

* Department of Housing.

stance, would carry significant tax liability from recapture of the credit, as well as from the tax on gain. A sale in year 16 for the remaining mortgage balance would involve *some* tax liability, while a sale for the original cost would provide sufficient proceeds to cover the full tax liability. The long-term objective of the partnership is to maintain its properties as low-income projects, and to transfer ownership to the sponsoring community organizations without incurring any tax liability.

ANNUAL INCREASES: Rents 5%; expenses 5%

INCOME	1995	1996	1997	1998	1998	2000	2001	2002
Gross Rental Income	$128,328	$134,744	$141,481	$148,555	$155,983	$163,702	$171,971	$180,570
Less: Vacancy (5%)	6,416	6,737	7,074	7,428	7,799	8,189	8,599	9,028
Effective Gross Income	$121,911	$128,007	$134,407	$141,127	$148,184	$155,593	$163,372	$171,541
EXPENSES								
Property Management (6% of effective gross income)	$ 7,315	$ 7,680	$ 8,064	$ 8,468	$ 8,891	$ 9,336	$ 9,802	$ 10,292
Utilities	30,956	32,504	34,129	35,836	37,627	39,509	41,484	43,558
Repairs/Maintenance	20,101	21,107	22,162	23,270	24,433	25,655	26,938	28,285
Real Estate Taxes	14,071	14,775	15,513	16,289	17,103	17,959	18,856	19,799
Insurance	11,257	11,820	12,411	13,031	13,683	14,367	15,085	15,839
Scavenger/Exterminating	2,111	2,216	2,327	2,443	2,566	2,694	2,828	2,970
Other Expenses	704	739	776	814	855	898	943	990
Total Expenses	$ 86,514	$ 90,840	$ 95,382	$100,151	$105,158	$110,417	$115,937	$121,734
Operating Income	$ 35,397	$ 37,167	$ 39,025	$ 40,976	$430,026	$ 45,176	$ 47,435	$ 49,807
DEBT SERVICE								
First Mortgage: $244,400 at 8% for 30 years								
Principal	$ 3,562	$ 3,857	$ 4,178	$ 4,524	$ 4,900	$ 5,306	$ 5,747	$ 6,224
Interest	17,923	17,627	17,307	16,960	16,585	16,178	15,738	15,261
Debt Coverage Ratio: 1.25								
Total Debt Service Payments	$ 21,485	$ 21,484	$ 21,485	$ 21,484	$ 21,485	$ 21,484	$ 21,485	$ 21,485
REPLACEMENT RESERVES	2,700	2,700	2,700	2,700	2,700	2,700	2,700	2,700
OPERATING CASH FLOW	$ 11,212	$ 12,983	$ 14,840	$ 16,792	$ 18,841	$ 20,992	$ 23,250	$ 25,622
Less: DOH* Interest (50% of cash flow)	5,606	6,491	7,420	8,396	9,420	10,496	11,625	12,811
Less: Partnership Management Fees	3,277	3,498	3,730	3,974	4,230	4,499	4,781	5,078
CASH FLOW AVAILABLE FOR DISTRIBUTION (accrued)	$ 2,329	$ 2,993	$ 3,690	$ 4,422	$ 5,190	$ 5,997	$ 6,844	$ 7,733

*Department of Housing

The National Equity Fund: The Chicago Equity Fund as a National Prototype

Although the Chicago Equity Fund was created as a vehicle for attracting corporate equity capital into the low-income housing sector under the tax shelter provisions of the old tax law, the tax credit project analyzed above—1500 West Washington—shows

Table 8.9
5700 West Washington:
Analysis of Taxable Income/Loss from Operations

	1987	1988	1989	1990	1991	1992	1993	1994
INCOME								
Gross Rental Income		$ 85,500	$ 95,760	$100,548	$105,575	$110,854	$116,397	$122,217
Less: Vacancy (5%)		4,275	4,788	5,027	5,279	5,543	5,820	6,111
Effective Gross Income		$ 81,225	$ 90,972	$ 95,521	$100,297	$105,311	$110,577	$116,106
EXPENSES								
Operating Expenses		$ 54,374	$ 64,558	$ 67,786	$ 71,176	$ 74,734	$ 78,471	$ 82,395
Interest Expense (debt service)		19,446	19,277	19,094	18,896	18,681	18,448	18,196
Interest Expense (DOH)*		1,333	1,115	1,775	2,468	3,196	3,961	4,763
Interest Expense (equity loan)	6,934	5,663	4,276	2,889	1,502	116		
Financial Consultation and Planning	3,500							
Partnership Management Fee	5,000	2,500	2,500	2,500	2,500	2,674	2,865	3,066
Accounting and Legal Fees	6,000							
Depreciation Basis:								
Building $103,500		3,764	3,764	3,764	3,764	3,764	3,764	3,764
Rehabilitation Costs $646,808		23,520	23,520	23,520	23,520	23,520	23,520	23,520
Personal Property $20,000		4,000	4,000	4,000	4,000	4,000		
Amortization Expenses:								
Organization Costs/Fees	2,500	2,500	2,500	2,500	2,500			
Equity Loan Fee	173	173	173	173	173			
Total Expenses	$ 24,107	$117,273	$125,683	$128,001	$130,499	$130,685	$131,029	$135,704
Taxable Income/Loss	$−24,107	$−36,048	$−34,711	$−32,480	$−30,202	$−25,373	$−20,452	$−19,598
GENERAL-PARTNER SHARE (1%)	$−241	$−360	$−347	$−325	$−302	$−254	$−205	$−196
LIMITED-PARTNER SHARE (99%)	$−23,866	$−35,687	$−34,364	$−32,156	$−29,900	$−25,120	$−20,247	$−19,402
Taxable Income Loss @ 37% Tax Rate	−8,830	−13,204	−12,715	−11,898	−11,063	−9,294	−7,492	−7,179
Low-Income Tax Credit		28,488	34,185	34,185	34,185	34,185	34,185	34,185
Total Tax Benefits	8,830	41,692	46,900	46,083	45,248	43,479	41,677	41,364
Capital Contribution (6,793)	32,126	36,142	35,514	34,872	33,508			
Net Benefits ($−6,793)	$−23,296	$5,550	$11,386	$11,211	$11,740	$43,479	$41,677	$41,364

* Department of Housing.

	1995	1996	1997	1998	1999	2000	2001	2002
INCOME								
Gross Rental								
Income	$128,328	$134,744	$141,481	$148,555	$155,983	$163,782	$171,971	$180,570
Less: Vacancy (5%)	6,416	6,737	7,074	7,428	7,799	8,189	8,599	9,028
Effective Gross								
Income	$121,911	$128,007	$134,407	$141,127	$148,184	$155,593	$163,373	$171,541
EXPENSES								
Operating Expenses	$ 86,514	$ 90,840	$ 95,382	$100,151	$105,159	$110,417	$115,937	$121,734
Interest Expense								
(debt service)	17,923	17,627	17,307	16,960	16,585	16,178	15,738	15,261
Interest Expense								
(DOH)*	5,606	6,491	7,420	8,396	9,420	10,496	11,625	12,811
Interest Expense								
(equity loan)								
Financial Consultation								
and Planning								
Partnership								
Management Fee	3,277	3,498	3,730	3,974	4,230	4,499	4,781	5,078
Accounting and								
Legal Fees								
Depreciation Basis:								
Building $103,500		3,764	3,764	3,764	3,764	3,764	3,764	3,764
Rehabilitation								
Costs $646,808		23,520	23,520	23,520	23,520	23,520	23,520	23,520
Personal								
Property $20,000								
Amortization Expenses:								
Organization								
Costs/Fees								
Equity Loan Fee								
Total Expenses	$140,604	$145,740	$151,123	$156,765	$162,678	$168,874	$175,365	$182,168
Taxable								
Income/Loss	$−18,693	$−17,733	$−16,716	$−15,637	$−14,494	$−13,281	$−11,992	$−10,627
GENERAL-								
PARTNER								
SHARE (1%)	$−187	$−177	$−167	$−156	$−145	$−133	$−120	$−106
LIMITED-								
PARTNER								
SHARE (99%)	$−18,506	$−17,556	$−16,549	$−15,481	$−14,349	$−13,148	$−11,872	$−10,520
Taxable Income								
Loss @ 37%								
Tax Rate	−6,847	−6,496	−6,123	−5,728	−5,309	−4,865	−4,393	−3,893
Low-Income								
Tax Credit	34,185	34,185	34,185	5,698				
Total Tax Benefits	41,032	40,681	40,308	11,426	5,309	4,865	4,393	3,893
Capital								
Contribution								
(6,793)								
Net Benefits								
($−6,793)	$41,032	$40,681	$40,308	$11,426	$5,309	$4,865	$4,393	$3,893

* Department of Housing.

Table 8.10
5700 West Washington:
Analysis of Projected Investment Summary*

Year (As of January)	Capital Contri- bution	Taxable Income/ Loss	Tax Savings/ Loss	Low- Income Tax Credit	Total Tax Benefits/ Costs	Potential Cash Flow Distribution
1987	$ 6,793	$−23,866	$ 8,830	–	$ 8,830	–
1988	32,126	−35,687	13,204	$28,488	41,692	–
1989	36,142	−34,364	12,715	34,185	46,900	–
1990	35,514	−32,156	11,898	34,185	46,083	–
1991	34,872	−29,900	11,063	34,185	45,248	–
1992	33,508	−25,120	9,294	34,185	43,479	–
1993	–	−20,247	7,492	34,185	41,677	–
1994	–	−19,402	7,179	34,185	41,364	–
1995	–	−18,506	6,847	34,185	41,032	–
1996	–	−17,556	6,496	34,185	40,681	$2,994
1997	–	−16,549	6,123	34,185	40,308	3,690
1998	–	−15,481	5,728	5,698	11,426	4,423
1999	–	−14,349	5,309	–	5,309	5,190
2000	–	−13,148	4,865	–	4,865	5,997
2001	–	−11,872	4,393	–	4,393	6,845
2002	–	−10,520	3,893	–	3,893	7,733

* Assumes a 37 percent tax-bracket investor entitled to a 99% share; a net present value (at 15 percent) of $69,471; an internal rate of return (IRR) of 46.41%; and a benefits/pay-in ratio of 1.30 (pay-in period) and of 2.66 (15-year investment period).

how a CEF-type entity can work under the new tax laws, as well. Deducing that tax reform will make corporations hungry for new shelters that can replace the investment tax credit and the other benefits of a now-bygone era, LISC has recently announced the creation of the National Equity Fund (NEF). In keeping with their roles in the Chicago Equity Fund model, corporations and businesses will now buy interests in a single large general partnership, to be re-formed each year (the National Equity Fund). The latter will then invest, as the sole limited partner, in individual limited partnerships set up by neighborhood-based organizations for the purposes of developing and managing projects as a general partner. (6p, p. 624)

LISC will market interests in the National Equity Fund to national corporations and local businesses in those localities where the projects will be sited. Plans are to raise as much as $25 million in equity commitments from 35 corporations. These commitments should support $100 million worth of low-income housing, to be developed in target states or cities such as Massachu-

Table 8.11
5700 West Washington:
Calculation of Low-Income Tax Credit

Acquisition Costs	$115,000
Basic Construction Costs	546,238
Other	171,817
TOTAL PROJECT COSTS	$833,055
Federal Funds toward Acquisition Costs	$115,000
Federal Funds toward Rehabilitation Costs	295,000
TOTAL FEDERAL FUNDS	$410,000
REHABILITATION CREDIT	
Eligible Basis (depreciables)	$666,808
Less: Federal Funds	295,000
Qualified Basis	371,808
(Multiply by)	9%
AMOUNT OF REHABILITATION CREDIT	$ 33,463
ACQUISITION CREDIT	
Building (less land)	$103,500
(Multiply by)	4%
AMOUNT OF ACQUISITION CREDIT	$ 4,140
AMOUNT OF TOTAL TAX CREDIT	
(Rehabilitation + Acquisition)	$ 37,603

setts, New York City, Chicago, Kansas City, and Denver. Judging by the Chicago Equity Fund's experience, LISC expects that the projects supported through the National Equity Fund will need major local financing assistance—in the form of subsidized second mortgages and bridge loans—because rents will only be high enough to support a 30 to 35 percent first mortgage. (6p, p. 624)

While it is too early to assess the long-term prospects of the National Equity Fund, we know enough about the new tax laws and corporate investment practices to identify the requisites for success. For major amounts of corporate capital to be attracted to the low-income housing sector, each deal or partnership must be structured so that the minimum assured return on investment reaches a competitive level. Under the new tax law, the minimum assured return is in the form of the tax credit, and this is nothing more than a 10-year annuity of known value whose price can be set at the negotiated or targeted level.

Thus, there are several requisites for the ultimate success of the NEF. First, the safety and security of the tax credit annuities must be assumed, and therefore, some kind of guarantee or indemnification fund might have to be created to attract corporate capital in the desired quantities into low-income housing. Second—if (other factors being equal) the higher the required return, the lower the corporate equity as a percentage of project

Table 8.12
5700 West Washington:
Analysis of Projected Sale of Property

	Year 10		Year 16	
	Mortgage	Original Cost	Mortgage	Original Cost
Sales Price	$628,226	$833,055	$597,347	$833,055
Less: Selling Expenses (3%)		24,992		24,992
Net Sales Proceeds	628,226	808,063	597,347	808,063
Less: Adjusted Basis of Property	542,554	542,554	395,050	395,050
TOTAL GAIN ON SALE	$ 85,672	$265,509	$202,297	$413,013
ALLOCATION OF GAIN				
General Partner (1%)	857	2,655	2,023	4,130
Limited Partner (99%)	84,815	262,854	200,274	408,883
TAX ON DISPOSITION				
Tax on Gain	$ 31,699	$ 98,238	$ 74,850	$152,815
Total Tax Credit Claimed	336,153	336,153	336,153	336,153
Less: Total Credit Earned				
(15-year compliance)	227,900	227,900	336,153	336,153
Amount Subject to Recapture	$108,253	$108,253	–	–
TOTAL TAX LIABILITY	$139,952	$206,491	$ 74,850	$152,815
ALLOCATION OF LIABILITY				
General Partner (1%)	1,400	2,065	748	1,528
Limited Partner (99%)	138,552	204,427	74,101	151,287
ALLOCATION OF NET SALES PROCEEDS				
Net Sales Proceeds	$628,226	$808,063	$597,347	$808,063
Less: First Mortgage	218,226	218,226	187,347	187,347
Less: Second Mortgage	410,000	410,000	410,000	410,000
NET PROCEEDS AVAILABLE				
FOR DISTRIBUTION	–	$179,837	–	$210,716
ALLOCATION OF				
DISTRIBUTIONS				
General Partner (1%)	–	$ 1,798	–	$ 2,107
Limited Partner (99%)	–	178,039	–	208,609

cost—then for the NEF to succeed, local participation in projects must be substantial. It must be even more substantial in higher-risk projects. This means that—in order to take full advantage of the new tax laws, as the NEF makes possible—communities might have to make major increases in their own-source revenues devoted to housing.

Third, as the Chicago experience illustrates, successful projects depend upon the existence of a strong and experienced cadre of community-based housing producers. And even where such producers are present, making them fully effective requires the presence of a strong technical assistance resource, such as the Community Equity Assistance Corporation (CEAC), and an informed and committed private lending community. One such informed and committed private lending community, the CEF—as our earlier analysis indicated—was just one element, albeit a critical one, in the Chicago Housing Partnership. How sophisticated and committed other such partners are in other communities across the country, and how committed the states and federal government are to helping them grow stronger and more sophisticated, will have a great deal to do with NEF's ultimate success.

The BRIDGE Housing Corporation

In 1981, a San Francisco Foundation task force on housing sought to attack the shortage of affordable housing in one of the highest-cost regions of the country. The BRIDGE Housing Corporation resulted. It is a new kind of public/private housing partnership with significant potential for widespread replication.

BRIDGE differs from the Boston and Chicago models in several important respects. First, BRIDGE is an organization that operates in the nine-county San Francisco Bay Area, and not just in a single political jurisdiction. This means that it must master complex land use and development regulations in many jurisdictions, and must maintain excellent relationships with many political bodies. A poorly planned or executed project, or a mismanaged community relationship in one locality could cause BRIDGE calamitous difficulties in other regional communities. This is especially true because BRIDGE—unlike its Chicago and Boston counterparts—acts not only as a facilitator of production by neighborhood-based organizations, but also as a direct producer in its own right.

As a producer, BRIDGE has an agenda that is easily as ambitious as those of its two inner-city counterparts. According to

BRIDGE President Don Terner, in order to make any difference at all,

> You must be able to provide housing in some volume, not just in token numbers. We are aiming to supply 5 percent of the area's multi-family housing—about 1,000 to 1,500 units yearly. (31a, p. 34)

Terner understands that such a volume could never be realized if BRIDGE were not sensitive to community concerns about high-density development and low-income housing projects. This is why BRIDGE places a premium on excellence in site planning and design. According to Terner,

> Every project has to be a showcase. You have to serve the consumer, but, just as importantly, you have to satisfy the nearby neighborhoods. (31a, p. 35)

Its diverse role in the production process, taken together with its varied portfolio, constitutes the second distinguishing feature of the BRIDGE enterprise. Since its inception in 1983, BRIDGE has participated in the development of over 3,000 houses, valued at $230 million (see Table 8.13). Unlike the Boston and Chicago Partnership projects, however, not all of BRIDGE's housing units are for low- and moderate-income families. Most projects mix below-market units with market-rate housing, with no design distinctions made between them. Since BRIDGE's inception, 44 percent of all the units it has produced or supported have been affordable to households with incomes between $12,000 and $25,000. This range makes the units eligible for Section 8 Existing Certificates in Bay Area communities. Indeed, this advantage is a particularly important one in a region with an extreme shortage of available low-income stock.

More specifically, BRIDGE's unusually diverse participation in affordable housing projects has been 1) as a private developer; 2) as the sole developer invited to develop city-owned land and surplus school properties into affordable housing; 3) as a codeveloper with the private sector's for-profit and local not-for-profit developers; 4) as an equity investor in nonprofit housing development; and 5) as a supplier of technical assistance and seed money to cover front-end and soft costs of projects that will be built by other local nonprofits (see Table 8.14).

The third difference between BRIDGE and the two inner-city partnerships concerns its location in one of the highest-cost and most restrictive development environments in the nation. The development review process in Bay Area communities averages, in duration, between 18 and 24 months, even for small, uncomplicated projects. Many Bay Area communities have adopted

Table 8.13
Summary of BRIDGE Activity
(Cumulative to May 1987)

Project/Location	Total Units	Below-Market Units	Rental/Ownership	Public/Private Investment	Project Value
OCCUPIED					
Diablo Vista Apartments, Livermore	135	34	Rental	$ 100,000	$ 6,900,000
Charles Hotel, Vallejo	24	24	Ownership	100,000	750,000
Marion Park Apartments, Novato	168	34	Rental	470,000	9,800,000
Center Street Rehabilitation, Oakland	10	10	Rental	51,000	320,000
Holloway Terrace, S.F.	42	42	Ownership	377,000	4,006,000
Amancio Ergina, S.F.	72	32	Ownership	138,000	5,440,000
Shared Leased Housing, Marin	30	30	Rental	–	1,125,000
Shared Purchased Housing, Marin	8	8	Rental	–	175,000
Swiss American Hotel, S.F.	67	67	Rental	2,000,000	2,500,000
The Meadows, Novato	99	20	Rental	275,000	5,000,000
Point Reyes Senior & Self-Help Housing	35	35	Elderly Rental/Ownership	661,400	1,800,000
Americana Apartments, Concord	200	40	Rental	140,000	10,400,000
Pickleweed, Mill Valley	32	32	Rental	1,200,000	2,700,000
Heritage Village, Fremont	192	39–67	Rental	200,000	14,000,000
SUBTOTAL	1,114	447			
IN CONSTRUCTION					
Magnolia Plaza, South San Francisco	125	62	Elderly Rental	TBD	$ 7,000,000
Peninsula Regent/Manor, Phase 1, San Mateo	207	–	Elderly Lifecare	$ 2,000,000	55,000,000
Richards Manor, Livermore	167	67	Elderly Rental	1,500,000	7,350,000
SUBTOTAL	374	67			
IN APPROVALS					
Morgan Heights, S.F.	63	63	Ownership	$ 1,100,000	$ 6,300,000
Pacifica Oaks	104	34	Elderly Rental	TBD	5,000,000
Frank G. Mar Community Housing, Oakland	119	119	Elderly/Family Rental	4,000,000	11,000,000
San Ramon School Site, Mountain View	202	60+	Elderly Rental/Ownership	300,000	16,500,000
Standard Brands, S.F.	49	49	Rental	TBD	3,700,000
Garrity Ridge, Pinole	225	45	Ownership	TBD	20,000,000
Peninsula Regent/Manor, Phase 2, San Mateo	106	106	Elderly Rental	200,000	6,000,000
Poly High Site, San Francisco	114	68	Ownership	3,000,000	13,900,000
Marin City School Site	220	88	Elderly/Family Rental/Ownership	TBD	TBD
Pope Street Site, Alameda	185	93	Elderly Rental	TBD	9,000,000
Hunt Avenue Affordable Housing, St. Helena	56	56	Rental	500,000	4,200,000
SUBTOTAL	1,568	843			
TOTAL	3,056	1,357		$18,312,400	$229,866,000

Source: BRIDGE Housing Corporation.

Table 8.14:
Status Summary for Selected BRIDGE Projects (As of May 1987)

Project/Location # Units/# Affordable Rental/Ownership	Project Description/BRIDGE Role
Diablo Vista Apts. Livermore, CA (Alameda County) 135/34 Rental Project Value: $6,900,000 Occupied	BRIDGE coordinated and implemented an innovative rental assistance fund that reduced rents on 34 units to the Section 8–eligible level. The developer, Lexington Homes, the city, and BRIDGE each contributed $50,000 to the fund, with interest used for monthly reduction payments. BRIDGE also assisted with tenant selection for the affordable units.
Marion Park Apts. Novato, CA (Marin County) 168/34 Rental Project Value: $9,800,000 Occupied	BRIDGE provided a $50,000 loan to the nonprofit sponsors, the Ecumenical Association for Housing and Novato Ecumenical Housing, to leverage a $520,000 pool for a loan to the developer, Davidson, Kavanagh & Brezzo. The 7 percent loan to the developer facilitated rent reductions beyond those required by bond-financing regulations.
Shared Purchased Housing Larkspur, CA (Marin County) 8/8 Rental Project Value: $175,000 Occupied	BRIDGE provided a loan to the nonprofit sponsor, Innovative Housing, to purchase a shared housing site. The loan money was used to cover the downpayment on the house. The loan will be repaid with proceeds from the rent-up on the units.
Holloway Terrace San Francisco, CA (San Francisco County) 42/42 Ownership Project Value: $4,006,000 Occupied	BRIDGE acted as codeveloper with HCDC, a locally based nonprofit, and provided predevelopment funds to expedite the project process. Reimbursement of BRIDGE funds, and of the cost of staff time, occurred at final closing.

BRIDGE Investment		Project Status
Expended	$50,000	Lexington Homes, BRIDGE, and the city completed a first-year evaluation of the rental assistance program and determined that the difference between the Section 8 payments received and the affordable rents exceeded the income derived from the assistance program as originally conceived. In order to continue to make all 34 units available to Section 8 certificate holders, Section 8 payments had to be increased to 120 percent. The housing authority approved the increase in June 1985.
Recovered	0	
Receivable	50,000	
Net	0	
Expended	$50,000	BRIDGE staff members are continuing to monitor the project informally. It is now 100 percent occupied.
Recovered	0	
Receivable	50,000	
Net	0	
Expended	$8,370	Innovative Housing requested an $8,370 loan for the purchase of a house located in Larkspur. The loan money was used as part of a downpayment for the purchase of the house, which would accommodate eight people. The loan was secured by a second deed of trust and was repaid in April 1987.
Recovered	8,370	
Receivable	0	
Net	0	
Expended	$272,490	All of the homes have been sold and are now occupied. BRIDGE has been repaid for all direct expenses and has received the full negotiated development fee. Because some excess funds remain, BRIDGE is now in the process of negotiating payment for 100 percent of staff costs. The project was awarded the Pacific Coast Builders' Conference Gold Nugget Award for the "Best in the West."
Recovered	322,890	
Receivable	0	
ʸ⸗t	50,400	

(Table 8.14: Cont'd.)
Status Summary for Selected BRIDGE Projects

Project/Location # Units/# Affordable Rental/Ownership	Project Description/BRIDGE Role
Marin City School Site Marin City, CA (Marin County) 220/88 Elderly/Family Rental/Ownership Project Value: TBD In Approvals	The Marin City Community Development Corporation and the Marin City Community Services District will jointly develop 220 units of housing (family and elderly, ownership and rental); a 200- to 250-room hotel; a park; a community center; and shopping and office space, on 42 acres in Marin City. BRIDGE will assume the primary development responsibility for the residential uses, and will assist in the development of the other aspects of the project.
Frank G. Mar Community Housing Oakland, CA (Alameda County) 119/119 Rental (Elderly/Family) Project Value: $9,000,000 In Approvals	The East Bay Asian Local Development Corporation is committed to providing replacement housing for the hundreds of Chinatown units lost to redevelopment over the past two decades. BRIDGE, acting as a codeveloper, has provided assistance with site identification and acquisition, design, and financial packaging. Escrow closed for purchase of the property on December 4, 1985.
Magnolia Plaza South San Francisco, CA (San Mateo County) 125/62 Rental (Elderly) Project Value: $7,000,000 In Approvals	BRIDGE and Adams & Graves (AG) have tentatively agreed to codevelop this three-acre surplus school site. This project will be coordinated with the city's efforts to rehabilitate the school into a senior center. BRIDGE, as a 25 percent partner, would be responsible for its percentage of predevelopment expenses, and would receive a similar percentage of the profits, which will be used to increase affordability levels.
Swiss American Hotel San Francisco, CA (San Francisco County) 67/67 Rental Project Value: $2,500,000 Occupied	The Chinese Community Housing Corporation purchased this single-resident occupancy (SRO) hotel at a price of $1,700,000 and rehabilitated it. BRIDGE assisted with structuring the proposed purchase terms and provided some gap financing for the purchase.

BRIDGE Investment		Project Status
Expended	$ 64,223	After many months of delay, the school district has fi-
Recovered	500,000	nally accepted the revised offer submitted by BRIDGE,
Receivable	0	the Marin CDC, and the CSD. BRIDGE staff and at-
Net	435,777	torneys are working with the school district to complete

the final details of the purchase agreement. Additionally, the San Francisco Foundation has approved a $500,000 interest-free, unsecured loan to option the property for 18 months, and has transferred first deeds of trust to BRIDGE for the Flea Market, Price, and gas station properties—all located adjacent to the school site. The total value is $577,000.

Expended	$69,170	EBALDC and BRIDGE have recently secured an ad-
Recovered	67,260	ditional $3.4 million from the city for the development
Receivable	0	of subterranean parking on the site; $5.5 million from
Net	(1,210)	HUD for development of the housing component; and

$500,000 from OCD for the commercial component. EBALDC and BRIDGE are in the process of finalizing design work, selecting a general contractor, and structuring the project to meet the requirements of each funding agency.

Expended	$162,362	The city has approved a sale/leaseback and taken title
Recovered	112,524	to the site. The city council will take final action in
Receivable	16,664	May on final terms for the lease and on the parcel
Net	(33,174)	map. The city staff has recommended a waiver of

several city fees that was considered by the city council in May 1987. The financing package, using tax-exempt bonds, was completed in May 1987; this was closely followed by the start of construction.

Expended	$48,000	The project has been completed and is fully occupied.
Recovered	50,226	BRIDGE staff will informally monitor the devel-
Receivable	0	opment.
Net	2,226	

Status Summary for Selected BRIDGE Projects

Project/Location # Units/# Affordable Rental/Ownership	Project Description/BRIDGE Role
Point Reyes Senior & Self-Help Housing Point Reyes Station, CA (Marin County) 35/35 Rental 25 (Elderly) Ownership 10 Project Value: $1,800,000 Occupied	BRIDGE provided a $56,500 land loan to the Ecumenical Association for Housing to help purchase the six-acre project site. BRIDGE also provided HUD a backup letter of credit of $95,696, to secure the off-site improvements.
Pickleweed Mill Valley, CA (Marin County) 32/32 Rental Project Value: $2,700,000 Occupied	BRIDGE was approached by the city of Mill Valley and the San Francisco Foundation in April 1985 regarding this project. The city had purchased the land and taken over the project in early 1984, after several attempts by private builders to construct it had failed. After initial analysis, BRIDGE agreed to work with the city to complete the development of the project.
Heritage Village Fremont, CA (Alameda County) 192/39–67 Rental Project Value: $14,000,000 Occupied	BRIDGE staff, in working with city staff, identified the nine-acre surplus Alameda County Water District property as appropriate for multiple-family housing. BRIDGE and Davidson, Kavanagh & Brezzo (DKB) formed a partnership to purchase and codevelop the site, with BRIDGE as a 25 percent partner. BRIDGE's proceeds from developing the project will be used to increase affordability levels.
Richards Manor Livermore, CA (Alameda County) 167/67 Rental (Elderly) Project Value: $7,350,000 In Construction	BRIDGE and Eden Housing, a local nonprofit, are codevelopers of this site, which was donated by the owner. BRIDGE provided predevelopment monies, negotiated the land donation, arranged financing, and worked with Eden to obtain the project approvals. Calmark, a for-profit partner, was selected to take over the project, through a lease guaranteeing affordability restrictions.

BRIDGE Investment		Project Status
Expended	$56,500	The BRIDGE loan was repaid with interest on September 5, 1985. The project was completed in May 1986 and is now 100 percent occupied.
Recovered	60,455	
Receivable	0	
Net	3,955	
Expended	$1,759,228	The project has been completed and is fully occupied. BRIDGE co-owns the development with the city of Mill Valley, and is working closely with the management company, the Ecumenical Association for Housing, to ensure that the project is operating smoothly.
Recovered	1,810,428	
Receivable	0	
Net	51,200	
Expended	$172,541	Construction was completed in March 1987. One hundred sixty-five units have been rented, well ahead of the projected rent-up schedule. BRIDGE will use its syndication proceeds to reimburse its direct costs, and to set up an account for project reserves and rent writedowns. BRIDGE will also retain a 15 percent interest in the project.
Recovered	263,194	
Receivable	0	
Net	90,653	
Expended	$765,436	Calmark's contractor is pouring foundations, with construction projected to last through early October 1987. Eden is negotiating with Calmark to manage the project upon completion.
Recovered	830,270	
Receivable	650,061	
Net	714,895	

(Table 8.14: Cont'd.)
Status Summary for Selected BRIDGE Projects

Project/Location # Units/# Affordable Rental/Ownership	Project Description/BRIDGE Role
Morgan Heights Hunters Point, CA (San Francisco County) 63/63 Ownership Project Value: $6,300,000 In Approvals	BRIDGE was asked by the San Francisco Redevelopment Agency to assess the feasibility of developing housing on their site, with a possible second phase on adjacent housing authority land. The agency has committed $490,000 toward site work for the first phase and has additional funds for the second. The structure and financing will be modeled after Holloway Terrace. BRIDGE will seek a private partner and may work with a local community group.
Garrity Ridge Pinole, CA (Contra Costa County) 225/45 Rental/Ownership Project Value: $20,000,000 In Approvals	BRIDGE has an option on this 32-acre vacant site, which has been declared surplus by the Richmond Unified School District. The site is designated primarily for single-family housing, with the westerly seven acres available for higher-density housing. BRIDGE, as a 25 percent partner, will codevelop the property with Davidson, Kavanagh & Brezzo, a private-sector developer.
Peninsula Regent/ Peninsula Manor San Mateo, CA (San Mateo County) 313/106 Rental Project Value: $61,000,000 In Approvals	The role of BASS, a BRIDGE affiliate in this project, has two facets: BASS will be the lead developer of the affordable component (Peninsula Manor), and will act as the lessee and operator for the market-rate component (Peninsula Regent). The two components are to be built on different sites but will be in close proximity so that certain facilities may be shared. The city of San Mateo has committed the tax increment from the Peninsula Regent to helping to subsidize the Peninsula Manor.
Poly High Site San Francisco, CA (San Francisco County) 114/68 Ownership Project Value: $13,900,000 In Approvals	BRIDGE and Pacific Union Development Company (PUDC) have formed a 50/50 partnership, which was selected by the city and a resident committee to lease and develop this former school site. BRIDGE's proceeds from developing the project will be used to increase affordability levels. The project will provide an exceptional number of homes for, and affordable to, families with children.

BRIDGE Investment		Project Status
Expended	$294,915	On the basis of expressions of interest by several construction lenders, the project design team has prepared working drawings to be submitted to the city by June 1, 1987, for building permits. Construction was expected to start in late July 1987. The Ecumenical Council will serve in an advisory capacity to help pre-sell the units.
Recovered	0	
Receivable	0	
Net	(294,915)	
Expended	$53,404	A site plan, which includes 112 single-family units and 108 condominium units, has been submitted, with the first public hearing scheduled for May 1987. Public hearings will be held over the next few months. The school district has agreed to revise the purchase agreement, allowing for partial releases of the site to accommodate phased development.
Recovered	37,500	
Receivable	2,553	
Net	(13,351)	
Expended	$1,183,801	BASS is negotiating an agreement pertaining to the market component of the project with BAC. The agreement provides for $200,000 to be made available by BAC to acquire a site for the affordable component. The staff has begun negotiations for sites that will accommodate approximately 100 units. Construction on the market-rate units began in November 1986. BASS is reviewing the documents associated with leasing and operating the Peninsula Regent, and has received a lifecare facility license from the state.
Recovered	1,183,801	
Receivable	0	
Net	0	
Expended	$390,322	The board of supervisors has placed the referendum on the ballot for a June special election (the earliest possible opportunity). BRIDGE and Pacific Union are working closely with the mayor and city departments to negotiate a lease, to demolish the existing buildings, and to process the required planning approvals. Campaigning against the referendum continues in the meantime.
Recovered	39,847	
Receivable	0	
Net	(350,474)	

Project/Location # Units/# Affordable Rental/Ownership	Project Description/BRIDGE Role
Pope Street Site Alameda, CA (Alameda County) 185/93 Rental (Elderly) Project Value: $9,000,000 In Approvals	The city of Alameda's housing authority has expressed an interest in having BRIDGE coordinate and develop a mixed-use project, to include 185 senior rental units and possible office space for the housing authority. The site history includes several failed attempts at development. BRIDGE has completed a preliminary analysis and has agreed to work with the housing authority to complete the project.

growth control ordinances that limit the number of building permits that can be issued each year. For example, the community of Pacifica issues a maximum of 70 building permits a year, and no single developer can receive more than 20 percent of the permits in any one year. BRIDGE had to take its 104-unit project to the voters to gain the first-ever (and, so far, the only) exemption to the city's growth control ordinance. The city of Livermore's growth management ordinance requires that all projects be reviewed during a given time period each year. If a developer misses this window of opportunity, his project is delayed for another year. So far, BRIDGE has done two projects in Livermore totaling 302 units.

Development fees also exert a heavy toll on project costs and affordability. In Pacifica, for instance, developer fees for thoroughfares, parks, and plan processing average $4,000 per unit, although in numerous cases, including Pacifica, BRIDGE has managed to get such fees waived or deferred. A crucial component of BRIDGE's operating strategy is the creation of value through the mastery of local land use regulatory systems—which frequently leads to density increases and sometimes to expedited project approvals or exemptions from onerous regulations. BRIDGE uses the resulting financial gains to write down occupancy costs to the end-users.

The importance of sound working relationships between BRIDGE and the communities in which it works cannot be overstated. As noted above, in the November 1985 elections, BRIDGE sought an exemption from the city of Pacifica's strict growth con-

BRIDGE Investment			Project Status
Expended	$	0	The Memorandum of Understanding between the
Recovered		0	housing authority and BRIDGE was approved by the
Receivable		0	housing authority commission in mid-November. A
Net		0	senior housing task force, composed of various individuals from civic and community groups, as well as city staff, has been established. The task force is now helping BRIDGE staff with the selection of consultants, and with refinement of the design/development process.

trol ordinance, and won 82 percent of the vote for its cause.* Other ways in which BRIDGE has created value-added in its projects are reflected in Table 8.14, and detailed below with respect to a specific development.

Richards Manor

How BRIDGE was able to generate additional subsidies for affordable housing by working local land use and development regulations is illustrated in a 167-unit project in Alameda County called Richards Manor. It began when a landowner in the city of Livermore, about an hour's drive east of San Francisco, proposed to donate 10 acres of land for senior citizens' housing. The site was zoned for eight units per acre and valued at $10,000 per unit, or $800,000. The city referred the landowner to a local nonprofit developer named Eden Housing, which, in turn, brought BRIDGE into the picture. Working together, BRIDGE and Eden secured the necessary project approvals.

First, the project had to receive special consideration under Livermore's growth control ordinance, which limits the number of building permits that can be issued each year. The project was allowed to use permits that had been allocated in previous years but had not been used. Next, BRIDGE and Eden obtained a density bonus in excess of 100 percent, according to the affordable-housing and special senior-citizens' housing incentives available under the law. These bonuses increased the planned

---

* BRIDGE Housing Corporation, *1985–86 Annual Report,* p. 8.

137

project in size from 80 to 167 units, and more than doubled the value of the site, to $1,670,000.

BRIDGE and Eden then joint-ventured the project with a for-profit partner, Calmark Development Corporation, a Southern California–based firm specializing in elderly housing that had shown interest in breaking into the Northern California market. Calmark is building the project, which is being financed with tax-exempt bonds issued by the Livermore Housing Authority. First Interstate provided credit enhancement for the bonds, in the form of a letter of credit.

Under federal law, bond-financed projects must set aside 20 percent of their units for low-income families. Because of the added land value created by the BRIDGE/Eden negotiation of development approvals, however, Richards Manor will have twice that number of low-income apartments. Project subsidies will come from payments on a land lease made by Calmark to BRIDGE/Eden, which maintains long-term ownership of the land. By pumping all available revenues back into the project, the participants will be able to keep its affordable rents below $400 per month.

The Anatomy of BRIDGE

The final difference between BRIDGE and the Boston and Chicago Partnerships lies in its internal organization. Like the other entities, BRIDGE has the strong backing of its locale's business community. The BRIDGE Campaign Committee—which is composed of the chairmen and CEOs of 17 national and Bay Area corporations—has raised nearly $6 million from corporations and foundations for the BRIDGE Development Trust Fund. The trust fund is a revolving, self-sustaining source of working capital for BRIDGE projects, but is not used to subsidize them. As indicated earlier, subsidies are earned by adding value to land through the development process, and are then funneled back into the project. This leaves the trust fund's revenues free to supply gap financing, to fund predevelopment costs, to provide for letters of credit, to secure options on sites or acquire sites outright, and to buy equity interests in promising projects that might not otherwise be built.

In contrast to the multiple-partner arrangements in Boston and Chicago, BRIDGE is a single nonprofit entity. It possesses all of the necessary project planning, packaging, financing, and management skills entirely within its corporate bounds. Given its major productivity, its staff is surprisingly modest in numbers: its professionals include only a president, vice president, comptroller, and five project managers. BRIDGE's president previously served as director of housing and community development for the state of California (four years), as a vice president of a private construction company, and as executive director of a nonprofit housing corporation in New York City. The organization's vice president has earlier been an executive director of a nonprofit housing corporation, for which he oversaw the completion of 12 projects totaling nearly 1,000 units; he also formerly worked on affordable housing for HUD and for several Bay Area communities. Typically, BRIDGE project managers have urban planning and business backgrounds and come to the corporation with previous housing experience.

A third-party evaluation of BRIDGE has concluded that

> BRIDGE has a sharp, lean staff uniquely qualified to assess what is needed to make Bay Area affordable housing projects work, and to supply the highly leveraged infusions of venture capital, gap financing, equity, and expertise to make them happen. [It has] the credibility to sway local elected officials and wary communities to undertake developments. [It has] the ability to act quickly and decisively, to commit funds flexibly, to draw on the expertise and "clout" of a potent set of directors and other supporters, and to deploy a network of high-quality architects, engineers, planners, designers, and other building professionals.*

The most important challenge facing BRIDGE in the future is to maintain its top managerial talent, and, should this prove impossible, to demonstrate that the organization can successfully survive a transition. The proper maintenance of this system, and its replication in other regions, would well serve the interests of affordable housing in the coming years.

---

* *The San Francisco Foundation Monitor's Report,* November 26, 1986, p. 2.

Bibliography

1) "A Housing Trust Fund for New York City: Background and Preliminary Recommendations." Citizens' Housing and Planning Council, July 1985.
2) Apgar, William C., Jr. "The Leaky Boat: How Much of a Housing Problem Remains?" 1985, unpublished.
   2a. The Boston Housing Partnership, Inc. "Program Summary." Undated.
   2b. The Boston Housing Partnership, Inc. "Program Description." Undated.
   2c. Boston Zoning Code, Article 26A, February 1986.
3) Arnold, Alvin L. *Real Estate Investment After the Tax Reform Act of 1986.* Boston: Warren, Gorham & Lamont, 1987.
4) BRIDGE Housing Corporation, *1985–86 Annual Report.*
5) Brown, H. James and Yinger, John. *Homeownership and Affordability in the United States 1963–1985.* Joint Center for Housing Studies of the Massachusetts Institute of Technology and Harvard University, 1986.
6) Brownstein, Zeidman, and Schower. "Summary of Certain Sections of the Tax Reform Act of 1986, September 23, 1986."
   6a. Volume 13, Number 32 (12/30/85).
   6b. Volume 13, Number 42 (3/10/86).
   6c. Volume 13, Number 44 (3/24/86).
   6d. Volume 13, Number 50 (5/5/86).
   6e. Volume 14, Number 8 (7/14/86).
   6f. Volume 14, Number 10 (7/28/86).

6g. Volume 14, Number 12 (8/11/86).

6h. Volume 14, Number 14 (8/25/86).

6i. Volume 14, Number 16 (9/8/86).

6j. Volume 14, Number 18 (9/22/86).

6k. Volume 14, Number 20 (10/6/86).

6l. Volume 14, Number 22 (10/20/86).

6m. Volume 14, Number 24 (11/3/86).

6n. Volume 14, Number 26 (11/17/86).

6o. Volume 14, Number 28 (12/1/86).

6p. Volume 14, Number 30 (12/15/86).

6q. Volume 14, Number 32 (12/29/86).

7) Bureau of National Affairs. *Housing Development Reporter:*

    7a. Cherry Hill, New Jersey. Amendments to Land Subdivision Ordinance of 1968, Ordinance 86–19. June 9, 1986.

    7b. City of Austin. *City Council Housing Task Force.* September 1986, draft.

    7c. City of Austin. "Report of the Mayor's Select Committee on Affordable Housing." February 20, 1986.

    7d. The Chicago Housing Partnership. Program Description. Undated.

    7e. The Chicago Equity Fund. "Basic Information." Undated.

    7f. City of Boulder. *Developer's Handbook for Low- and Moderate-Income Housing.* July 1985.

8) California Department of Housing and Community Development. "Model Inclusionary Zoning Ordinance." Undated; p. 2.

    8a. Chattanooga Venture, Inc. *The Chattanooga Ten-Year Program to Make All Housing Fit and Livable.* September 1986.

    8b. ULI–the Urban Land Institute. *Urban Land,* Vol. 45, No. 10 (October 1986).

9) City and County of San Francisco. "Office Affordable Housing Production Program." August 16, 1985.

    9a. Chicago Tribune. *The American Millstone.* Chicago: Contemporary Books, 1986.

10) City of New York. *Ten-Year Capital Plan Fiscal Year 1987–1996: Overview.* May 1986.

11) City of New York, Office of Management and the Budget. *Executive Budget, Fiscal Year 1987.*

12) *Coalition for Affordable Housing Report.* Austin, Texas: Peat Marwick Mitchell & Company, May 1986.

13) Community Development Services. *Housing Affairs Letter:*

    13a. No. 86–34 (8/22/86).

    13b. No. 86–36 (9/5/86).

    13c. No. 86–37 (9/12/86).

    13d. No. 86–38 (9/19/86).

    13e. No. 86–40 (10/3/86).

    13f. No. 86–47 (11/21/86).

14) "Corporate Funds to Fuel Community Programs," *Urban Land,* Vol. 45, No. 10 (October 1986).

15) Council of Large Public Housing Agencies. *Newsletter,* October 30, 1986.
   15a. Sidor, John. *State Housing Initiatives: A Compendium.* Council of State Community Affairs Agencies, 1986.
16) Cullick, R. "Affordable Housing Plan to Include Builder Fee," *Austin American-Statesman* (February 12, 1986).
17) Cullick, R. "Firm Urged in Report on Housing," *Austin American-Statesman* (May 22, 1986), p. B4.
18) DePalma, A. "Building Boom Is Near an End," *New York Times* (November 23, 1986).
19) Federal Home Loan Mortgage Corporation. "Tax Reform, 1986," *Freddie Mac Reports* (October 1986).
   19a. Green, Marcia Slacum. "D.C. Holds Rent Subsidies Lottery," *Washington Post* (August 20, 1986).
20) Guggenheim, J. *Tax Credits for Low-Income Housing.* Washington, D.C.: Simon Publishing, 1986.
   20a. Hawaii Housing Authority. *Rental Assistance Program Procedural Handbook.* June 20, 1986.
21) *Housing and Community Development Guidelines, 1986–87.* Pennsylvania Department of Community Affairs.
   21a. Keating, W. Dennis. "Housing/CD Linkages: A Tested Strategy," *Journal of Housing,* Vol. 43, No. 3 (May/June 1986).
22) Keating, W. Dennis. "Linking Downtown Development to Broader Community Goals: An Analysis of Linkage Policy in Three Cities," *Journal of the American Planning Association,* Vol. 52, No. 2 (Spring 1986).
   22a. Lee County, Florida, Board of County Commissioners. Ordinance 85-4. January 22, 1986.
   22b. "Experimental Housing Policy for Jersey City." Department of Housing and Economic Development, 1986.
   22c. Levy, Marilyn W. *Stimulating Middle-Income Housing Production.* New York University Real Estate Institute, 1987.
23) Low-Income Housing Information Service. *Low-Income Housing Round-Up,* No. 105 (September 1986).
24) Lublin, Joann S. "Uncertain Solution: Vouchers for Housing Help Some of the Poor, Fail to Benefit Others," *The Wall Street Journal* (November 19, 1986), p. 1.
   24a. Letter to Michael A. Stegman from Linda L. Conroy, director of research and program development for the Massachusetts Housing Finance Agency. July 15, 1986.
25) Merriam, Dwight; Brower, David J.; and Tegeler, Phillip D., editors. *Inclusionary Zoning Moves Downtown.* Washington, D.C.: American Planning Association (APA) Press, 1985.
   25a. Maryland Department of Economic and Community Development. "Rental Allowance Program Regulations." November 15, 1986, draft.
   25b. Miami Zoning Ordinance, Section 1556.2.2.

26) "Municipal Legislative Goals and Policy regarding Housing, Community Development, and Redevelopment Issues." North Carolina League of Municipalities, 1987.

27) National Association of Home Builders. *Low- and Moderate-Income Housing: Progress, Problems, and Prospects.* Washington, D.C.: 1986.

28) National Association of Housing and Redevelopment Officials. *NAHRO Monitor:*
   28a. Volume 8, Number 11 (8/31/86).
   28b. Volume 8, Number 19 (10/15/86).
   28c. Volume 8, Number 21 (11/15/86).
   28d. Volume 8, Number 22 (11/30/86).
   28e. Volume 9, Number 23 (12/15/86).

29) Nenno, Mary K. *New Money and New Methods: A Catalog of State and Local Initiatives in Housing and Community Development.* National Association of Housing and Redevelopment Officials, September 1986.

30) ———. "Reagan's Plans for HUD: More than Short-Term Cuts," *Journal of Housing,* Vol. 43, No. 3 (May/June 1986).
   30a. National Trust for Historic Preservation, Inner City Ventures Fund. Program Brochure. Undated.

31) Nenno, Mary K. "Affordable Housing: Housing for Low- and Moderate-Income Families." Mimeographed, January 1986.
   31a. Bradford, W. O'Hearn. "Bridging the Housing Gap," Part III, *Newsday* (March 8, 1986).

32) Peers, A. "Municipals May Still Be Good Bets, If You Can Decipher the Tax Bill," *Wall Street Journal* (September 10, 1986), p. 35.
   32a. Pennsylvania Department of Community Affairs. *Housing and Community Development Guidelines, 1986–87.*
   32b. Boston Redevelopment Authority. *Parcel-to-Parcel Linkage Program, Interim Report: Project 7, Kingston/Bedford, Parcel 18.* March 1986.
   32c. City of Hartford. "Ordinance Providing for Employment on Assisted Projects." June 1986.
   32d. City of Honolulu. "Community Benefit Assessment Program." Department of Land Utilization, June 1986.
   32e. Princeton Township. Affordable Housing Ordinance. November 1984.

33) *Raleigh Housing Task Force Report.* April 1986.

34) Salins, Peter D. "America's Permanent Housing Problem." Mimeographed, 1986; p. 6.
   34a. Smith, R. Marlin. "From Subdivision Improvements to Community Benefit Assessments and Linkage Payments: A Brief History of Land Development Exactions." Mimeographed, 1985.
   34b. SHARP Guidelines, Revised. Massachusetts Housing Finance Agency, January 17, 1986.

35) *Section 312 Loan Program Handbook.* Washington, D.C.: 1986.

35a. State of North Carolina, Office of the Governor. Press Release No. T-00876, May 29, 1986.

36) "Study Says 1987 to Be Taxing Year in Real Estate," *Raleigh News and Observer* (October 15, 1986), p. B6.

37) Talansky, Alan. "Syndication after Tax Reform: A Financing Option in the Developer's Favor," *Urban Land,* Vol. 45, No. 10 (October 1986), pp. 36–37.

37a. District of Columbia. "Tenant Assistance Program" [TAP]. 1986.

38) *The House We Live In.* The Commission to Study Housing Programs in North Carolina, January 1983.

39) *The Wall Street Journal* (October 22, 1986), p. 20.

40) John C. Weicher. "Private-Sector Housing Production: Has the Rising Tide Lifted All Boats?" Mimeographed, 1986; p. 69.

41) Werner, Frances E. "Linkage Programs as an Anti-Development Tool," *Housing Law Bulletin,* Vol. 16, No. 6 (November/December 1986).

Appendix 1
Selected State Abstracts

California Department of Housing and Community Development

921 Tenth Street
Sacramento, CA 95814-2774
Leslye Corsigia
(916) 322-1560

California Homeownership Assistance Plan (CHAP)

The CHAP provides up to 49 percent of the purchase price of a home, in the form of a mortgage participation loan with an institutional lender. The loan enables eligible households to purchase housing that they would otherwise be unable to acquire. Upon sale of the property, the state will receive a share in the equity, in an amount proportionate to the original investment. Under this program, the department assists 1) renters who would otherwise be displaced by condominium conversions to purchase their units; 2) mobile-home park residents to purchase their spaces, if the park is converted into a stock cooperative; 3) eligible households to purchase mobile-homes placed on permanent foundations; and 4) stock cooperatives or nonprofit corporations to develop or purchase mobile-home parks. This program was funded at $7.5 million in 1980.

California Self-Help Housing Program

The CSHHP provides grants and loans to local government agencies and nonprofit corporations that assist low- and moderate-income families to build or rehabilitate their homes with their own labor. Mortgage and technical assistance funds are available. Technical assistance grants are used to cover training and supervision of self-help builders; to aid in project planning; to offer loan packaging and counseling services; and to provide workshops. Mortgage assistance funds are used to reduce the cost of the self-help units.

This program was originally funded at $200,000 per year, starting in 1978. The mortgage assistance component was added in 1984 and received a larger appropriation. The 1986 appropriation was for $2.2 million, but the total funds available are approximately $4.4 million. Mortgage payments are based on a 7 percent rate and partially amortized over 10 years. For each year over 10 years, the remaining principal is reduced by 10 percent, so that after 20 years, the mortgage is completely amortized.

Mobile-Home Park Assistance Program

The MPAP provides financial and technical assistance to low-income mobile-home park residents, or to organizations formed by park residents who wish to own and/or operate their mobile-home parks. The financial assistance component of the program is a revolving loan fund with a 7 percent rate. This program was funded by a $2.5 million appropriation, plus $2.4 million from other sources. Other sources include a tax on mobile-home sales.

Rental Housing Construction Program

This program received initial funding of $82 million in 1979. Program funds are used through three basic financing approaches:
1) direct financing to local entities;
2) rural rental assistance, which uses RHCP funds to write down rents on projects financed through FmHA; and
3) the CaHFA set-aside.

Special-User Housing Rehabilitation Program

This program was enacted in 1983. It uses a 3 percent, 30-year deferred payment loan, which provides upfront subsidies for the rehabilitation and/or acquisition of substandard housing. Funds may be used for the acquisition and/or rehabilitation of apartments to be occupied by the elderly; by the physically, mentally, or developmentally handicapped; and by the low- and very-low-income persons who might live in residential hotels. This program was funded at $5 million in 1984, $3 million in 1985, and $2.5 million in 1986.

Predevelopment Loan Program

The PLP provides 7 percent loans to local government agencies and nonprofit corporations. The loans can be used for a variety of predevelopment expenses incurred in securing the long-term financing for the production or rehabilitation of subsidized low-income housing in both urban and rural areas. Loan terms range from one to three years. Loan fees are for architecture, engineering, consultant, and legal services, or for permits, pay bonding, and application fees, etc. ... Loans are also made to eligible borrowers for land purchases in order to accumulate a land bank of sites for future development of low-income housing. This program uses a revolving fund of $4 to $5 million per year. It was funded at $5 million in 1979 and 1980.

California Housing Finance Agency

1121 L Street, 7th Floor
Sacramento, CA 95814
Karney Hodge
(916) 322-3991

80/20 State/Local Pilot Rental-Housing Finance Program

This program was initiated in March of 1986. The program requires that 80 percent of the rental units must be rented to low-income families, and 20 percent rented to very-low-income families. A contribution by a sponsoring local government must minimally be in the 20 to 30 percent range. Local contributions can be in the form of CDBG funds, city parcels, tax increment financing, or general revenue.

This program is feasible by virtue of a $1 million allocation to be used to "buy down" the interest rate on a project's takeout financing, which is also provided by the CaHFA. The buydown, referred to as a feasibility loan—not to exceed $150,000 per project—will reduce monthly rents and make housing available to low- and very-low-income households.

Interest rates are as low as 5 percent in the first year. Each year, rents will increase an average of 4 to 5 percent, allowing an increase in mortgage interest rates up to 10.5 percent—the current rate for CHFA fixed-rate, 30-year loans. One project is under construction, and six others are in various stages under this program.

80/10/10 Rental-Housing Mortgage Loan Program

This program was also initiated in 1986. It provides that 10 percent of the units must be for low-income and 10 percent for very-low-income families. The remaining 80 percent of the units may be rented at market rates.

Multifamily Rehabilitation and Infill New Construction Program

This innovative financing approach provides for the new construction and rehabilitation of existing apartments, focusing on projects of five to 20 units.

This source of below-market capital enables localities to rehabilitate older neighborhoods, as well as to infill undeveloped lots with affordable-rental structures. A unique feature of this program is that it enables builders/developers to utilize existing infrastructure, thereby reducing potential development costs.

Colorado Division of Housing

John Maldonado
1313 Sherman Street
419 Centennial Building
Denver, CO 80203
(303) 866-2033

The Colorado DOH was created in 1970 to promote cooperation and coordination in the development, production, and conservation of housing for low-income residents. The housing development grant program received an appropriation of $1.45 million in FY'85–86. The program does not have any strict guidelines. The objectives are to assist a maximum number of low-income households to obtain safe, sanitary, affordable, and decent housing; and to encourage municipal and county governments, as well as the private sector, to get involved in the development and rehabilitation of housing for low-income households.

Financial assistance is provided to eligible applicants for the costs of development, production, and conservation of low-income housing projects and programs. Eligible applicants are public entities and private, federal-income-tax-exempt nonprofit corporations. The grant amount requested must be at least matched with nonstate funds. Low-income households are defined as those earning less than 80 percent of the area median.

Revolving Loan Program

The purpose of this loan program is to provide short-term loans to eligible sponsors for costs generally associated with housing predevelopment activities or with front-end costs. The loans are provided for development and redevelopment costs associated with the construction of new housing or with the rehabilitation of existing housing for low- and moderate-income households. "Low-income" is defined as 80 percent, and "moderate" is defined as 100 percent of the median.

Interest rates on loans range to a maximum of one point below prime, depending on the applicants' abilities to pay, their needs for assistance, the level of risk, and other circumstances. The maximum loan amount is $60,000 to any one applicant. For FY'85–86, the fund received $450,000 from state appropriations. Currently, the fund has approximately $1 million outstanding.

Delaware Department of Community Affairs

Kay Walter
18 The Green
P.O. Box 1401
Dover, DE 19903
(302) 736-4263

In 1968, the state established the housing development fund (HDF) with an initial appropriation of $8 million. This appropriation was put into a revolving fund and used primarily for seed and construction loans to nonprofit and limited-profit housing developers. Over 3,200 units of housing were assisted, with loans totaling more than $38 million. In 1986, the state legislature passed bills to broaden the financial base and flexibility of the HDF:

- The amount of $2.5 million was added, bringing the total fund balance over $11 million.
- The fund may now retain interest and other earnings on idle balances.
- A $3.00 document surcharge on all recorder-of-deeds filings is established. Ninety-five percent of the funds collected (estimated at $400,000 annually) flow to the HDF.
- Grants, as well as loans of indefinite term, are authorized.
- The council on housing and community development must approve all uses of the HDF.

Housing Rehabilitation Loan Program

Initiated in April 1985, the HRLP provides low-interest loans, up to $15,000, for up to 10 years, to bring owner-occupied and investor-owned properties (rented to low- and moderate-income families) up to standard conditions. Loans are made at 3 percent. The three county governments and three larger cities in Delaware were allocated the funds. Loans are administered locally, and can only finance 75 percent or less of the actual cost of the rehabilitation work done. The program was funded by a $2 million allocation from the governor.

Delaware Assisted-Loan Program

This program was funded with a $5 million set-aside from an $83.5 million single-family mortgage bond issue. Eligible borrowers have incomes less than $21,600, and have not owned a home in the past three years. The state housing authority writes down the mortgage interest rate by one point, to 8.75 percent. This is an origination fee of 3 percent of the amount borrowed.

Transitional Living Facility for Women

The sum of $250,000 was included in the FY'86 Capital Improvement Act, to provide a shelter with support services for female-headed households. The present plan is to rehabilitate a vacant 18-unit public housing project to move these households toward self-sufficiency.

Florida Department of Community Affairs

Douglas A. Lees
Housing Resource Planning
FL DCA
2571 Executive Center Circle East
Tallahassee, FL 32301
(904) 488-1536

While the proposed housing initiatives for 1985 to 1986 recommended an annual commitment of $30 million to low- and moderate-income housing, the final legislation signed by the governor on July 1, 1986, only appropriated a total of $3.3 million to address the problem. The legislation establishes the following:

- The creation of the Florida Affordable Housing Demonstration Program, to be administered by the department of community affairs. This is a two-year pilot program to encourage the construction and rehabilitation of low-cost housing units affordable for very-low-, low-, and moderate-income persons in four to seven demonstration areas. Selection of the sites is based on 1) level of need; 2) commitment of the local government to providing cost-saving incentives to developers; 3) the existence of active community-based organizations in the area to be served; 4) geographic distribution of demonstration areas, to include urban and rural, coastal and noncoastal, and high and low growth rates; and 5) counties with various population sizes.

    Applications will be ranked according to: proposed costs; benefit to low-/moderate-income persons; the capacity of the applicant to carry out the proposal; and the extent to which the applicant demonstrates potential cost savings.
- The creation of the affordable housing loan program: funded by the Florida Affordable Housing Trust Fund to encourage, through zero-interest or low-interest loans, the construction or rehabilitation of housing units affordable to persons earning less than 120 percent of the median income. At least 60 percent of the units in a project must be sold or rented to very-low-income, low-income, or moderate-income persons. The maximum loan amount shall not exceed one-third of the total project cost.

- The creation of the Florida Affordable Housing Trust Fund, to be "administered as a non-lapsing, revolving fund by the department of community affairs, for the provision of affordable housing to very-low-, low-, and moderate-income persons, and to otherwise carry out the purposes of this part. ..." (Section 5, Florida Affordable Housing Act of 1986)
- The sponsoring of a community-based organization loan program: a revolving loan program to assist community-based organizations in developing affordable housing. Community-based organizations can be assisted in covering predevelopment expenses with these funds. Loans of up to $5,000 per unit, with a maximum of $100,000 per project, are available.
- The creation of the affordable housing study commission, to analyze solutions and programs that could begin to address the state's acute need for housing for low-income persons. An interim report will be submitted to the governor by March 1, 1987, describing its progress.
- The setting-up of a mobile-home relocation, site acquisition, and development trust fund, which will be established and authorized to make loans to sponsors for the acquisition and development of suitable sites for mobile homes for low-income persons who must relocate their homes. The loans are available provided that: 1) a need for such sites exists; and 2) funding is not otherwise available from private sources. Loans will be made at 3 percent per year, with a term not to exceed three years. The land acquired for the purpose of a mobile-home relocation park must be maintained in this use for at least 10 years.
- In addition, an appropriation of $2.7 million from the general revenue fund to the Florida Affordable Housing Trust Fund, to be allocated as follows:
  –$2,100,000 for the affordable housing loan program;
  –$1,600,000 for the affordable housing demonstration program (no more than $500,000 may be loaned directly to very-low- or low-income persons);
  –$120,000 for the community-based organization training and technical assistance program;
  –$400,000 for the community-based organization loan program;
  –$50,000 for the inventory of public lands and buildings; and
  –$30,000 to establish an affordable housing study commission.

Hawaii Housing Authority

Adelbert Green
1002 No. School Street
P.O. Box 17907
Honolulu, HI 96817
(808) 848-3285

Rental Assistance Program

The purpose of this program is to encourage private developers to develop multifamily rental housing by providing rent subsidies to defray operating costs. The program is patterned after HUD's Section 8 program, except that rent subsidies are limited to $175 per unit per month. Each project must maintain at least 20 percent of its units as rentals for low- and moderate-income tenants.

The rent subsidy payments are made from the interest earnings generated from the investment of the rental assistance revolving fund. The revolving fund may receive funds from any government program or grant, from private grants or contributions, and from appropriations by the state legislature. Funds realized by the authority from its share of the appreciation in the value of an eligible project may also capitalize the revolving fund.

The rental assistance contract cannot be less than 10 years, or greater than the period for which the authority has invested the principal amount of the fund that is committed to the eligible project, at a known rate of return. The assistance payments cannot exceed the amount available through investment of the fund. For government- and nonprofit-sponsored owners, the term cannot exceed 25 years or the term of the mortgage, whichever is less; and for limited-dividend owners, the term cannot exceed 15 years or the term of the mortgage, whichever is less.

"Hula Mae" Special Assistance Program

"Hula Mae" was a homeownership program that provided a monthly subsidy to reduce eligible borrowers' monthly mortgage payments during the first four years of their loans. Eligible borrowers were households earning 80 percent or less of the median. The subsidy amount was based on qualifying the borrower's housing cost–to-income ratio, and on total debt-to-income ratio—28 percent and 36 percent, respectively. The average subsidy ($4,000) was placed in an interest-bearing account, and phased out over four years, so that the full payment was required in the fifth year.

The program was capitalized by collecting one point of each sales price from developers. Homeownership opportunities were provided to borrowers with incomes as low as 58 percent of the median income. This program was in effect from 1982 through 1984, and then discontinued with the decline in interest rates.

Illinois Housing Development Authority

130 E. Randolph Street
Chicago, IL 60601
(312) 565-5200
Kendall Jackson
Maryanne Giustino
Public Relations Coordinator

"Build Illinois" is a new program that includes two grants modeled after federal programs: the Illinois Development Action Grant (IDAG), a state version of UDAG; and a housing opportunities grant.

The IDAG program was initiated in 1985, with a focus on stimulating economic activity to benefit low- and moderate-income individuals and families. Eligible projects include housing, commercial, and industrial development. Currently, the IDAG is only available to the city of Chicago; $20 million has been appropriated for projects in the city. Developers must apply for the state funds through the city.

The program limits the grants to no more than $1 million per year per project, and no less than a $30,000 minimum funding level. Some applications have been approved. Next year, the legislature may consider extending the program to give it a statewide scope.

Kentucky Housing Corporation

Patti Perry
1231 Louisville Road
Frankfort, KY 40601
(502) 564-7630

Excess Reserves

The Kentucky Housing Corporation is permitted to make "prudent" transfers of excesses in the debt-service reserve fund. These transfers are to provide funds for additional insured loans to eligible borrowers at interest rates substantially below the normal market borrowing rate. In 1984, the transfer was $5 million; in 1985, $6 million; and in 1986, $5 million was transferred from reserve.

The funds are used to write down interest rates, to as low as 1 percent, on loans for home purchases and improvements. The amount of subsidy provided is determined on a case-by-case basis. In general, the eligible household income is less than $15,000. An estimated $650 million to $1 billion in assets is expected to accumulate in the fund over the next 25 years.

Maine State Housing Authority

Curt Swinehart
Assistant to the Director
295 Water Street
PO Box 2669
Augusta, ME 04330
(207) 623-2981

Real Estate Transfer Tax

State legislation enacted in 1985 created a dedicated real estate transfer tax, replacing a state appropriation. The new transfer tax will continue to generate revenue for the MSHA Housing Opportunities for Maine (HOME) Fund. This fund is used to lower interest rates on bond-financed programs, and to finance special housing programs, as well as innovative new programs for affordable housing and community initiatives.

The legislature created the HOME fund in 1982. Over the four-year period of 1982 through 1985, $8.25 million was appropriated to the HOME fund. The fund is now capitalized by an increase in the title transfer tax assessment, in the range of $2.20 per $1,000 of valuation. The transfer tax is on both the buyer and the seller, at $2.20 to each. The funds generated from the transfer tax are divided between general state revenue funds and the HOME program. Approximately $4 to $5 million is expected to flow into the HOME fund annually.

Apartment Improvement Program

This program provides below-market-rate loans to encourage rehabilitation of existing rental properties that: are non-owner-occupied; have five or more units, with the owner the resident manager; or are not owned by a limited partnership, a corporation, or a trust. All work must be of a nonluxury nature.

The interest rate is 9 7/8 percent; the term of the loan may be five, 10, or 15 years. Loan proceeds cannot be used for more than 10 percent commercial purposes. Properties must remain in rental units for 10 years, with at least 20 percent of the units for households with low incomes (80 percent of the median). There is a provision that requires the property owner to limit rent increases for each tenant below the income guidelines, for one year from the date of the loan closing, to a total rent that is the greater of:
1) Ten percent of the existing pre-loan rent; or
2) Twenty-five percent of the monthly income of the household at the time of certification.

Homeless Shelter Financing Program

This program provides financing for the purchase, rehabilitation, or refinancing of the existing debts on emergency shelters, transitional housing, or extended temporary shelters. The housing authority has set aside approximately $300,000 in HOME funds for this program. Loan requests should not exceed $100,000. Proposals will be ranked according to the need, experience, capability, and stability of the sponsor; project feasibility; project cost; project quality; the degree of leveraging; and the degree of community involvement.

Maryland Department of Economic and Community Development
Community Development Administration

45 Calvert Street
Annapolis, MD 21401
Marc Burford
(301) 269-2468

Homeowners' Emergency Mortgage Assistance Program. This program was created in 1984. The general assembly provided CDA with $500,000 to assist involuntarily unemployed homeowners in paying off their delinquent mortgages. The program is a partnership between CDA, cooperating lenders, and housing counseling agencies, on a statewide basis. Delinquent accounts are brought up to date, and then assistance is provided for a period of up to 24 months. The average assistance amount is $7,000. Repayment of assistance begins when the homeowner is reemployed. The terms of repayment are flexible, based on income and other debts. A 6 percent interest rate is charged, and the term may be up to 10 years.

Maryland Housing Rehabilitation Program. Funded by the sale of state general obligation bonds, loans are made by CDA for the rehabilitation of existing single-family, rental, and commercial properties. This program permits the use of flexible interest rates to better serve low-income persons.

The Governor's Housing Initiatives of 1986

Low-Income Rental Housing Production Program. Will provide low-interest, deferred-payment loans to construct or substantially rehabilitate rental housing for lower-income households (generally well below $20,000), dedicated to at least a 15-year occupancy. Loans are available either for capital cost assistance (mortgage loans, project development costs) or mortgage assistance (use of loan proceeds to establish an escrow fund, from which earned interest is used to subsidize rents). Households served will have incomes below 60 percent of the state median; at least 20 percent of households will have incomes below 30 percent of the median.

Loans will be repaid at maturity, at sale of project, or when the project no longer serves low-income households. Repayments will be deposited into a revolving fund, used for additional low-rent housing loans. Twenty percent of funds will be reserved for nonprofits for a period of six months. The local government in whose jurisdiction the project is located will be required to make a contribution as a condition of approval. Legislation is proposed, and $9 million is budgeted, to produce 1,000 low-rent units, with subsidies continuing for 15 years.

Low-Income Rental Allowance Pilot Program. Will provide a rent subsidy to a target population (typically single, low-income, homeless, moderately impaired or disabled or generally disadvantaged but capable of independent living, and ineligible for federally funded housing assistance programs). Allowances will be predetermined and dependent on regional cost variables and other factors. Seventy-five percent of funds will be allocated to target jurisdictions on a competitive basis. Local housing agencies will provide assistance for housing aid and inspections.

Allowances will be provided for existing housing, selected by the recipient, if the housing meets minimum standards. Allowance payment levels will be predetermined (estimated to be about $85 per month) but will depend on regional cost variables and other factors, such as whether the housing includes cooking facilities. One million dollars is budgeted for 1,000 renter allowances for one year.

Indoor Plumbing. Will provide low-interest, deferred-payment loans to enable low-income persons (owner/occupants or owners of rental properties in which two-thirds of the units are occupied by limited-income residents) to finance the repair and installation of or connection to, the appropriate water and wastewater system(s). Legislation will amend the code. The amount of $700,000 is budgeted to improve 100 housing units.

Accessory, Shared, and Sheltered Housing. Will provide low-interest, deferred-payment loans, primarily to low-income borrowers, to make improvements, modifications, and additions to existing housing for accessory units or for homesharing or sheltered-care use especially for low-income persons (elderly, handicapped, or otherwise disadvantaged). Average loans are as follows:

- To modify for shared use: $1,500
- To provide sheltered care: $6,000
- To create an accessory unit: $15,000

Legislation will amend the code.

Available funds come to $300,000, which will be used to help finance 40 projects, housing 110 households.

Group Home Acquisition. Will provide low-interest or deferred-payment loans to nonprofit organizations, and preferred–income rate loans to other sponsors, to acquire homes for use as group homes and shelters for low-income special populations (developmentally disabled, handicapped, or abused children and spouses, and the homeless). Potential borrowers must demonstrate the capacity to manage the housing, to provide necessary support services, and to pay back the loan. Legislation will amend the existing Maryland Home Financing Program Law to allow nonprofits to borrow funds for group homes.

Two million dollars has been set aside from existing funds in the MDHFA program, to provide 25 loans serving up to 250 individuals.

Nonprofit Housing Rehabilitation. Will provide low-interest, deferred-payment loans to nonprofits for the rehabilitation of housing serving low-income special populations. This program will enable nonprofits to provide low-cost rental housing for low-income individuals; temporary shelters for displaced individuals; and half-way houses and group homes for handicapped, disabled, or elderly individuals. Loan funds could also be used to make accessibility modifications and minor repairs to homes owned and occupied by these special populations. A nonprofit organization must own each property and demonstrate repayment and project-management capabilities. Interest rates will be determined according to project feasibility and needs, and repayment may be deferred.

Legislation will amend the Maryland Housing Rehabilitation Program Law to allow loans to nonprofits for this purpose.

Two million dollars has been budgeted to support 25 projects per year, housing 150 households.

Nonprofit Home Maintenance and Repair Program. Will provide a small number of matching grants to nonprofit organizations to provide basic safety repairs and minor home maintenance services on behalf of low-income elderly and handicapped homeowners and at an affordable cost. This program will operate as a demonstration over two years. The average grant is expected to be $20,000 per year. Legislation will not be necessary.

The amount of $250,000 has been budgeted for 12 nonprofits, serving a minimum of 500 households.

Nonprofit Project Operating Assistance. Will authorize matching grants to community action agencies and other nonprofits, to pay for the project-specific administrative and operating expenses associated with the development of low-income housing projects. Will cover project-specific administrative expenses (staff or consultant services).

No legislation will be necessary.

The sum of $200,000 has been budgeted for 15 nonprofits.

Construction Loan Fund. Will provide below-market-rate preconstruction and construction loan funds to nonprofits and local governments, to construct rental and owner-occupied housing for low-income households. Loans will typically be for no longer than two years, and interest rates will approximate 8 percent.

No legislation will be necessary.

Up to $2 million in existing CDA reserves will assist the construction of 40 units of housing.

Homeownership Programs

Mortgages for Low-Income Buyers. Will provide mortgage loans as low as 4 percent for households of two or more earning $18,000 or less per year, and for single persons earning less than $15,000 per year.

No legislation will be required.

Ten million dollars from the Maryland Home Financing Program's revolving fund (beginning in February 1986) will finance 250 mortgage loans to low-income households.

Homeownership Incentive Program. "Using a pool of funds realized from prepayments from previous CDA revenue-bond issues, CDA will offer below-market-rate mortgage loans to Marylanders with annual incomes primarily less than $20,000, with adjustments for large families (five or more)." Loans will be made at 7.75 percent and will require participation on the part of local governments or nonprofits to maximize their effectiveness. CDA will competitively award the commitments to local governments and nonprofits from a set-aside of permanent mortgage financing.

No legislation will be needed.

Three million dollars in existing CDA prepayments will finance 75 mortgages.

Reduction of Closing Costs. Will reduce closing costs for *all* homebuyers, making ownership more affordable. The program will:

- Prohibit lenders from imposing a collection fee on escrow points;
- Prohibit lenders from charging, at the time of closing, prepaid interest on the loan;
- Implement disclosure procedures for lender-required attorney fees for residential property loans;
- Limit attorney review fees to $100, unless there is a full explanation of and justification for higher fees; and
- Prohibit lender inspection fees.

Legislation is proposed to amend the Commercial Law Article. No funds will be necessary.

AFDC Rent Leveraging Demonstration. Will determine the willingness of landlords to provide better standards of housing at affordable levels for poor people, in exchange for a reliable income stream and access to improvement programs (such as weatherization assistance and low-interest rehabilitation loans). The program will leverage some of the estimated $70 to $100 million in state general funds, paid annually by AFDC recipients for rent, to achieve better housing conditions. One to three jurisdictions will be targeted, for a total of 100 units.

The total size of the demonstration will be about 100 units. Participants will voluntarily have the rent portion of their benefits withheld and paid directly to the landlord quarterly, in advance. In return, the landlord will repair and maintain the property to an agreed-upon standard at an agreed-upon rent. The department of human resources will continue to pay the rent, if the unit becomes vacant through no fault of the landlord.

The sum of $100,000 will be available to cover the first quarter's rents, and will be replenished by funds withheld from participants' grants.

Care Homes. Will provide financial assistance to "care-homes providers," who will in turn provide supported housing for disabled adults who require supervision and assistance but not skilled housekeeping or professional care. Includes the chronically mentally ill; disabled foster children reaching the age of 18; multiply handicapped persons who cannot be accommodated by other residential programs; and those frail elderly persons who need a higher level of care than that provided by sheltered elderly housing. Care-home providers will receive training and a one-time startup grant of $500, as needed, to purchase or install necessary equipment. A monthly subsidy of $500 per client will be provided, supplementing other income.

One million dollars would provide startup costs and support payments for 200 beds, and would hire the staff who would monitor the program.

Emergency Shelters. Will double state support of emergency shelters/housing. All funds will go directly toward providing emergency shelter services, and will not cover administrative costs.

The amount of $500,000 is proposed, to provide an additional 25,000 nights of shelter.

Transitional Housing for Women. Will aim to enable women to achieve self-sufficiency. The program proposes the establishment of three four-unit homes in new or rehabilitated buildings, and includes support services for the women and their children.

Program funding should come to $25,000 for operation costs (as part of FY'87).

A $90,000 loan from DCA is expected to be matched by a low-interest loan from the McAuley Institute, for acquisition of the three homes.

Sheltered Housing for the Frail Elderly. Will increase state support for supervised housing costs for approximately 150 low-income frail elderly persons. Payments averaging $200 per month per participant will be made to qualified single-family private providers and nonprofits that will provide housing to eligible low-income individuals living in certified, small congregate housing.

The sum of $360,000 is proposed to assist 150 additional frail elderly persons in single-family and nonprofit-sponsored residential-sheltered housing.

State general obligation bonds ($79.2 million) will fund: the Maryland Housing Rehabilitation Program, the Maryland Home Financing Program, and the Maryland Homeowners' Emergency Mortgage Assistance Program.

State appropriations should come to $22.5 million.

Massachusetts Housing Finance Authority

Marvin Siflinger
Executive Director
50 Milk Street
Boston, MA 02109
(617) 451-3480

State Housing Assistance for Rental Housing (SHARP)

The SHARP program was created in 1983 and has committed funds to 64 competition-winning developments, with a total of 7,813 units. SHARP is a state-funded subsidy loan program designed to stimulate privately owned rental housing in Massachusetts in which at least 25 percent of the units are to be occupied by lower-income households—households earning 80 percent of the areawide median-income limits.

This is a shallow-subsidy program that combines construction and permanent financing from the sale of tax-exempt bonds through the MHFA with a state-funded subsidy loan that writes down the interest rate on the MHFA loan to as low as 5 percent for a term of up to 15 years. It is expected that most SHARP projects should become self-sustaining over this 15-year time frame. The state subsidy is a loan, not a grant, and must be repaid to the MHFA at a rate of 5 percent.

The interest-reduction subsidy is designed to bridge the gap between cost-based rent and attainable rent. The subsidy is the "minimum amount necessary to make the proposed rental housing project feasible, and to ensure that 25 percent of the units are available to low-income households." "Cost-based" rent is defined as the rent needed to support the mortgage loan and the operating cost of a project. "Attainable rent" is defined as the maximum rent at which units can be rented on the open market. In the case of low-income units, the attainable rent cannot be higher than the published Section 8 existing fair market rent.

In 1986, $15 million was appropriated for new and existing projects, while $22 million was authorized and may still be forthcoming.

Massachusetts Housing Partnership

This partnership was formed in 1985 as a public/private effort to meet housing needs and broaden local opportunities. The first initiative was the homeownership opportunity program, to enable moderate-income individuals and families to purchase their first homes. A total of $225 million will be available through this program to finance the construction of 2,500 new housing units over a two-year period. Units can be created using new construction, rehabilitation of abandoned structures, or conversion of nonhousing structures. Communities will offer incentives that will facilitate development and reduce costs.

The assembled resources include:
1) $200 million in below-market-rate mortgages from the MHFA.
2) The Massachusetts Housing Partnership Fund's provision of $35 million to reduce financing costs. This fund is capitalized by an excise tax on savings and loans that are switching from private insurance to federal. Due to the switch, the S&Ls have decreased reserve requirements, and are withdrawing funds from these reserves. The tax is on the withdrawal of reserve funds. These funds will be used to buy down the interest rate of the MHFA BMIR loan by approximately 3.5 percent. Funds used to reduce the interest rate will be repaid to the MHP fund, at the time when the house is sold, by requiring 20 percent of the appreciation to be recycled to the fund.
3) Up to $5 million in Community Development Action Grant funds, to construct sewers, roads, and other infrastructure associated with housing development. Affordability of these units will be preserved over the long term by deed restrictions.

Michigan State Housing Development Authority

Plaza One, 4th Floor
401 So. Washington Square
P.O. Box 30044
Lansing, MI 48909
Terrence R. Suvernay
(517) 373-8018

Direct Lending Program (80/20 Program)

Established in 1984, this is a $100 million production program to finance new or rehabilitated rental housing without federal subsidies. The authority directly underwrites and funds the construction and permanent mortgage loan of each development. Twenty percent of the units are rented at market rates, and 60 percent are for residents with incomes up to 125 percent of the area median (150 percent in distressed areas). Twenty percent of the units must be set aside for households with incomes less than 80 percent of the area median.

The authority has pledged up to $1.2 million annually to subsidize rents on 8 percent of the units to make them affordable to households earning less than 50 percent of the median income. To accomplish this, the authority will establish an annual fund equal to $300 times the total number of units within a development. This amount will then be paid or credited to the owner, on behalf of those units occupied by very-low-income tenants. In addition, the authority contributes reserves to underwrite mortgage interest rates to 8.5 percent (6.5 percent for distressed-area developments).

At the end of 1985, $29.3 million in loans had been closed, to develop 1,045 units in 11 developments.

The Pass-Through Program

MSHDA received statutory authority in 1984 to issue tax-exempt bonds that are secured solely by the properties being financed and by some form of credit enhancement provided by the borrowers. The bonds are supported by letters of credit and by mortgage or bond insurance. This pass-through program's obligations are limited obligations, rather than general obligations of the agency; they are not secured by the authority's capital reserve account, and are therefore not backed by the moral obligation of the state. At least 25 percent of the amount authorized must be used in eligible distressed areas.

This program works on behalf of privately-secured rental developments that will not use the credit backing of MSHDA or of the state. Eligible borrowers include limited-dividend housing associations or corporations, consumer housing cooperatives, and nonprofit housing corporations, as designated under the authority's Act.

Interest rates are determined by the private market, based on the security of the credit enhancement. While income limits are higher than in the 80/20 program, at least 20 percent of the units must be rented to families at or below 80 percent of the median income in distressed areas. In other areas, 20 percent of the units must be occupied by families with incomes at or below 80 percent of the median. The next 15 percent of the units must be occupied by families earning less than 125 percent of the median or by elderly, and another 15 percent of the units must be occupied by families with incomes at or below 150 percent of the median. The last 50 percent of the units may be rented at market rates.

In 1985, $54.8 million was loaned to finance 1,368 rental units in seven developments.

Homeownership Assistance

Mortgage Set-Asides

The authority has agreed to set aside up to $9.1 million in end loans for 10 community groups that are renovating and reselling homes, and for Detroit Nonprofit Housing Corporation's project to build eight new houses.

Home Improvement Loans

Since 1978, this program has offered loans to homeowners to improve their dwellings—primarily structures more than 20 years old. The loans are financed from bond proceeds. The interest rates are underwritten by a $3 million contribution from MSHDA reserves, and by $12.1 million in state appropriations received prior to 1981.

Competitive Grant Program

Originated in 1984, the three-year pilot competitive grant program allows the authority to make grants to community organizations and non-profit housing agencies on a competitive basis. Applications are scored according to a point system that is based on need, administrative competence, project feasibility, efficient use of funds, the equal-opportunity eligibility of the recipient, and the nature of the special populations served. The maximum grant is $50,000, and no agency will be awarded a grant for two years in a row.

In awarding the funds, emphasis is placed on expanding the options of low- and moderate-income individuals in obtaining and maintaining affordable, decent housing. These funds therefore must be used to provide loans to persons and families whose incomes do not exceed 80 percent of the median. Eligible activities include:

- Rehabilitation of low- and moderate-income owner-occupied dwelling units;
- Acquisition/rehabilitation of real property for resale to low- and moderate-income persons;
- Home improvement programs; and
- Support services related to housing research activities that evaluate ways of meeting the housing needs of low- and moderate-income residents.

At least 75 percent of the funds must be used for tangible housing improvements to real property, or for housing acquisition. This program is funded by $1 million in earnings from the housing development fund. In 1985, grants totaling $330,000 were awarded to nine groups, out of 74 applicants. The awards were to be leveraged with $2.1 million in local contributions, federal funds, and foundation grants.

The 1986 Housing-Cost Reduction Competition

The authority is sponsoring a national competition, with up to $27,000 in prizes, for new ideas for cutting the cost of residential housing construction. This program aims to encourage construction methods, design alternatives, and products that result in the greatest cost savings in multifamily or single-family housing for low- and moderate-income people.

Minnesota Housing Finance Agency

Jack Jenkins
400 Sibley Street
Suite 300
St. Paul, MN 55101
(612) 296-9828

Market-Rate Elderly Interest-Writedown Rental Program

The purpose of this program is to provide financing that enables the construction of $4 to $7 million worth of elderly housing, at rents affordable to moderate incomes. The program consists of three parts:

1) The agency has issued $9 million of 30-year fixed-rate bonds, to provide 30-year fixed-rate mortgages.
2) The agency will use $1 million of its own funds as second mortgages, to provide a 30-year interest-rate writedown.
3) The agency will provide a shallow-subsidy payment for 20 percent of tenants. The subsidy is approximately $150 per month.

At least 20 percent of the units in the development must be occupied by persons or families whose incomes do not exceed 80 percent of the median income for the area.

Market-Rate, Family, Graduated-Payment Mortgage/Rental Program

This program aims to provide financing for the construction of approximately $5 to $10 million worth of moderate-income housing. The agency would issue 30-year fixed-rate bonds, and provide a mortgage with graduated payments for the first five years of the 30-year term. If necessary, the difference in debt service between the mortgage's graduated rate and the fixed bond rate will be paid from the interest of a portion of the agency's reserves that has been invested for five years. Assuming $10 million in mortgages the program would finance 260 family units. (Twenty percent of units must be occupied by households earning 80 percent or less of median.)

New Jersey Housing and Mortgage Finance Agency

Susan Kimball
3625 Quakerbridge Road
CN 18550
Trenton, NJ 08650-2085
(609) 890-8900

In 1985, the New Jersey Fair Housing Act created the New Jersey Council on Affordable Housing, and appropriated funds to support the implementation of affordable housing programs. The housing and mortgage finance agency was appropriated $15 million and charged with establishing "affordable housing programs to assist municipalities in meeting the obligation of developing communities to provide low- and moderate-income housing." The agency is specifically authorized to award assistance to programs in municipalities whose housing elements have received substantive certification from the council on affordable housing. Affordable housing programs that may be financed or assisted under the agency include, but are not limited to the following:

- Assistance for home purchases and improvements, including interest-rate assistance, downpayments, and closing-cost assistance, and direct grants for principal reductions;
- Rental programs, including loans or grants for developments containing low- and moderate-income housing, moderate rehabilitation of existing housing, and congregate care and retirement facilities;
- Financial assistance for the conversion of nonresidential space into residences; and
- Other assistance, including grants or loans for infrastructure, or construction loans to be taken out with permanent financing provided by the agency.

The Fair Housing Act also provides an appropriation of $2 million, plus an estimated $8 million annually from an increase in the real estate transfer tax dedicated to the department of community affairs' neighborhood preservation/balanced housing program. The program will be expanded to provide grants and loans to municipalities for such purposes as:

- Rehabilitation of substandard units, and construction of new units or conversion of nonresidential units for low- and moderate-income households;
- Costs of studies, plans, architectural and engineering and other technical services; costs of land or property acquisition; and costs of demolition, infrastructure projects, and other activities related to the creation of low- and moderate-income units.

North Carolina Housing Finance Agency

424 North Blount Street
P.O. Box 28066
Raleigh, NC 27611
(919) 781-6115

Elderly Rent Subsidy Program. Offers FmHA 1 percent permanent
financing and an NCHFA monthly subsidy of up to $100 per apartment,
to provide affordable housing for low-income senior citizens. Sixty percent of the units are reserved for occupants earning 50 percent or less of
the area median income, and the remaining for those meeting FmHA's
moderate-income requirements.) The agency will subsidize a portion of
four apartment projects located in counties with median incomes of
$20,000 or less. The subsidy is renewable after five years.

Single-Family Subsidies Program. Offers first-time low-income
homebuyers a combined reduced-interest-rate mortgage loan and monthly mortgage contribution. The base interest rate is reduced up to 4.5
percent, depending on a borrower's annual income. The subsidy payment decreases, and the interest rate increases, as a borrower's income
increases. A 5 percent cash downpayment is required to qualify for a
loan. Upon sale of the property, the agency recaptures the amount of
subsidy payments from up to 30 percent of the house's appreciated
value.

Multifamily Subsidy Program. Offers below-market, fixed-rate financing, as well as up to $100 per month per unit, to help low-income
renters earning in the low to mid-teens. The rent subsidy is available for
the full term of the mortgage, and is funded by the income produced
from the 1985 pilot program's appropriation of $2 million. This subsidy
maintains rent costs (including utilities) at 30 percent of a household's
monthly income.

Home Improvement Loan Subsidy Program. This program uses
agency funds to lower borrower interest rates to 3 percent; local governments have the option to reduce the 3 percent rate further. This program will be available statewide. The maximum loan amount is $15,000;
loan terms are five, 10, or 15 years. The program is scheduled to begin
in late 1986.

Pennsylvania Department of Community Affairs

Dave Chittister
Chief, Community Development Division
Bureau of Housing and Development
Box 155
Harrisburg, PA 17120
(717) 787-7156

SRO and Homeless Programs

In December 1985, Governor Thornburgh signed a bill making appropriations to the department of public welfare and to the department of community affairs, to establish a low-cost SRO housing program for the homeless. The legislation establishing the homeless assistance program creates a $2 million bridge housing program to be administered by the department of welfare, and a $3.5 million SRO program to be administered by the department of community affairs. The SRO housing program is intended to create low-cost single-room-occupancy housing facilities for the homeless and for other low-income individuals. The SRO units will be established in existing buildings. No new structures may be constructed with the grant monies.

Priority will be given to those projects that demonstrate an ability to coordinate the SRO with established social service networks, and that use effective public/private partnerships to initiate creative leveraging techniques in order to maximize available public funds. It is anticipated that the department will fund four to six demonstration projects. No single grant will exceed $1 million. Grantees must provide 25 percent matching funds to any SRO state, federal, local, or public/private source. State SRO funds may not be used for social services or operating subsidies.

Income eligibility standards are set by the grantee, based on the project and the community. A majority of the units must maintain monthly rents of $150 or less. This program is currently active in nine communities.

The 1986–1987 budget contains $10 million for homeless programs. Three million dollars has been appropriated to continue the emergency shelter program. In addition, $7 million has been appropriated for services to the homeless, such as bridge housing, SRO, residences for the mentally-ill homeless, and housing assistance—but excluding emergency shelters.

Of the $7 million, $2 million has been committed to continue operation of 27 bridge housing programs, which were started in April 1986. The sum of $750,000 will be used to fund a demonstration for the housing assistance program. New bridge housing will receive $1 million, and SRO projects will receive over $2 million in new funding. An additional $1 million will be used to fund between three and five specialized residential programs for the mentally-ill homeless.

Bridge housing is a program that assists homeless individuals for as long as a year, providing and arranging supportive services, with the goal of returning clients to the most independent life situation possible. It is a transitional service that allows homeless clients who are in temporary housing to move to supportive living arrangements while preparing to live independently. To be eligible, a client must be a low-income individual residing in a group shelter, a domestic-violence shelter, a safe home, a motel paid for with public funds, a jail, a mental-health facility, or a drug or alcohol facility. Eligible clients may include families facing foster-care placement of their children solely because of lack of housing.

A total of $750,000 will be used to fund a housing assistance demonstration program in approximately five counties. Housing assistance is payment for rent, security, or utilities to an individual or family, to prevent and/or end homelessness by maintaining these persons in their own residences. Payments are limited to $750 per applicant, or no more than four months' rent.

Housing and Redevelopment Assistance Program

Two major categories of funding assistance under this program are housing assistance and economic development. For 1986–1987, $20 million has been appropriated for this program. In general, 60 percent of the funds are being used for housing.

Housing assistance grants are available for local programs that support one or more of the following goals:

- Rehabilitation of owner-occupied low- and moderate-income residential properties;
- Rehabilitation of investor-owned properties whose tenants meet low- or moderate-income guidelines; and
- Provision of predevelopment or development expenses for the new construction or rehabilitation of subsidized housing projects—if such funds are essential but unavailable from other sources.

Eligible activities for grants include those entailed in:

- Combining grants with other funding sources;
- Providing housing seed-money loans, to assist with predevelopment or development expenses of HUD, FmHA, PHFA, or assisted-housing projects;
- Providing interest subsidies on housing rehabilitation loans;
- Making site improvements to support the rehabilitation of housing units; and
- Assisting in the rehabilitation of rental units used for low- and moderate-income persons.

Pennsylvania Housing Finance Agency

2101 No. Front Street
Harrisburg, PA 17105
(717) 780-3800
Robert Bobincheck
Director, Homeowners' Emergency Mortgage Assistance Program

Homeowners' Emergency Mortgage Assistance Program

Created in 1983 to offer assistance to homeowners who were threatened with the loss of their homes through foreclosure, this program permits the PHFA to bring delinquent mortgages current; in many cases, it provides continuing payments for qualified applicants. All assistance is in the form of a loan. The program received an appropriation of $25.7 million from the commonwealth for funding in each year of the program. To date, $50 million has been committed to mortgage relief.

Eligibility is based on the property, the mortgage, the lender, and the homeowner. The property must be owner-occupied and located in Pennsylvania, and must be the principal residence of the homeowner. Eligible homeowners must be permanent residents of Pennsylvania and be suffering financial hardships beyond their control—such that they are unable to correct their mortgage delinquencies. Homeowners must be at least 60 days delinquent in mortgage payments. They must have a reasonable prospect of resuming full mortgage payments within 36 months of the time the assistance was initially awarded, and be able to pay the mortgage in full by its maturity date.

The assistance provided is based on a percentage of income. Thirty-five percent of net income is dedicated to principal, interest, taxes, insurance, and utilities. Assisted homeowners are evaluated each year, and are expected to repay the loan at a 9 percent rate. A lien is placed on the property.

Rhode Island Housing and Mortgage Finance Corporation

Mike Rylant
Financial Director
60 Eddy Street
Providence, RI 02903
(401) 751-5566

The Rhode Island HMFC has developed 10 new programs to make housing opportunities more available to low- and moderate-income Rhode Islanders. The first of the 10 programs will be implemented by fall of 1986; all will be implemented over an 18-month period. Together, the 10 programs represent a commitment of over $120 million, and should provide new housing opportunities for an estimated 6,000 Rhode Islanders. Based on the corporation's most recent audited financial statement (FY'85), it is determined that $32,760,000 in surplus funds can be used immediately to address critical housing needs.

The programs are as follows:

1) Homeownership opportunity program. To assist low- and moderate-income first-home buyers. Source: $50 million in tax-exempt mortgage revenue bonds, and $1 million in RIH funds.

2) Home improvement revolving loan program. Low-interest loans to improve units. Source: $6 million from RIH; $6 million from participating banks.

3) Affordable housing partnership program. Low-interest loans [RIH] for housing initiatives developed in partnership with cities and towns and nonprofit entities. For rehabilitation or new construction on vacant land, or for special-needs housing. Source: $9 million in RIH funds.

4) Municipal-government housing investment program [RIH]. Recycling UDAGs: RIH will invest a limited portion of its credit reserves to purchase for its investment portfolio "secured promissory notes held by municipal corporations; these notes represent the borrowings by third parties of federal grants." The repayments will be dedicated to a neighborhood housing fund, to improve housing for low- and moderate-income people.

For example, the city of Providence has proposed that RIH purchase its $5.8 million Fleet Center UDAG note, and that the proceeds from the purchase be used by the city to help finance housing and retail development in the downtown area. The RIH would then commit itself to dedicating the UDAG payments to a Providence neighborhood housing fund. The payments would be $500,000 per year for 28 years. This could also be used with other municipalities that are interested in earmarking their UDAG payments for housing programs.

5) Family rental housing production assistance program. To encourage developers to build or substantially rehabilitate affordable housing for low- and moderate-income renters. Source: $30 million in tax-exempt revenue bonds, $1 million in RIH funds.

6) Elderly homeownership assistance program [RIH]. Homeowners use the equity in their property as a source of monthly, tax-free cash income over a 10-year period. Source: A $5 million trust fund that will be established to support this program permanently.

7) Elderly congregate-care facility program [bond-financed].

8) Congregate-care demonstration program [RIH].

9) Emergency housing and shelter trust fund [RIH]. To provide immediate physical improvements to existing shelters, and to establish a permanent trust fund that can make resources available to nonprofit groups that provide emergency housing assistance. Source: $1 million in RIH funds for grants to make improvements, and a $3 mil-

lion RIH contribution to a permanent "emergency housing and shelter trust fund."

10) Research agenda. To commence public policy research on: 1) a comprehensive plan for identifying housing demand and needs throughout the state on a multiyear basis; and 2) the relationship between the RIH and local public-housing agencies. Source: $150,000 in RIH funds. *(Rhode Island Housing—A New Beginning,* April 1986).

Appendix 2
Selected Local Abstracts

Arlington County Planning Department

Bob Brosnan
2100 No. 14th Street
Arlington, VA 22201
(703) 558-2291

Density Bonuses

Arlington County uses a passive approach to providing low-income housing. Beginning in 1973, the county provided a 10 percent density bonus for projects that provided low- and moderate-income housing. This was changed in 1981 to a 15 percent density bonus or an additional height of up to six stories. This allowance has only been used once, and resulted in the developer transferring ownership of a 60-unit apartment complex to a local nonprofit—the Arlington Housing Corporation.

The other approach the county uses is to require low-income housing provisions from developers during the site-plan negotiation process. This applies only to large-scale projects and has not had a significant impact.

The county also provides income subsidies from county appropriations. These funds are provided to low-income families required to pay more than 30 percent of their incomes for rent. The funds are provided directly to the beneficiary, and they are expected to be used for housing.

Casino Reinvestment Development Authority (CRDA)

Patrick O'Such
227 No. Vermont Avenue
Atlantic City, NJ 08401
(609) 347-0500

In 1978, the state of New Jersey instituted a 2 percent tax on gross casino revenues, to finance affordable housing for low- to middle-income households (up to 150 percent of the median). The original requirement called for payments to be made within five years, at the end of each fiscal year. The issue of enforcement responsibility was addressed in December 1984, with the creation of the CRDA.

After the establishment of the CRDA, casinos had the option of paying 1.25 percent of gross revenues or constructing an amount of low-income housing equivalent to 2.5 percent of gross revenues. The actual construction option includes a potential credit or a break on future taxes.

The funds received in the first four years after 1984 will go to Atlantic City, then they will be allocated to the rest of the state. Pre-1984 funds will be used solely to produce housing in Atlantic City.

To date (July 15), receipts amount to $51 million (since 1984) and $9.2 million (before 1984).

Because of the provision in the pre-1984 law for casinos to pay over a period of five years, this fund will continue to grow considerably over the next three years. After 1984, the law requires upfront payment of the revenue percentage.

To date, one project has received approval, and one has received preliminary approval. The project with final approval consists of 201 units of "multi-income-level," multifamily rental dwelling units. The project with preliminary approval has three phases: I: rental rehabilitation, 19 units; II: condominium construction (homeownership or rental), 47 units; and III: rental of three complexes (110 units).

The rehabilitation component of the authority's activities provides direct loans to property owners at the following interest rates:

Fund	Rate
1978–1983	7 percent
1984	Two-thirds of AAA bonds' average rate

The decision on which fund to use is based on the interest rate needed to make a project feasible, and is considered on a project-by-project basis.

For a development to be considered by CRDA, the developers must own the land and have a development plan and a financing plan. CRDA will then provide the financing for the proposed housing project.

City of Austin Housing and Community Services

Eliseo Garza
P.O. Box 1088
Austin, TX 78767
(512) 442-7200

Proposed Linkage, and Proposed General Obligation Bonds to Capitalize Superfund

During the late summer of 1985, in response to rapid growth in Austin and to the federal withdrawal of housing funding, the city of Austin began considering alternatives for the production of low-income housing. Although no programs have yet been implemented, there are four main ideas proposed:

1) Housing "superfund." Similar to the San Francisco and Boston approaches of capitalizing a housing trust fund with developer contributions toward financing affordable housing. This is the most controversial approach considered, and probably will not be implemented. State legislation may preclude this option without an amendment.
2) Affordable housing coalition. Proposed issuance of housing bonds for multi- and single-family housing.
3) Interfaith housing coalition. Church-based efforts to develop low- and moderate-income housing.
4) Cooperation between builders and businesses to find alternatives to the superfund idea (primarily tax-exempt bonds).

In addition to these efforts, the city is in the process of streamlining the development process to speed up permit approvals and reduce costs to the developer. The previous average was 1.5 to 2.0 years' lag time. The new figures are, so far, unknown.

Report of the Mayor's Select Committee on Affordable Housing (February 20, 1986)

This report recommends a land use clearinghouse, plus legislation allowing the city to pursue: city equity share programs; land banking; city involvement in mortgage lending; revenue bonds to create rental units; and the development of a special tax to fund housing programs.

The report also recommends a "housing and shelter program" targeted toward families earning 80 percent or less of the median income. (Twenty percent of the funds would go to families earning 60 to 80 percent of the median income, and 80 percent of the funds to families earning less than 60 percent of the median income.) The source of funds would be a per-square-foot levy on all new nonresidential construction, payable within the 12 months following the issuance of the certificate of occupancy. It also calls for a bond election of $35 million in general obligation bonds with which to start the fund.

Report of the Coalition for Affordable Housing (May 29, 1986)

This report is the product of a consultant's study commissioned by the coalition, which is "a group supported by commercial developers, bankers, and other business leaders" *(Austin American Statesman,* May 22, 1986).

The report recommends the formation of a nonprofit housing corporation that would administer housing production programs. The corporation would be funded by a one-time loan of $6 million to establish a revolving loan fund, and by $75 million in bond money ($25 million in city general obligation bonds, $15 million in revenue bonds for multifamily housing, and $35 million in state-issued bonds used to reduce mortgage rates for first-time homebuyers).

Boston Housing Partnership
Carol Glazer
106 Bedford Street
Boston, MA 02111
(617) 423-1221

The Boston Housing Partnership is a public/private partnership (private nonprofit corporation) formed in 1983. The partnership addresses the problems of deterioration and abandonment, to create affordable housing for households with limited incomes. Initial funding for the partnership's operations came from grants from the city of Boston, local corporations, and private foundations. The agency puts together the financial resources necessary for viable projects, and makes them available to community-based sponsors. The actual ownership of the properties is held by locally based community development organizations. The major activities of the partnership are to:

- Secure funding commitments to make the projects financially viable;
- Provide seed money to community sponsors for upfront development costs;
- Work with the city to expedite the tax foreclosure process, the property transfers, and the possible abatements of water and sewer fees; and
- Oversee the development planning and rehabilitation of the property, as well as its sound long-term management.

The major responsibilities of the community-based organizations are to:

- Determine the type of housing program appropriate for the particular neighborhood;
- Submit detailed information on the project sponsor, buildings, budget, project operation, management, marketing, and tenant selection;
- Select consultants and review architectural, engineering, and legal work;
- Supervise the renovation and construction work for the housing projects;
- Prepare the marketing plan and the tenant selection process; and
- Prepare and implement the property management and operation guidelines and procedures.

The first project is a multifamily rehabilitation. Sixty-nine deteriorated or abandoned buildings in scattered locations will be rehabilitated, creating 700 units of low- and moderate-income housing. Ten neighborhood-based community organizations are directing the work. These organizations will own the buildings through the partnership in 15 years.

Financing for Program I

Amount	Source
$4.1 million	CDBG grants
430,000	Private foundation grants
22.3 million	HFA tax-exempt bonds
8.8 million	Equity from investors in limited partnerships
6.4 million*	Interim loans to meet current costs (construction, working capital, . . .), to be repaid out of the series of installments of equity financing
3.4 million/year for 15 years	SHARP, state, and federal rental assistance programs

* A $4.5 million low-interest loan secured by a bank's letter of credit, and $1.9 million from LISC, Ford, and MCDFC.

The second major multifamily project will purchase and renovate 1,100 HUD-foreclosed units in 62 buildings presently in severely deteriorated condition. Funding will come from HUD Section 8 rental assistance, from the state, from the city of Boston, and from limited-partner investors.

Boston Redevelopment Authority

Greg Perkins
Assistant Director of Research
One City Hall Square
Boston, MA 02201
(617) 722-4300

Linkage/Neighborhood Housing Trust Fund

In December 1983, the Boston Zoning Commission established a linkage mechanism, under Boston's zoning code, to create low- and moderate-income housing. The linkage formula required developers to pay $5.00 per square foot for every square foot over 100,000 square feet of new or substantially rehabilitated commercial space. Payments were made in equal installments over 12 years, beginning two years after the issuance of the building permit or upon issuance of the certificate of occupancy, whichever came first.

New linkage policies were proposed by the mayor and adopted by the zoning commission on February 26, 1986. The new policies are targeted to benefit neighborhoods, and will provide the first job-training trust fund in the nation. Under the job-training linkage program, developers of commercial buildings throughout the city will make payments of $1.00 per square foot for each square foot of floor area over 100,000 square feet. The new regulations also reduce the payment period for downtown projects from 12 to seven years, and require that payments begin at the issuance of the building permit. This is expected to approximately double the value of linkage payments. Developers of commercial buildings outside the downtown will continue to be covered under the original regulations. Impacted neighborhoods are targeted to receive 10 percent of the housing contribution made for downtown projects, and 20 percent of that for neighborhood projects.

Developers have a choice of contributing to a neighborhood housing trust or to the actual construction of units. The latter kind of payment is called the "housing creation exaction." Units must be "for occupancy exclusively by low- and moderate-income residents of the city, at a cost at least equal to the amount of the appropriate housing payment exaction." The "development impact project exactions" apply to: office, retail business and service, institutional and educational, and hotel and motel uses, but do not include apartment hotel uses. The estimated revenues from this program are $3 to $5 million per year for the next 15 years, or $37 to $52 million over the next 10 years.

The initiative called Downtown Guidelines introduced to Boston the concept of parcel-to-parcel linkage. Parcel-to-parcel linkage is a land disposition policy that makes the critical connection between economic growth and community needs and values. Boston has several valuable parcels of land downtown, in the hearts of areas undergoing substantial development. Some of the land is city-owned parking lots or garage sites. Some of it, long abandoned, is owned by state and federal agencies. In addition, the city and state own a number of parcels in Boston's most depressed neighborhoods. Under the program, participating governments must link the development of publicly owned downtown parcels with that of publicly owned parcels in the neighborhoods. The connecting of prime downtown sites with less lucrative neighborhood opportunities will produce new enterprise opportunities in Boston.

Boulder Housing Authority

City of Boulder
Cathy McCormick
Department of Housing and Human Services
Boulder, CO 80306
(303) 441-3140

Inclusionary Zoning

The city of Boulder has placed a high priority on the production of moderate-income housing. Toward this end, the city has several programs requiring and encouraging the production of moderate-income housing.

Ordinance #4638 requires all developments of 10 or more units to provide for rental or sale of at least 10 percent of the units for moderate-income households. If a development is annexed to the city after December 18, 1973, the developer is required to provide a minimum of 15 percent of the units to moderate-income households. Rental units are affordable to households earning between 80 percent and 100 percent of the Boulder median income. For-sale units are affordable to households earning between 80 percent and 120 percent of the median income.

Developers may offer an alternative program that is approved by the housing authority, that accomplishes the purpose of this program, and that imposes a similar duty on the developer. Units are to be provided within the boundaries of the project, unless the housing authority finds that this would not be feasible.

Rental units must be rented for at least 10 years at or below the rents established annually by the housing authority. Sales units are sold at or below prices also established by the authority. All purchasers of moderate-income sales units must sign an agreement that controls the second sales price of the unit for 10 years. Purchasers are allowed appreciation on their units, based on the base price of the unit, plus the value of permanent improvements. This value is multiplied by the percentage of increase in the median income for Boulder for each year of ownership.

The ordinance also contains a bedroom conversion factor. This factor determines the number of moderate-income units to be provided, based on number of bedrooms per unit. The following bedroom-configuration equivalency conversion table is used:

Efficiency living unit	0.50 unit
One-bedroom apartment	0.75 unit
Two-bedroom apartment	1.00 unit
Three-bedroom apartment	1.25 units
Four-bedroom apartment	1.50 units

For example, a project with 100 units has a moderate-income commitment of 15 units. If all of the units are three-bedroom ones, the number of moderate-income units to be built would be 15/1.25, or 12. Developers who produce more moderate-income units than required may "bank" the extra units for five years, up to a maximum of 25 units.

Developers are required to submit a report indicating name(s), address(es), incomes, and family sizes of households who purchase the moderate-income units, and the price paid for each home. Rental projects are required to submit similar reports, including information on rent paid and number of bedrooms in each unit.

The planning department often grants density increases in exchange for the provision of moderate-income housing above the moderate-income housing requirements. This program has created approximately 800 units since 1978.

Community Development Department

Mary Flynn
Deputy Director
City Hall Annex
Inman and Broadway
Cambridge, MA 02139
(617) 498-9034

Voluntary Linkage

Cambridge has formally considered a mandatory inclusionary-housing and linkage-zoning proposal twice in the recent past. These specific zoning efforts failed to gather sufficient support to be adopted. The many discussions surrounding the proposals indicated strong support among the business and development community for a linkage program that was reasonable and fair, and through which these interests could make a positive contribution to the city's housing assistance effort.

Despite the absence of a formal, mandatory requirement for linkage as previously proposed, commercial and residential developers in Cambridge are continually pressed to make some contribution, in the form of money or housing units, to assist the city in providing affordable housing. Currently, the city is exploring the development of a set of guidelines that could serve to define a reasonable means of voluntary participation in a linkage program. Such guidelines could serve as a framework for linkage discussions among the development community, the city, and the neighborhoods affected by the new developments.

Three projects to date (June 24) have been negotiated on a project-by-project basis. All three are housing projects; two are relatively large projects in an economic development area that the city is working on in terms of infrastructure and the like. The two large projects have made contributions to the city's linkage fund—$500,000 for a 390-unit project, and $200,000 for a 75-unit project. In the third project, the developer agreed to provide three affordable units in a 30-unit project. These concessions have been made by the developers as a means of gaining community support for their projects, which would otherwise not have been approved.

Department of Community Development

Township of Cherry Hill
David Benedetti
Cherry Hill, NJ 08034
(609) 488-7800

Affordable Housing Impact Fee and Inclusionary Zoning

Cherry Hill, in an effort to meet its obligation to provide an opportunity for low- and moderate-income families to live in the township, has enacted an ordinance that requires payment of a housing impact fee prior to the issuance of any building permits, and requires developers of multifamily housing to set aside 10 to 20 percent of each project's units to be sold to families of low and moderate incomes. Multifamily projects are required to include a certain percentage of modest-priced units, as defined by the township. However, the developer of a multifamily project may elect to pay the impact fee in lieu of making the modest-priced unit set-aside, subject to approval by the planning board.

Housing Impact Fee

The amount of the housing impact fee is calculated differently for residential and nonresidential developments. The impact fee may be paid in five equal installments; the first is required before issuance of the building permit, and the second before issuance of the certificate of occupancy. The balance of the installments is due each year on the same date as the second payment. These fees are placed in an escrow account of the township, to be used for the sole purpose of aiding in the provision or rehabilitation of modest-priced housing.

For residential projects requiring major subdivision approvals, the impact fee will be an amount equal to 1.5 percent (0.015) of the square footage of the unit, multiplied by the median price per square foot of new housing in the Northeast region, as contained in the *Characteristics of New Housing,* published annually by the census bureau. This is currently $45.15, and will be raised to $49.80 in January 1987.

Nonresidential projects (except those of nonprofit institutions) will pay a fee of either 3 percent of the construction cost as noted on the construction permit application, or $1.00 per square foot of building area, whichever is greater.

The following are exempt from impact fees:

- Any unit approved as part of a development requiring a set-aside for modest-priced housing;
- Any unit of single-family detached housing that is less than 1,500 square feet in size and that has sold for an amount equal to or less than the square footage multiplied by the median price-per-square-foot of new housing in the Northeast region.

Modest-Priced Housing Program

Cherry Hill's original inclusionary zoning ordinance was adopted in 1973, and required every multifamily development to set aside 5 percent of the total number of units as modest-priced units. The income of prospective purchasers was not to exceed the median family income for the Philadelphia MSA. In 1984, the unit requirement was increased to 10 percent, with 5 percent to be allocated for sale, and 5 percent for rental. The incomes of the prospective rental occupants were not to exceed 80 percent of the median income for the Philadelphia MSA. Under the 1973 ordinance, 200 modest-priced units were constructed. An additional 200 units have been approved under the 1984 ordinance.

In July 1986, the modest-priced unit requirement was raised to 20 percent of the total units, with half of the units for sale and half for rent. In addition, the units that will be for sale now have the same income requirements as do the rental units (80 percent of the median). Several other conditions are also stipulated.

Units offered for sale are to be sold at a maximum price equal to the square footage of the floor area times 80 percent of the median price-per-square-foot of new housing for the Northeast region (as contained in the *Characteristics of Housing,* published by the census bureau). Rental units are to be sold at 65 percent of the median price-per-square-foot. If a modest-priced unit is offered for resale, the maximum price is determined as follows: Original purchase price, adjusted by the percentage change of the CPI, minus housing component for the Philadelphia MSA as of January in the year of the sale, plus the increase in value as a result of any improvements, as determined by the township tax assessor. (Another way of stating this is: the maximum price is calculated by increasing the original purchase price by the percentage change in the eligible owner's income from the date of purchase to the date of sale.) All units offered for resale must be offered in conformance with the deed restrictions of those units.

The ordinance includes requirements for:

- The number of bedrooms and the sizes of the units;
- The dispersion of units in the project;
- The facades of modest-priced units (these cannot be distinguishable from those of other units);
- The rate of completion of the modest-priced units (this must be the same rate as that of the rest of the project); and
- Deed restrictions specifying that the modest-priced units remain as such.

Based on past records of building activity, the township expects to receive approximately $6 million over the next six years, and an additional $9 million in the following six-year period. The reasoning behind this program is completely tied to the state mandate under *Mt. Laurel II* that requires localities to provide their "fair share" of affordable housing. In addition, the township has a homeownership rehabilitation program (CDBG), and a rental rehabilitation program.

Department of Housing

Joel T. Werth
City of Chicago
318 South Michigan Avenue
Chicago, IL
(312) 922-7922, ext. 707
or
Patrick Johnson
National Equity Fund

Chicago Housing Partnership

The Chicago Housing Partnership is a new public/private collaboration that has generated $50 million between 1985 and 1987 and rehabilitated 1,250 low- to moderate-income apartments. The partners are the city of Chicago's DOH, the Chicago Equity Fund (CEF), the Community Equity Assistance Corporation (CEAC), local lenders, neighborhood-based housing development organizations, and LISC. The program has leveraged $16 million in private investments and has reached two-thirds of its three-year goal of $10 million in corporate equity. Between 1985 and 1987, major banks will provide $25 million in first mortgages; the Chicago DOH will contribute $15 million in second mortgages; the CEF will invest $10 million in equity; and LISC will add bridge financing when necessary. The CHP generates predictable financing through the CEF, and streamlines the financial packaging and brokering process by creating a "one-stop" center—the CEAC—to help nonprofit housing developers package their projects and build their technical skills.

Chicago Equity Fund

The Chicago Equity Fund (CEF) is a series of partnerships to be formed annually by Chicago's major corporations for the purpose of investing in housing rehabilitation projects for low-income residents of Chicago neighborhoods. The initial goal of the CEF was to raise $10 million in capital over three years, and to rehabilitate $50 million worth of apartments. This goal will be exceeded in two years. CEF investments are made exclusively in low-income neighborhood revitalization projects, and cover a large part (20 to 30 percent) of the costs of rehabilitation. The structure of the CHP and of the CEF allows the nonprofit sponsors to syndicate their developments and raise 20 to 30 percent of the costs through limited partnerships.

Thirteen of Chicago's most prominent companies joined the first investor partnership in mid-1985, with an average investment of $500,000 and a total of $6.4 million. The companies that participate in the CEF earn a modest profit from their investments, mostly realized through tax advantages, as well as by sharing in the cash flow from the project. If a project is sold, the corporations and the nonprofit share the proceeds. The CEF has invested this equity in 12 projects totaling $26 million, which will produce 521 affordable rehabilitated apartments. The resulting apartments will rent for $325 per month, with a minimum federal operating subsidy.

These projects are located in neighborhoods throughout Chicago, and are selected and sponsored by nonprofit, community-based groups representing each of these neighborhoods. The Community Equity Assistance Corporation, a LISC subsidiary, offers valuable technical assistance to the nonprofits organizing the projects.

In 1986, the CEF expected at least $5 million in commitments from new companies, which will produce another 500 or more apartments at a total cost of $25 million. Organizers are working to expand the CEF into a nationwide operation that pools capital from investors all over the country, combines it with technical expertise and investment management services, and provides "one-stop" equity financing to project sponsors in areas lacking strong local investor communities.

Housing Abandonment Prevention Program

This program halts abandonment in selected neighborhoods by intervening in the operation and management of occupied properties and by providing technical and financial assistance to correct dangerous conditions that may cause the building to be vacated and subsequently abandoned. The focus is on early intervention, by empowering 10 neighborhood organizations to identify troubled buildings and work with property owners, the city, and the courts to save the buildings. To date, 963 dwelling units in 41 buildings have been saved from abandonment, at an average cost of $981 per unit. Overall services have been extended to 1,100 dwelling units through intervention and technical assistance.

This program was initially funded by $1 million in CDBG funds. The DOH is considering a research proposal to develop an early-warning data base to help organizations identify buildings earlier in the cycle than is now possible, by accessing tax, utility, and water records.

Chicago Neighborhood Housing Program

The DOH plans to construct moderate-income housing on large vacant lots owned by the city. With $10 million, the DOH will build 400 to 500 townhouses for sale between $55,000 and $60,000. These two- and three-bedroom townhouses are to be affordable to four- and five-person households in a $20,000-to-$27,000 income range.

The townhouses are built on a site-by-site basis as funds become available through revenues from urban renewal land sales, fees from tax-exempt bond financing, and other sources. In addition to the land, the DOH will provide site improvements, low-interest mortgages, and equity participation loans. These loans will be zero-percent-interest, deferred-payment loans due upon sale or refinancing during the first five years, and contingent upon the retirement of the first mortgage and the return of the homeowner equity. The loan would be forgiven after five years, to avoid speculation and neighborhood instability.

The DOH will work with community-based organizations and churches to generate a non–interest bearing trust fund of $10 to $12 million, to provide construction financing at no cost to the developer. This will reduce costs by $4,000 to $6,000 per unit.

Housing Facade Program

The DOH will provide funds on a 50/50 matching basis to property owners of one- to four-unit buildings for facade improvements. Zero-interest, deferred loans will be provided, up to $1,000 per unit, on city blocks where more than one-half of the property owners have applied for assistance.

Illinois Housing Partnership Program
Five million dollars will go each year to the city, for rehabilitation financing for low- and moderate-income housing rehabilitation.

Illinois Development Action Grant Program
Up to $10 million a year will go to the city for residential, commercial, and industrial projects.

Surtax Program

Peter Kopentis
Surtax Program Manager
Dade County, FL
(305) 643-9800

Real Estate Transfer Tax

From the fact sheet on the documentary stamp surtax: "In 1983, the Florida legislature passed legislation allowing certain counties the power to levy a discretionary surtax on documents recording the sale of property. The surtax is for establishing and financing a homeownership assistance loan trust fund to assist in the construction, rehabilitation, or purchase of housing for low- and moderate-income families. Single-family residences were exempted from the tax. The amount of funds available for administration is limited by the Act to 5 percent."

Soon after the Florida state legislature passed this law, the Metropolitan Dade County Commissioners enacted a local ordinance that established a surtax of 45 cents per $100 value on deed transfers. The ordinance was adopted in October 1983. The county was sued by realtors, who claimed that the surtax was discriminatory because it only taxed commercial property. The state supreme court ruled in the county's favor. In December 1983, the county began collecting revenues. The law has been amended to allow the funds to be used for rental developments. The funds are only used for loans that are returned to the trust fund.

Current status: To date, there is roughly $27 million in the fund, all of which is committed to various projects. The revenues are coming in at a rate of $750,000 per month, or $9 million per year. To date, the payback on the loans is approximately $75,000.

The homeownership assistance loan program is designed to provide opportunities for low- and moderate-income families to purchase homes, using a combination of private financing for first mortgages and public funds for second mortgages. The second mortgage makes up the difference between what the family can afford (and qualify for) and the cost of the home. Second mortgages have an interest rate of 3 percent for low-income and 6 percent for moderate-income families. The maximum second mortgage amount is $35,000.

The single-family rehabilitation assistance loan program is funded by the homeownership assistance loan trust fund and provides low-interest-rate loan funds (interest rates at either 3 percent for low-income or 6 percent for moderate-income, or deferred loans due at the time of sales or transfers), to enable low- and moderate-income owner/occupants to finance the rehabilitation of their homes. Up to $20,000 is available for each loan.

The state law requires the county to allocate 50 percent of the funds to low-income housing. ("Low-income" is defined as 80 percent of the median, and "moderate-income" is defined as 140 percent of the median.) But the local decision was to allocate a minimum of 75 percent of the funds to low-income households. The actual proportion provided to low-income families is currently 85 percent.

Distribution of rehabilitation loans
Low-income	$2,812,281
Moderate-income	2,952,131

Distribution of homeownership loans
Low-income	$6,324,733
Moderate-income	7,847,918

It is estimated that 420 families will become homeowners, and that an additional 150 families will receive rehabilitation loans each year.

Department of Housing

Steve Gordon
Housing Planner
1445 Cleveland Place Room 400
Denver, CO 80202
(303) 575-2736

Denver Housing Initiatives

Denver Housing Initiatives represents the cooperative efforts of the city and county of Denver, the Colorado Housing Finance Authority, the Piton Foundation, and the Colorado Division of Housing to promote the construction and rehabilitation of housing in Denver, particularly for low- and moderate-income households; to make the most of available resources by using them more efficiently; and to make it easier to access funds by establishing a single application process. Multiple sources of funds are loaned and sometimes granted to nonprofit organizations.

The types of projects that will be considered include: the acquisition and rehabilitation of housing, the adaptive re-use of nonresidential buildings, and new construction. Both rental and sale housing will be considered. Funds may be used to offset project costs, or for letters of credit, or as reserves, in order to make it possible for projects to obtain other sources of financing. There are four types of assistance available from the four sponsoring organizations:

- technical assistance;
- upfront development costs;
- construction financing; and
- permanent financing.

The minimum requirement is that 20 percent of the units be available for low- and moderate-income households (earning no more than

80 percent of the median). One of the criteria for selection is the benefit to low- and moderate-income people. Priority will be placed on projects benefiting low-income people, defined as earning 50 percent or less of the SMSA's median family income. The period of time for which it is assured that the units will be inhabited by low- and moderate-income households is an important consideration in determining if this criterion has been met.

Other criteria for selection are: the extent to which a project will revitalize a deteriorated neighborhood; the impact of the project on people with special, unmet housing needs; the extent to which the project expands housing opportunities for low- and moderate-income families and promotes the establishment of walk-in schools; and the extent to which moderate-priced housing is preserved.

Applications must also address: the capacity of the organization to achieve the specific project; (for rehabilitation projects) the seriousness of the problems to be corrected; the compatibility of the site plans and designs with the surrounding neighborhood; the length of time it takes to pay off any secondary financing; the number of dollars needed per low-income unit; and the feasibility of the specific project.

This program is relatively new, beginning in January 1986. Applications are taken quarterly, and to date (June 25), there is tentative approval for five projects.

Department of City Planning
Ed Meehan
550 Main Street
Hartford, CT 06103
(203) 722 6635

Voluntary Density Bonuses

History

Linkage was first proposed in September 1983. But in February 1984, the corporation counsel recommended that linkage be illegal unless the state law was changed. In March 1984, a linkage task force was created.

July 1985 saw consultants recommending that the city council seek state legislation allowing a commercial lease tax. Political proponents of the linkage task force report were elected in November 1985. And in February 1986, the city council concluded that linkage is necessary, and asked for ordinances to enact the policy.

Current Status

On June 23, 1986, the city council defeated an ordinance based on exaction taxes (similar to the Boston and San Francisco programs). The defeated ordinance would have imposed a $1.90 fee on every square foot of new office space. However, the council did adopt an ordinance that:

- Creates a linkage trust fund for the specific purpose of providing funds for job training, and housing and economic development assistance. Expenditures of the fund are made based on recommendations by the city manager, with approval by the council.
- Establishes employment requirements for publicly assisted projects. A publicly assisted project is defined as one receiving tax abatements, public bonds, public land, and easements. Any such projects are required to meet minimum construction-employment criteria for Hartford resident tradeworkers (40 percent), minority tradeworkers (25 percent), and female tradeworkers (6.9 percent). Failure to meet these requirements will terminate all tax benefits and require the developer to pay $10,000 for each job below the required percentage for Hartford and minority residents.
- Provides bonus floor space for certain proposed uses, facilities, or improvements. The bonus ratio is the ratio of the area in square feet of the bonus use to the floor area permitted the bonus projects in *excess* of an FAR of 10. The FAR includes the area allocated to parking.

For example, a bonus ratio of one-to-three (1:3) means that for each square foot of bonus use, the project is eligible for three additional square feet of floor area for permitted uses. Each eligible use has a bonus ratio and a maximum allowable FAR increase, or an FAR cap. The eligible projects include: residential (there are no affordability requirements); pedestrian-oriented retail; transient parking; cultural and entertainment facilities; visitor and convention-related housing; pedestrian circulation improvements; day care/nurseries, and employment.

Sample Use	*Bonus Ratio*	*FAR Cap*
Residential use	1 : 8	4
Pedestrian-oriented retail	1 : 3	2
Transient parking	1 : 4	2
Employment	1 : 625	6

- Provides floor area bonuses for provision of job-training or employment programs for Hartford residents during the construction or occupancy phase of a project. The agreement requires that Hartford residents be employed in 25 percent of the total of permanent jobs, and that each job above this amount is equal to 625 square feet of bonus floor area.

In lieu of meeting the employment requirements or of providing an eligible bonus use, developers may contribute $5.00 per square foot for each square foot of bonus area to the linkage trust fund.

Since the mid-1970s, Hartford has been requiring publicly assisted developers of mixed-use projects to set aside at least 20 percent of the units as affordable housing. "Affordable" is defined using HUD's 80 percent of the median. "Publicly assisted" means that a project has benefited from: urban renewal land, rezonings, urban mass transit funds, or any other related public incentives.

Department of Land Utilization

John Whalen
650 South King Street
Honolulu, HI 96813
(808) 523-4432

Community Benefit Assessment

For the past several years, the city and county of Honolulu have invoked the conditional zoning provisions of its zoning code for various purposes, including the provision of affordable housing. This has been accomplished through "unilateral agreements" with developers of residential projects. The unilateral agreements are conditions that are attached to approvals for rezoning. In general, these conditions have required 10 percent of the units to be set aside for households with incomes that are less than 80 percent of the median. Approximately 1,000 units of affordable housing have been produced under this system, with an additional 1,000 currently owed to the city as part of the development agreements.

The system of unilateral agreements has not worked well because the same requirements were applied to all residential rezonings; minor rezonings were affected to the same extent as major changes in designated land uses. The variety of land costs throughout the city was not considered, and the definition of a low-income unit was not clearly stated.

To bring more order, fairness, and predictability to the practice of "conditional zoning," the city is developing a community benefit assessment (CBA), to be tied to the rezoning of land for all types of development. The CBA method is based on a broader view of the "rational nexus" between new development and community costs. In this system, a developer can earn credits for providing any combination of community benefits, such as the dedication of land or the construction of low-income housing,or the provision of oversized infrastructure, of child-care facilities, of public facilities such as police/fire stations, and so forth. The purpose of the CBA is to avoid the "opportunity cost" borne by government when private lands are rezoned to higher uses. The CBA is intended to cover the "lag time" or gap between new property tax assessments on rezoned properties and the actual appreciation in land values. The increase in land value resulting from a zone change is the basis for its assessment amount. A location factor is included, to adjust for rural/urban land-value differences.

Zone changes involving projects in residential districts with 25 dwelling units or less are exempt. Projects in other zoning districts involving 25,000 square feet of floor area or less are also exempt. Rather than imposing a fee on the developer, this voluntary arrangement has the developer and the city creating a "unilateral agreement," in exchange for a zone change for higher-density development. The developer must satisfy the agreement before building permits are given for the proposed development. The assessment is based on a formula that gives credits for the type and amount of benefits that the developer agrees to give to the city. One of the aims of this program is to reduce the risk of the developer in a very unpredictable development environment.

Housing contributions must remain rental units for 10 years. Each unit represents a credit of $10,000 (adjusted by the CPI). Units rededicated for an additional 10 years receive an additional credit of $5,000.

Hawaii has recently passed enabling legislation similar to the California laws allowing development agreements to be made. The community benefit assessment will be considered by the city council in 1987.

The following factors are used in determining the amount of the assessment:

- LA (land area, in acres or square feet);
- MD (maximum density for a new zoning district);
- LF (location factor, ranging from 0.463 to 1.944 in the central business district);
- ZF (zoning factor, ranging from 0.3 for rural districts to 5.9 for the resort district); and
- CPI (a CPI adjustment factor that was set at 1,000 in 1986, with an annual increase or decrease to be equivalent to the percentage change in the Honolulu CPI).

Exemptions from the assessment are available:

- If the area where the new zoning has been assigned has an equal or lower zoning factor than the original zoning;
- If LA × MD = 25 units or less, and constitutes the entire zone-change request; and
- If LA × FAR = 25,000 square feet or less, and is the entire zone change.

To calculate the assessment when the new zoning is for a residential district, the following formula is used:

Assessment = LA × MD × LF × (ZF new − ZF original) × CPI × $1,000

And to calculate the assessment when the new zoning is for other than residential, agricultural, or preservation use, this formula is applied:

Assessment = LA × FAR × LF × (ZF new − ZF original) × CPI × $0.25

Housing and Community Development Office

Howard County, Maryland
Ron Davis/Rochelle Brown
3450 Courthouse Drive
Carroll Building
Ellicott City, MD 21043
(301) 992-2024

Real Estate Transfer Tax and Community Renewal Fund

Howard County has a real estate transfer tax. The tax is 1 percent of the sale price of *all* property transferred in the county. Since 1970, revenue from this tax has been used as a source of revenue for housing programs. From the funds collected by the tax, 12.5 percent is contributed to the county's community renewal fund. This fund is used for the housing programs of the county. The majority of the fund exists to cover shortages incurred by the two county housing projects, but it is also used for staff, for emergency shelter facilities, and for special studies. Currently, $1.5 to $1.6 million is in the fund. The two housing projects are:

1) Hilltop Housing. Subsidized and operated completely with county funds. A 94-unit county-built complex that provides units to low-income families for 30 percent of their adjusted monthly incomes. The costs not covered by the 30 percent rent requirement are subsidized by the fund.
2) Guilford Gardens. Recently completed. One hundred units, 50 percent of which is Section 8 new construction. Since 1981, the complex has been operated as a rental cooperative. Residents have established their own rents, and they direct management of the complex.

In addition, the county is in the process of completing the Nordan Homeownership Project, which was begun in 1980 with a block grant award, to develop affordable housing for first-time homebuyers. The project was built in three phases. The county purchased, improved, and subdivided the land into 14 lots. Homes were built to sell for $42,500, $45,000, and $50,900. The county provided a second mortgage for the cost of the lot, construction financing, building permit fees, and connection fees.

Four of the units were built by a cooperative effort among the state, the county, the Enterprise Social Investment Corporation (ESIC), and the Ryland Group. The state provided low-cost mortgages; Ryland was the builder; and the ESIC facilitated the negotiations between Ryland and the county. The houses sell for $29,600; this price buys a down-sized three-bedroom modular home for a family earning between $8,000 and $15,000 per year. Mortgages are given at 4 percent interest over a 30-year term.

This program won an award from the National Association of Counties.

The Rehabilitation Loan Fund

Part of the community renewal fund, this loan fund currently has a balance of approximately $450,000. Homeowners are given interest rates of 3 to 9 percent for rehabilitation costs. The maximum loan amount is usually $15,000, although exceptions have been made by combining CDBG funds with county funds.

The Vacant Housing Rehabilitation Fund

Recently receiving approval for CDBG funds, this program will make available rehabilitation funds and vacant buildings for persons and families on the waiting list for Section 8 and public housing. Approximate projected costs per structure are $30,000 to $31,000.

Industrial Revenue Bonds

These bonds are used for affordable housing construction. Two to three years ago, apartments were built with IDB funds. Twenty percent of the units were required to be set aside for low- and moderate-income (Section 8–eligible) families. But it was discovered that developers were skimming the list to find applicants at the 80 percent-of-median-income level, and not renting to lower-income applicants. Thus, about one year ago, a board resolution was passed that requires that, of the IRB set-aside, units must be rented to families earning from 60 to 80 percent of the median income. Families will pay 30 percent of their monthly adjusted income for rent (minus a utility allowance).

Department of Housing and Economic Development

Gerard Cotrone
26 Journal Square, 16th Floor
Jersey City, NJ 07306
(201) 547-5070

Negotiated Linkage

Jersey City is proposing a mechanism to help generate the resources necessary to create affordable housing, by linking the market-rate housing and commercial development throughout the city to the subsidization of inner-city affordable housing units. The program is flexible, using three mechanisms to create affordable housing:

1) Developers may build or rehabilitate low- and moderate-income housing themselves.
2) Developers may participate in the financing or sponsorship of affordable housing elsewhere in Jersey City, through providing payments to the subsidization of specific projects; or
3) Developers may contribute payments to a municipally established housing trust fund, which will be used by the department of housing and economic development to sponsor affordable housing throughout the city.

The policy for new or substantially rehabilitated commercial development is based on a calculation of the likely impact of such projects on the demand for housing in Jersey City. The formula for determining developers' contributions is as follows:

- A generally accepted figure is that every 250 net rentable square feet of new office space generates one new employee.
- The average Jersey City household contains 1.09 adults who are employed full time.
- Forty-two percent of Jersey City residents work in Jersey City.
- Approximately 30 percent of the members of the Jersey City workforce are employed in commercial and office occupations.

This formula is used only to determine the amount of square footage over 100,000 square feet. Developments below 100,000 square feet are allowed to negotiate in-lieu contributions to a municipal trust fund. An average subsidy cost of $12,000 per unit is used. Based on these factors, the need for housing generated by new office development can be estimated as follows:

$$\frac{\text{Square feet of office space}}{250 \text{ square feet}} \times \frac{0.30 \times 0.42}{1.09} = \text{Number of units}$$

Because construction of actual units is preferable to financial contributions, incentives are offered to commercial developers who wish to

196

provide units rather than cash. Developers can reduce their trust-fund contribution by 20 percent by providing below-market financing to low- and moderate-income purchasers, or by providing financing for the construction of affordable housing. Developers can reduce their housing responsibilities by 80 percent by providing actual housing units rather than cash.

Residential developments are required to set aside 10 percent of all new or substantially rehabilitated housing for low- and moderate-income households. This set-aside comprises units that are rented *or* sold as affordable. Developers have three options for meeting inclusionary guidelines:

1) To make in-lieu cash contributions, calculated at the amount necessary to subsidize 10 percent of the units to make them affordable to low- and moderate-income households;
2) To provide the required 10 percent of units off-site, within the same neighborhood; or
3) To provide the required 10 percent of units on-site, within the same development.

The city provides a number of resources to developers who are willing to comply with these guidelines. These resources include the waiving of fees, the provision of land, and tax-exempt financing from the New Jersey Housing and Mortgage Finance Agency. In almost two years of operation, this program has received commitments from developers for 1,300 units.

Division of Housing, Lee County, Florida

Dennis Simon
P.O. Box 398
Ft. Myers, FL 33902
(813) 335-2138

Housing Density Bonus

Under the density bonus program, a developer may be eligible to exceed the standard density range for a particular land use category, if the developer either makes the additional dwelling units available to low- and moderate-income persons in a site-specific manner, or makes a cash contribution to the low- and moderate-income housing fund. "Low-" and "moderate-income" are defined as 50 percent and 80 percent, respectively, of the Lee County median income.

Developers have the choice of either a site-specific density bonus (SSDB), or a cash-contribution density bonus (CCDB). Maximum density bonuses are set for different categories of land use, as designated by Lee County's land use categories:

	Density Range (units/acre)	Maximum Density Bonus
Intensive Development Area	Eight to 14	8
Central Urban Area	Five to 10	5
Urban Community	One-half to 6	4
Fringe Area	One-half to 6	4

The actual bonuses that developers receive are determined by the degree to which the developers meet the following seven criteria. A project must have:

1) A location in a state-approved enterprise zone;
2) Fifty percent or more of the bonus density units set aside for low-income families;
3) A minimum 10 percent of bonus units in three-bedroom apartments;
4) Direct access to two or more public-collector or arterial streets;
5) Availability of public, central sewer and water;
6) Compatibility with the density and intensity of surrounding land use; and
7) No acreage contained within the development site that exhibits "resource protection area" or "transitional zone" criteria.

Developers selecting the construction option (SSDB) must meet all seven of these criteria to be eligible for the maximum density bonus. Developers opting for the cash contribution must meet all of the criteria, except numbers 2 and 3, to be eligible for the maximum bonus. See following chart:

	Bonus Received (percent)	Number of Criteria Fulfilled
SSDB	100	7
	75	6
	50	5
		(Minimum criteria for bonus eligibility: fulfillment of criterion #2 plus four others.)
CCDB	100	5
	75	4
	50	3

The SSDB requires developers to provide that percentage of low- and moderate-income units that equals the actual density bonus the developer is applying for. A minimum of 10 percent of the total units of the proposed development must be designated for low- and moderate-income families for a period of at least 10 years.

The CCDB option requires the developer to pay the contribution in full before a building permit is issued. Density bonuses run with the development order, not with the land. The standard contribution rate is $6,000 per unit for units selling for $100,000 or less. For units selling for more than $100,000, contributions should equal 10 percent of the selling price.

Contributions are made to the low- and moderate-income housing fund, which may be used to provide rental assistance, mortgage assistance, housing rehabilitation, demolitions of dilapidated housing, and relocations of residents to safe, sanitary, and decent housing. The major purpose of the fund is to promote homeownership opportunities for low- and moderate-income families. At least 75 percent of the funds must be spent on low-income persons in any given fiscal year.

City of Los Angeles Community Redevelopment Agency

John Maguire
354 South Spring Street
Los Angeles, CA 90013
(213) 977-1815

Tax Increment Financing

California state law requires that 20 percent of the annual flow of tax increment financing funds be used for housing purposes, whether the projects are existing or new ones. The city of Los Angeles has established two tax increment financing districts, Bunker Hill and the central business district, which generate funds for the production of low-income housing in the city.

Tax increment funds can be used for two types of housing: 1) housing found to be of benefit; and 2) replacement housing, which is always of benefit. For this reason, two separate trust funds were established to differentiate replacement housing from housing of benefit.

Bunker Hill was an urban renewal area, and by law, the state requires a one-to-one replacement of housing units "within the project area or within the territorial jurisdiction of the agency." The Bunker Hill program uses a *replacement housing trust fund,* which finances the one-to-one replacement of units, and assists low- and moderate-income units outside the project area—if the units are of benefit to the project. The replacement housing trust funds are used in three ways:

1) As feasibility or gap loans, to provide loan funds for costs not covered by first mortgage and developer equity of 10 to 15 percent.
2) As direct aid, to provide assistance in meeting approved development costs not supportable by a first mortgage—based on rents affordable to low- and moderate-income households.
3) As homeownership loans—deferred, "soft" second loans—due upon sale or refinancing, to make homeownership of units located in CRA

condominium projects available to low- and moderate-income home-buyers.

Generally, the agency's loans are secured by second deeds of trust, are repayable from residual receipts (excess project income), and bear simple interest (2 to 8 percent per annum). Loans are due on sale or refinancing. Except for homeownership loans, it is required that CRA relocatees be given priority for occupancy in at least 50 percent of the units assisted. The CRA approves the management plan, design, and construction drawings, and ensures that a deed restriction is recorded on the property to limit the occupancy of the units to low- and moderate-income persons and families (those earning up to 120 percent of the median income).

Between 1978 and April 1986, $110 million was spent or committed to the production of 5,833 units in Bunker Hill. In addition to these units, 1,678 units were produced outside the project area, for a cost of $22 million. The Bunker Hill project has produced a total of 7,511 units, and has spent or committed approximately $132 million. (Average subsidy per unit is $17,678—low, because of past use of Section 8 federal funding.)

In the central-business-district (CBD) project, $23 million was spent for 2,400 units, at an average cost of $9,800 per unit. This cost is skewed low because of the high numbers of SRO units produced through this project.

The homeless shelter trust fund has produced 420 beds for the homeless. This fund is capitalized by the CBD housing trust fund, and is administered by the redevelopment agency. An annual capitalization of this fund ($1.8 million last year) maintains this program.

City of Miami Planning Department

Joyce Meyers
275 Northwest Second Street
Miami, FL 33128
(305) 579-6086

Voluntary Linkage

The city of Miami provides a density bonus to developers in return for low- and moderate-income housing. This provision is available in two "special public-interest" districts located in a fast-growing area adjacent to the CBD. The ordinance provides developers with a choice of building housing on the site or off the site, or of contributing to a housing trust fund.

SPI-5 District

The floor/area ratio may be increased for any permitted use, up to a total increase of FAR 1.0, provided that for every one square foot of increase there shall be either:

- A nonrefundable developer contribution of $4.00 to the city of Miami's affordable housing fund; or
- Developer-sponsored construction of 0.15 gross square feet of affordable housing, defined as sales housing with a retail sales price not in excess of 90 percent of the gross median for Dade County's new-housing sales prices, or rental rates (project average) not in excess of 30 percent of the gross median for Dade County's monthly income.

All affordable housing units constructed under the ordinance must be located within one mile of the district's boundaries, or be located in another community redevelopment area.

SPI-7 District

For residential uses, the floor area shall be increased according to either of the alternatives below; however, in no case shall the increase in nonresidential floor area exceed 2.75 times the gross land area. The two alternative approaches are as follows:

- For every square foot of residential floor area provided on-site, the maximum nonresidential floor area shall be increased by one square foot. Such residential floor area shall be constructed concurrently with any uses receiving this bonus.
- Or, for every $6.67 contributed to an affordable housing fund established and administered by the city of Miami, an increase of one square foot of nonresidential floor area shall be permitted. All funds so contributed shall be expended solely within the SPI-7 District.

Minneapolis/St. Paul Family Housing Fund

3608 IDS Tower
Minneapolis, MN 55402
(612) 338-3693
Tom Fulton, Executive Director

The Minneapolis/St. Paul Family Housing Fund is a private, nonprofit housing finance corporation that was formed in 1980 for the purpose of helping the cities to provide affordable housing for low- and moderate-income families. The McKnight Foundation was the impetus for the creation of the fund. The foundation contributed a total of $17 million, with $10 million set aside for what it called "program-related investments" (funds that would ultimately be returned to the foundation). The remaining $7 million took the form of grant money that would be used to carry out family housing fund programs.

For their part, Minneapolis and St. Paul have sold $270 million of single-family mortgage revenue bonds in three separate bond issues beginning in June 1981. Urban Development Action Grant (UDAG) funds have also been allocated to support the housing effort. In its first five years of existence, the fund helped finance 5,419 units—ownership, rental, and cooperative—that were either newly constructed, rehabilitated, or secured for future ownership by the mortgagee.

Family Housing Program

Stage I

The first bond sale in June 1981 was for $120 million, and was expected to provide 1,800 home mortgages, with more to follow in a second bond sale. The program emphasized first-time mortgages for young families with low to middle incomes. When regular bank mortgages were in the 16 to 17 percent range, the program offered 30-year assumable mortgages at 11⅞ percent. Buyers had to pay 5 percent downpayment, but the program offered special loans—made possible through McKnight and UDAG funds—for about one-third of the qualifying buyers, who were unable to afford homes at the 11⅞ percent mortgage rate. These loans, called equity participation loans (EPLs), and equity contribution loans (ECLs) rendered the payments affordable by paying up to 20 percent of the purchase price of a home as an additional downpayment. Graduated payment loans were also available, if equity loans were not sufficient. The loans are repaid when the house is sold.

EPLs have an interest rate equal to a home's appreciation. ECLs and GPLs have zero interest, and are repayable only after the owners have recovered their own downpayments and paid their selling costs. The fund's loans have reduced the income requirements from the $25,000 to $35,000 range to the $15,000 to $25,000 range, depending on the price of a given home.

Stage II

In May 1984, the cities sold $125 million in tax-exempt mortgage revenue bonds. Stage II—with emphasis on home recycling—provided 2,000 home mortgage loans at a low 9¾ percent to young families who could then buy homes costing less than $77,500 from sellers who were more than 50 years old. Buyers snapped up Stage II's allocation for recycled homes within two months of the program's inception in July 1984.

In February 1985, the fund announced the family assistance program, a smaller program funded by $24.5 million in bonds because of new federal restrictions. The program continues to emphasize the recycling of empty-nester houses to young families. It also offers buyers with incomes of $29,500 or less the additional assistance of a no-interest loan that would temporarily buy down the interest rate to 9.5 percent during the first years of the mortgage.

Multifamily Housing Programs

As of January 1986, the fund had made loans to 51 multifamily housing developments containing a total of 1,214 units. The fund has assisted each of these projects with one of three different vehicles:

1) Equity loans, which generally mature when the project is sold or when the first mortgage is repaid. In some projects, the fund also receives a portion of new cash flow.
2) Graduated assistance payments, by which the fund provides monthly subsidy payments to cover the difference between what the occupants can afford to pay and the cost of financing and operating the project. This program is similar to Section 8, except that the fund's subsidy is phased out as income increases, relative to the fixed debt-service payments. The fund's subsidies are structured as loans, repayable if a project is sold, or when individual shares are sold in a cooperative project.
3) Special loans, which are tailored to the special needs of individual projects. For example, the fund loaned one nonprofit sponsor $364,332 to pay the reservation fee for an $11.7 million mortgage loan through GNMA's Tandem Plan.

These projects involved more than $41.9 million of mortgage financing from a variety of sources (mostly tax-exempt bonds), and the fund used $4,693,634 of McKnight money to fund its loans. Of the 51 projects, 16 were new-construction projects, and 35 were rehabilitations. Eighteen of the projects were cooperatives; 38 involved Section 8 rent subsidies; and 24 were developed by nonprofit sponsors, most of them neighborhood-based. Most of the units are affordable to low- and very-low-income families.

Twin Cities Housing Development Corporation

The fund has created and capitalized a separate nonprofit development corporation, the Twin Cities Housing Development Corporation, to cosponsor the development or acquisition of low-income housing with neighborhood-based nonprofit developers. The TCHDC is working on three new projects, containing 74 low-income units.

Recycle Account

The fund uses loan repayments to make additional "recycle" loans. The source of new money represents loan repayments made on earlier fund financings, valued at a total of $7 million. Loan repayments will be used to help preserve the livability and affordability of existing low-income housing developments, as well as to help produce additional low-income units for families.

Problems

Some developers have concerns about the family housing program's restrictions. Income ceilings make it difficult to find qualified buyers. "We had to build a certain quality of home—$60,000 to $70,000. With the income restrictions, the window for qualified buyers was about $1,000, from about $27,000 to $28,000. Such tight restrictions took time and cost money."

Because of their design, fund loans have not been assumable. This restriction has inhibited a fund mortgagee from selling easily because the special financing enjoyed by the first buyer could not be fully transferred to the second buyer.

Some problems have stemmed from Stage I guidelines, and the fund tried to address these in Stage II. The program board took the position that neither the cities nor the fund were responsible for remedying construction defects, for instance, and developer requirements were tightened for Stage II.

Monroe County Planning Department
Ty Symroski
Key West, FL 33040
(305) 294-9614

Density Bonus and Impact Fee Exemption

Monroe County, which includes the Florida Keys, has attracted an affluent retirement community, as well as keen interest from South American investors. The county is designated a critical area of concern by the state department of community affairs because of its unique environmental attributes. This designation requires that the county revise its comprehensive plan and development regulations. In revising its comprehensive plan, the county has added incentives for construction of affordable housing that are structured around a transfer-of-development-rights (TDR) program. Each parcel has an allocated density and a maximum net density that can be received by transfer. These numbers vary throughout the zoning districts.

Types of housing eligible for density bonuses include:

- Multifamily housing. Developers can increase density up to the maximum net density for the site under the TDR program, as long as the increased density is consistent with the other components of the land use plan, such as environmental protection and capital facilities. In one zoning district, this could result in a fivefold increase. Any bonus units that are permitted must meet the affordability requirements.
- Single-family housing. This bonus is designed to provide housing ownership opportunities for middle-income residents who are employed in the county. To be eligible for the bonus, developers must guarantee that their units will be sold to households that receive 70

percent of their incomes from employment in Monroe County. The bonus will allow for development on sites that are zoned so as to be otherwise unbuildable. For example, a one-acre site that has a minimum lot size of two acres.

- Employee housing. This provides a density bonus in certain districts for employers who develop employee housing, such as dormitories.

The county is also interested in providing very-low-income housing but does not expect the density bonus program to facilitate this.

Affordable housing is defined as the "total cost of the shelter being accessible to households with incomes up to 125 percent of the median, and at a cost of no greater than 30 percent of their incomes." Projects that include affordable housing may be exempt from the impact fees that are required for capital-facilities improvements. The requirements for exemption are currently being developed, and should be finalized by the end of September 1986. The revised comprehensive plan was approved by the county and by the state in July 1986, and will go into effect in September.

Housing and Community Development

Scott Reilly
Montgomery County
100 Maryland Avenue
Rockville, MD 20850
(301) 279-1325

The condominium conversion tax was created in 1981, in response to the large number of condominium conversions that were then taking place in the county. Its purpose is to preserve rental housing for low- and moderate-income residents.

The only change that has taken place since the inception of the program has been an amendment to the original, broader bill to limit the beneficiaries to low- and moderate-income people. The county levies a 4 percent tax on the initial sales of rental units into condominium use, and by law, the proceeds from this tax are used for any activity related to preserving low- and moderate-income rental housing.

A new activity of the county is its right-of-first-refusal on rental apartment sales; the county can match an offer and buy a project. Two apartment complexes are being bought by the county for about $4.3 million; together, they contain 83 units of rental housing.

This program had accumulated approximately $18 million before the county began spending this year on the major purchases of rental housing. As the condominium market in Montgomery County has become relatively soft in the recent past, the county has had to take a longer-term perspective on the use of these funds.

The county also works in conjunction with the housing opportunities commission, which floats tax-exempt bonds to help finance affordable housing.

Housing Development Corporation

Charles Brass
Program Development Director
75 Maiden Lane
8th Floor
New York, NY 10038
(212) 344-8080

City Planning Commission

Dana Driskell
Department of Development
2 Lafayette Street
New York, NY 10001
(212) 566-3978

Housing Preservation and Development

Roz Post
General Affairs
100 Gold Street
New York, NY 10038
(212) 566-4440

The Housing Development Corporation

This is the city's multifamily housing finance agency. In 1985 alone, HDC accomplished the sale of nine individual bond issues. Five more were structured and completed in November and December 1985. Ten of HDC's financings, which were in fact bond issues totaling $640 million, involved its 80/20 program.

In most cases, low-income units in the 80/20 program are solely supported by internal subsidies generated from project revenues. The 20 percent portion is for tenants with incomes that do not exceed 80 percent of the area median income. Since 1984, the 80/20 program has created approximately 2,200 low-income units, while benefiting from $962 million in HDC notes and bonds issued.

HDC's moderate-income rental housing assistance program is using surplus earnings generated by the municipal assistance corporation to leverage tax-exempt bond proceeds to produce affordable rental housing. At least 20 percent of the units have to be occupied by low-income tenants, with the remaining tenant incomes at 175 percent of the median ($48,000 per year). Developers are able to obtain tax-exempt-funded mortgages for up to 90 percent of their costs.

In conjunction with HPD, HDC undertook a new initiative to fund the moderate rehabilitation of occupied low-income projects. HDC provided tax-exempt-funded first mortgages, in combination with second mortgages made by HPD at a 1 percent interest rate, pursuant to its participation loan program.

The Housing New York Program (HDC subsidiary)

The state legislature recently created the "Housing New York" program. The Housing New York Corporation was created and authorized to issue up to $400 million in notes or bonds, backed by excess reserves generated by the Battery Park City Authority, from its market-rate commercial and residential projects.

At least 75 percent of the $400 million in proceeds that the Housing New York Corporation anticipates raising over the next four to five years must be spent on housing for families earning less than 90 percent of the median ($25,000 per year). No more than 25 percent of the monies can be spent for households between 90 percent and 175 percent of the median ($48,000). Families with incomes over $48,000 per year are not eligible.

The $4.2 Billion Housing Program

New York City projects capital spending to increase by $2.1 billion. In addition, $700 million is expected from the housing trust fund; $200 million from HDC excess funds; $1.2 billion from the Battery Park City Authority's funds; and also, increased "payments in lieu of taxes" for the World Trade Center. In 1985, $60 to $70 million was appropriated.

Over the next 10 years, New York City seeks to create 126,000 low-income units: 16,000 "gut" rehabilitations; 36,000 city-owned rehabilitations; and 74,000 to be "preserved" from abandonment.

The City Housing Trust Fund

A mortgage recording tax is levied on a percentage of the sale or transfer of existing or new property. This tax is used to finance the administration of the state of New York's (SONYMA's) mortgage agency. Recently, there has been a surplus, so that the excess above the administrative needs of SONYMA has gone to the housing trust fund.

Advance Planning Division

Bob Aldrich
County of Orange
12 Civic Center Plaza
P.O. Box 4048
Santa Ana, CA 92702
(714) 834-5380

Inclusionary Zoning

Orange County has developed two programs to address low-income housing needs: the affordable housing program (AHP) and the housing opportunities program (HOP). Established in 1979, AHP consists of controls on new residential development to allow for a minimum percentage of low-income units in Orange County. The government's rationale was that, if it could provide affordable housing in Orange County, fewer people would have to commute from neighboring Riverside County, where less expensive homes were available, and thus air pollution would be reduced.

Although subject, since 1983, to the housing opportunity program's new requirements, the projects signed off prior to 1983 must still meet AHP requirements. These entail that a minimum of 25 percent of all new housing should be priced affordably for families earning 80 to 120 percent of the county's median income.

The housing opportunity program was established in 1983 and essentially grew out of the AHP, modifying somewhat the inclusionary requirements, and phasing out the mandatory element after three years. The objective of the HOP is that 25 percent or more of the new for-sale or rental housing built in the unincorporated area should be affordable to households earning 120 percent or less of the county's median income, and should be allocated as follows: 10 percent low-income, 10 percent moderate-income, and 5 percent middle-income.

The mandatory component requires developers of projects of 30 or more units to commit themselves to the provision of 10 percent of such units as affordable for households earning 80 percent or less of the county's median income. Developers may transfer vested excess affordable-unit credits of any income category from other projects that have produced vested excess affordable credits. Developers may also dedicate land, or write it down, in an amount equivalent to the value of the excess credit.

Developers voluntarily agreeing to provide more than 10 percent of the units within a project as affordable (80 percent or less of the median income) will receive county incentives. Incentives include access to the county's housing revenue-bond financing for all affordable units to be constructed; density bonuses; reductions in mandatory parking; land writedowns; and the county's participation in acquiring available federal monies.

Since 1979, both programs have produced approximately 6,500 units. In addition, 20,000 affordable units are expected to be built in 22 planned communities—based on future growth projections. These are projects already signed off. The two combined programs are scheduled for phaseout in late 1986 because of developer pressures. One major problem is the very loose resale protections on the affordable units; buyers, in fact, are selling units off after five years for profits.

Planning Department

Toby Kramer
City of Palo Alto
P.O. Box 10250
Palo Alto, CA 94303
(415) 329-2170

Inclusionary Zoning and Density Bonus

Palo Alto's low-income housing objectives, goals, and specific programs are reflected in its comprehensive plan. The plan emphasizes increasing the housing supply, especially for low- and moderate-income individuals, and maintaining a diversity of housing types and sizes, a mixture of ownership and rental housing, and a full range of housing costs. Programs related to low-income households include:

The Below-Market-Rate Program

Established as part of the housing element of the comprehensive plan in 1976, the BMR has resulted in 137 units being committed to date, serving 172 families. The BMR program requires that, in housing developments of 10 or more units, not less than 10 percent of the units should be provided at rates affordable to low- and moderate-income households. For each BMR unit provided, a developer is permitted to build one additional market-rate unit, up to a maximum unit increase over the allowable zoning of 15 percent, and consistent with all other zoning requirements. The requirement applies to both rental and ownership development.

Units can be provided on-site or off-site. If they are built off-site, then not less than one BMR unit for each nine units developed is allowed. In addition, the city will consider an in-lieu payment alternative. The in-lieu payment is to be 3 percent of the actual sales price of each unit sold. The initial sales price of BMR units is based on payments affordable to families whose incomes are no higher than 120 percent of the median income, as related to household size, as established by HUD for Santa Clara County. Eligibility for BMR rental units is restricted to households having gross incomes below the current maximum levels allowed by Section 8 or by successor federal housing-assistance programs. Each BMR household pays 30 percent of its adjusted income on rent.

The Housing Improvement Program

Offers low-interest-rate loans, citywide, to households earning 80 percent or less of the median income for the county, as established by HUD. Since 1974, 282 loans have been committed. The maximum loan is $25,000. The loan terms are 5 percent interest for a maximum of 20 years. Up to $7,500 of any loan may have a repayment deferred until the sale of the property, if the loan committee determines that hardship exists, and if the applicant is "very-low-income." Eighty percent of the loan's proceeds must be used for code deficiencies.

The Mortgage Revenue Bond Program

Since 1982, Palo Alto has participated in four single-family bond issues for ownership housing, and six multifamily issues for rental housing. For single-family ownership, below-market-rate, 30-year, fixed-rate mortgages are provided to first-time homebuyers who earn less than 150 percent of the county's median income. Twenty percent of the units in the multifamily rental program must be made affordable to households earning from 50 percent to 80 percent of the county's median income.

The Condominium Conversion Ordinance

To maintain affordable rental housing, Palo Alto has restricted certain conversions of rental units to condominiums. The ordinance applies to conversions involving a change of ownership of three or more rental units. For an application for conversion to be accepted, there must exist a surplus of vacant rental units offered for rent or lease, in excess of three percent of the available rental stock. In addition, the conversion must provide one below-market-rate rental for every two market-rate units to be converted.

The Rental Housing Acquisition Program

RHAP is managed and operated by the Palo Alto Housing Corporation. The city acquires, rehabilitates, and operates existing rental housing for low- and moderate-income households. Palo Alto allocates upfront purchasing and rehabilitation financing only.

Financing

Funding for the range of affordable housing programs is provided: by available CDBG funds; from the city general fund; from the housing reserve fund, which receives in-lieu payments from the BMR program; and from the environmental mitigation payments program, which collects from commercial and industrial developers. The EMPP has generated $1.8 million.

The formula linking low-income housing to commercial and industrial development rests on the foundation of a housing requirement: developments must provide the number of low-income and moderate-income housing units determined by the following formula, or provide an in-lieu fee:

$$\frac{\text{Gross square feet}}{350} \times 0.017 = \text{Number of units required}$$

This formula is based on an estimate of the amount of housing necessary to satisfy 10 percent of the demand for low- and moderate-income housing. This considers the number of low- and moderate-income employees generated per household by the average commercial and/or industrial development.

Alternatively, a developer can make an in-lieu payment to the city's special housing fund of $50,000 per required unit, as a reasonable approximation of the cost of constructing an average below-market-rate unit. This payment equals $2.43 per square foot of the proposed development. Rates fluctuate with the consumer price index (CPI).

Housing Programs

Alex Jaegerman
Room 211, City Hall
389 Congress Street
Portland, ME 04101
(207) 775-5451

Housing Development Fund

Patterned after the UDAG program, this fund was allocated $400,000 from the housing rehabilitation revolving loan fund. The city is currently soliciting proposals for the first round of loans from this fund.

At least 51 percent of the units developed must serve low- and moderate-income families. A competitive point system is in place that will determine awards for funding. Other point-winning characteristics include: leveraging ratio, impact on the neighborhood, and property taxes generated. This revolving fund will also be capitalized by paybacks from UDAGs and CD funds.

Tax Title Properties

Primarily vacant properties that have been received by the city for taxes due, these structures have been selected for low- income housing development. On a request-for-proposal basis, the city has chosen developers to develop these properties for low- and moderate-income housing. Currently, four to five properties are being pursued, toward producing approximately 30 units for low- and moderate-income purposes. The developers of these properties may use the housing development fund to help finance their projects. The program includes land writedowns, or deferred payments for the properties, as received from the city.

Housing Programs

Duggan Kimball, Planning Director
369 Witherspoon Street
Princeton, NJ 08540
(609) 924-5366
Alan Mallach, Financial Advisor
(609) 448-4616

Background of the Affordable Housing System in Princeton

Princeton's affordability ordinance was enacted in November 1984 in response to the *Mount Laurel* court decision, which provided a concrete formula for the determination of a community's "fair share" of affordable housing. This determination is based on the growth of jobs in the community. It was further provided by the court that New Jersey's localities had a constitutional obligation to affirmatively provide for affordable housing to meet their fair shares. Structured to take advantage of Princeton's high land values and strong housing market, Princeton's program encourages an entrepreneurial approach by the municipality to low-income housing production. Thus, the Mount Laurel court decision, and the recently enacted Fair Housing Act (New Jersey), are the legislative and regulatory bases of the township's approach.

Two separate entities have been formed, to serve two different functions: the Princeton Township Housing Board is the policy branch of the program, setting rules and providing technical assistance for the operation of the program. The Princeton Township Housing Fund is a separate corporate entity whose members are appointed by the housing board. The fund is able to act in an entrepreneurial fashion, by purchasing land and developing half of a residential project for market-rate sale, which subsidizes the other 50 percent (lower-income residential development) through its profits. Other funds are also used to help in this effort: the state has contributed to this fund, and efforts are underway to encourage the university's participation.

An "affordable housing unit" is defined as a dwelling unit for which a household pays, with regard to a unit for sale, not more than 20 percent of its gross income for PITI and for homeowners' association fees, and with regard to a rental unit, not more than 30 percent of its gross income for all shelter costs, including utilities. "Low-income" is defined as 0 to 50 percent of the median income established by HUD; "moderate- income" is 50 to 80 percent; and "middle-income" is between 80 and 150 percent of the median.

Zoning for RM and RH Districts

The ordinance establishes a residential market program district (RM). The RM district is medium-density residential (3.25 units per acre). In the RM district, subdivision and site-plan approvals are contingent on a developer's complying with the affordable-housing set-aside requirements. At least 22 percent of the units in each development must be set aside to be sold or rented at prices qualifying the units as lower-income units. The 22 percent requirement is considered to be the highest percentage allowed by case law *(Mount Laurel)*. A higher low-income unit set-aside would be feasible for developers, due to the fact that Princeton is a premium market area, and that very high profit margins have been earned in the past.

Developments in the RM are considered to be receiving a built-in density bonus, because the surrounding parcels are predominantly zoned for two units per acre. The requirement for the set-aside is that 50 percent of the units must be affordable for those earning 50 percent of the median income, and that the other 50 percent of the set-aside must be affordable for those with 80 percent of the median income. Provisions for the siting and completion of low-income units, as for the numbers of bedrooms and the minimum floor areas, are also included.

Additionally, the developer cannot design for and market to households in which one primary wage earner is 62 years old or older; this would result in a greater percentage of the units being lower-income units than would represent the percentage of such households in the lower-income population of the region. The initial sales prices and rents of the units must not exceed the applicable maximums established periodically by written regulation of the housing board. Sales prices for resales of the lower-income units will also be established by the housing board, which will limit increases to the percentage of increase in the median household income in the region.

The developer may construct the low-income units on an alternate site, provided that the following conditions are met:

- The alternate site is zoned RH;
- The number of required low-income units will be increased by 36 percent;
- The number of non–lower income units permitted on the RM site does not exceed the sum of: 1) the non–lower income units that would have been permitted if the low-income units had been built on-site, plus 2) the number of lower-income units that would have been built on-site multiplied by 0.65. So, on a 100-acre tract, the number of non–lower income units permitted cannot exceed: $325 \times 0.22 = 72$; $253 + (72 \times 0.65) = 47$; $253 + 47 = 300$.

Approval by the Planning Board

An RH zone is a high-density residential zone, with up to 12 units per acre. The RH zone is an overlay zone that allows a much higher-density use than would otherwise be permitted. If not developed as RH, most sites would have a density of four units per acre.

This second component of the zoning program allows the township to take advantage of the Princeton housing market in order to benefit low-income residents. The township's housing fund may, by itself or in conjunction with another applicant, develop in the RH district, provided that one-half of the units are middle-income, and one-half are low-income. RH-density development can only be done either by the township or jointly with the township.

Development Fee for All Zones but RM and RH

Developers of residential projects in all zones but RM and RH are required to pay a development fee based on the square footage of each unit. The funds collected by this fee are intended to support program administration. The fee for each proposed unit is calculated as follows:

0–999 square feet	$0.25 per square foot
1,000–1,999 square feet	$249.75, plus $0.50 per square foot for each square foot over 999
2,000 or more square feet	$749.75, plus $0.75 per square foot for each square foot over 1,999

Affordable Housing Contribution for Nonresidential Construction

An affordable housing contribution is required for all construction creating new nonresidential floor space, including additions or conversions of existing residential floor space. Projects that convert nonresidential floor area from one category to another one that generates more employment than the previous category are also required to make a contribution based on the net increase in employment. The formula is designed to reflect the increased need for lower-income housing that will result from the jobs to be added as a result of that development. The coefficients used for determining the extent of each applicant's contribution are as follows:

- Gross floor area per job created (GFA/J):

Office uses (includes banks and S&Ls)	250
Research uses, laboratories, and educational uses (other than as part of a nonprofit)	500
Retail/commercial uses (hotels, motels, light industry)	600
Warehouse/storage and parking garages	1,000
Nonprofit institutions	5,000

- Number of households per jobholder   0.775
- Percentage of job-linked lower-income households   0.22
- Nonresidential developer obligation   0.25

Based on these coefficients, the amount to be paid is determined from the following formula, where "GFA" is the gross floor area in the structure:

$$\frac{GFA}{GFA/J} \times 0.775 \times 0.219 \times 0.25 \times \$20,000$$

One project that is currently in progress has a total of 280 units of residential development, at a density of 10.5 units per acre. This project will provide 140 units of affordable housing.

There are currently six tracts of land zoned for the RH use, only two of which are owned privately. One of these privately owned parcels is now under contract for sale.

The present target for the affordable housing production level is 550 affordable units within 12 years.

San Diego Housing Commission

Dan W. Conway
Administrative Analyst
1625 Newton Avenue
San Diego, CA 92113
(619) 231-9400

Affordable Housing Density Bonus Program

This program was implemented with the adoption of an ordinance amending the municipal code, and became effective on April 24, 1981. A density bonus of up to 25 percent is available to developers who agree to make bonus units affordable to low- and moderate-income households. "Low-income" is defined as 80 percent or less of the median; "moderate" is defined as 80 percent to 120 percent of the median. "Affordability" is defined as a monthly housing cost, including utilities, of not more than 30 percent of the gross monthly income for low-income households, and not more than 35 percent of the gross monthly income for moderate-income households. More than 12,000 affordable rental units have been built.

The ordinance includes the following provisions:

- At least 20 percent of the total units, or the number of bonus units, whichever is less, will be affordable for persons and families of low and moderate income.
- The affordable units will remain available and affordable to persons and families of low and moderate income for a period of not less than 20 years.
- The units affordable to persons and families of low or moderate income must be so identified, and described.

Coastal Affordable Housing Compliance Permit

Under Senate Bill 626 and Policy 600-3, developers of proposed new housing projects within the city's coastal zone must, whenever feasible, provide dwelling units affordable to persons and families of low or moderate income. Projects of 25 units or less are exempt. Developers have three options:

1) To provide the restricted units for rent or sale at affordable prices for five years;
2) To pay an in-lieu fee for each unit, transferring the responsibility for providing the affordable unit(s) to the commission; or
3) To make a contribution of real property, acceptable to the executive director of the housing commission.

As to the construction of a given project, if the commission determines that it is feasible for a developer to provide affordable units, the developer can decide among the following mechanisms:

- To build affordable rental or sale units that will remain affordable for five years;
- To engage in new construction, or to write down rents on existing units that were not previously affordable; or
- To contract with other developers to build the units, with the approval of the commission.

Also acceptable to the commission is payment of an in-lieu fee, as shown:

Sale projects	$10,000 per affordable unit, or 2 percent of gross selling price of entire project, whichever is higher
Rental projects	$10,000 per affordable unit or 2 percent of appraised value of total project, whichever is higher.

Condominium Conversion and Demolition

Developers of coastal housing projects are required to replace those units, proposed for conversion or demolition, that are occupied by low- and moderate-income households. Replacement units may be provided on or off the site, and may be for rental or for sale, as long as they remain affordable for five years. Here, too, a developer may opt for an in-lieu fee, due upon the date when sales commence. Sample in-lieu fees include:

Studio	$ 8,040
One-bedroom apartment	9,300
Two-bedroom apartment	10,080
Three-bedroom apartment	8,640

Conditional Use Permits
for Senior-Citizen Developments

The city allows senior-citizen housing developments a 50 percent increase in density over that permitted by the underlying zone. The rationale behind this incentive is that the average senior citizen's household size is significantly less than the citywide average household size. All bonus units are subject to affordability requirements as administered by the housing commission.

Rehabilitation Assistance

This program leverages limited public funds to provide below-market-rate loans to owners of single-family homes and rental properties, to improve their properties. Public funds are placed on deposit to leverage six times their value in bank loans for property owners. The result is a blended-rate loan that reduces the overall costs of rehabilitation.

Leveraged and direct loans are offered to qualified borrowers at 1.5 percent to 8 percent, depending on the characteristics of a property. Technical assistance is also provided, to identify needed repairs, to oversee the contractors' bidding process, and to monitor the quality of workmanship. In 1985, 300 homes were rehabilitated, with a total investment of $3 million. In the past seven years, a total of 2,500 homes have been rehabilitated.

City Planning Department

Ed Goetz
Housing Assistant
450 McAllister Street
San Francisco, CA 94102
(415) 558-2881

Linkage/Housing Trust Fund

The residence element of the San Francisco Master Plan calls for the provision of additional housing to accommodate the demands of new residents attracted by the expanding employment opportunities made available by the growth of office uses in the city. To promote this policy, the city planning commission proposed the office housing production program (OHPP) guidelines in 1981. These guidelines were revised and adopted as an ordinance in 1985, to create the office affordable housing production program.

The OAHPP applies to new or substantially rehabilitated downtown office projects exceeding 50,000 square feet. Developers have the option of providing housing or contributing an in-lieu fee of $5.34 per square foot. Although the city's economic study recommended charging from $9.47 to $10.47 per square foot, the more conservative figure was selected.

If a developer elects to construct housing units, or to participate in a joint venture to meet the requirement, 62 percent of the units constructed must remain affordable to low- and moderate-income households for 20 years. The following formula is used to calculate the number of units required:

Net additional square feet of office space × 0.000386

The developer can also satisfy the housing requirement by providing a combination of a partial number of the required units, and payment of an in-lieu fee of $13,834 per unit for the remaining balance of units. In-lieu fees are due prior to the issuance of the certificate of occupancy. The funds received by the OAHPP are deposited in the affordable housing fund, which is used solely to increase the supply of housing for low- and moderate-income households. This program has generated $27 million in contributions and produced almost 4,000 housing units.

Community Housing and Resources, Inc.

Dorothy Newman
Director
P.O. Drawer Q
Sanibel, FL 33957
(813) 472-4136

Below-Market-Rate Housing

Sanibel's below-market-rate housing program is completely voluntary and does not have any strict requirements. The city has an agreement with the Community Housing and Resources Corporation, a nonprofit, to administer the program. The nonprofit organization receives direct assistance and loans from the city. Households earning 120 percent or less of the Lee County median income are eligible for the program.

Projects are negotiated on a case-by-case basis. The planning commission can relax density limitations or allow conditional uses, based on negotiations with developers who agree to provide below-market-rate units or to make in-lieu contributions. Four affordable units are currently being constructed, and five more have been approved. The nonprofit housing corporation has also received an in-lieu contribution of land that will provide three units.

Community and Economic Development Department

Ann Sewill
Santa Monica, CA 90401
(213) 458-8701

Linkage Program

The Santa Monica City Council approved implementation of its "project mitigation measures" program in April 1986. This program links large-scale office development to low-income housing generation. The measure has been approved by the mayor. Since the late 1970s, Santa Monica has had an office/housing linkage program in effect that has dealt with developments on a case-by-case basis.

Project mitigation measures are conditions for approval of office development, including medical office buildings, in excess of 15,000 square feet (new construction) or of 10,000 square feet (additions to existing development). A developer may satisfy the requirements either by contributing an in-lieu fee to the city, or by providing housing on-site or off-site.

In-Lieu Fees

The amount of the fee is $2.25 per square foot for the first 15,000 square feet of net rentable square feet, and $5.00 per square foot for the remainder of the net rentable square feet. Payment of at least 25 percent of the total obligation is due prior to issuance of the certificate of occupancy. The remainder is due within three years. Forty-five percent of the in-lieu fees are deposited into a housing mitigation fund for the development of low- and moderate-income housing. Another 45 percent are deposited in a parks mitigation fund. And 10 percent are deposited in an account that can be transferred to the housing fund or to a park mitigation fund.

On-Site or Off-Site Development

The number of units to be provided by a developer is equal to the comparable amount of his in-lieu payment. As of April 1986, the in-lieu payment for each housing unit was $30,060. The in-lieu payment (and consequently the value of each housing unit on-site and off-site) is adjusted for inflation by the consumer price index. All units must be affordable to households earning no more than 80 percent of the area median income. Units are deed-restricted for at least 50 years, to remain affordable to low- and moderate-income persons.

Inclusionary Housing Element
of the City General Plan

Since January 1983, all residential developments of three or more units are required to provide 25 percent of their units as affordable. Inclusionary units are available to households with incomes less than 120 percent of the county's median income. The planning department is drafting a report that recommends reducing the inclusionary housing requirement to 15 percent, and increasing the minimum development size to five units.

Department of Housing
and Urban Development
1133 North Capitol Street, NE
Washington, DC 20002
(202) 535-1000

The department is implementing four major programs in 1986. Of the $98.2 million in general operating funds available to the department in 1985, $20.15 million were provided by appropriations.

Land Acquisition for Housing
Development Opportunities

LAHDO is designed to respond to the need to stimulate private investment in the rehabilitation of vacant housing, and in the construction of new housing for low- and moderate-income residents. Specifically, the program provides for developers' land-sale leaseback arrangements with the District of Columbia, in order to eliminate land costs as a component of the total development debt. This program provides an incentive for investment in the production of low- and moderate-income housing by offsetting the effect of land costs, the termination of federal assistance programs, and market and regulatory constraints on rents.

The objective of the program is to improve the economic feasibility of developing low- and moderate-income housing, by eliminating, as a mortgageable development cost, the value of the land on which assisted projects are located and by funding certain related site improvements. Land purchased by the District through the program would be leased back to the project owner/developer on a long-term basis, with a predetermined buyback provision. Projects being developed within this program must set aside at least 20 percent of the units for lower-income occupancy. In addition to this minimum criterion, projects will be considered for assistance under this program if a variety of other demonstrations of public benefit can be made to the satisfaction of the DHCD. Funds for initiating this program will come from D.C.'s capital improvement program.

Distressed Properties Improvement Program

Established by the D.C. Rental Housing Act of 1985, this program will aid the owners of financially troubled but otherwise stable rental properties. The program will allow participating landlords to write off delinquent taxes and water and sewer bills, and to abate future property taxes, in order to make these properties available to low-income residents.

Tenant Assistance Program

Also established by the D.C. Rental Housing Act of 1985, tenant assistance was implemented in fiscal year 1986 with $5 million in D.C.-appropriated funds. This is a D.C.-sponsored and -operated voucher program that will provide rental subsidies to low-income individuals and families in existing rehabilitated housing. Priorities will be given to the elderly, to the handicapped, and to female heads of households. To qualify, families must have an income of less than 80 percent of the median for the area, adjusted for family size.

The program enables low-income families and individuals to search for standard housing in the private market within the District. Landlords participating in the program will have their units inspected by a DHCD representative, to ensure that the units meet D.C.'s housing code. The DHCD guarantees payment of monthly contributions toward the contracted rent. Under the program, families and individuals generally pay 30 percent of their adjusted monthly incomes for rent and utilities. If the head of a household is elderly or handicapped, they pay 25 percent of their income. A tenant may pay more than 25 percent or 30 percent if his or her rent exceeds the payment standard schedule.

Current monthly payment standards are:

Unit Size by Bedrooms	Payment Standard
0	$370
1	450
2	530
3	665
4	745
5	857
6	969

Applications were taken in May 1986 for qualified low-income families, and are no longer being solicited. The DHCD is currently seeking landlords to participate in the program. (DHCD Annual Report, 1985)

Appendix 3
Selected Nonprofit/Community-Based Program Abstracts

BRIDGE Housing Corporation

J. Donald Terner
150 California Street
Suite 200
San Francisco, CA 94111
(415) 989-1111

In 1981, the San Francisco Foundation received an anonymous gift of $600,000 and appointed a "blue-ribbon" task force to address the housing crisis. The formation of BRIDGE was recommended as an aggressive nonprofit regional development corporation. BRIDGE incorporated in June 1982, and in that same year, the San Francisco Foundation added another $100,000 to the initial gift. BRIDGE was then sufficiently capitalized to operate for a year, and to undertake its first group of development projects. In 1983, BRIDGE received its nonprofit tax-exempt status. It is dedicated to the production of large volumes of high-quality homes for families earning $12,000 to $25,000 annually.

BRIDGE links the resources and expertise of business, government, and philanthropy to achieve its goals of low-income housing production. Every development involves the active participation of community residents, through negotiations, technical assistance, and financial assistance.

BRIDGE takes advantage of three tax provisions to reduce housing costs, including: equity financing/syndication; debt financing/tax-exempt bonds; and tax-deductible gifts. Non–tax related techniques include: the use of surplus public lands; a deferred-return investment/direct investment; land cost reductions; the achievement of maximum densities through inclusionary bonuses; and risk reductions through positive community relations.

The activities of BRIDGE are financed through a development trust fund that can be used to provide equity capital, venture capital for predevelopment activities such as land acquisition, architectural and engineering studies, rent subsidies,and guarantees to secure project financing. Expected to reach $5 million, the size of the fund determines the number of units BRIDGE will be able to produce. To date, the fund is capitalized at $4.8 million. BRIDGE investments have typically generated eight to 10 times their face amounts in value added to property.

To capitalize the trust fund, BRIDGE seeks tax-deductible contributions from corporations and foundations. When fully capitalized, the fund will serve as a revolving and virtually self-sustaining source of working capital. (1984–1985 Annual Report)

As of May 1986, BRIDGE had developed the following housing opportunities:

	Number of Projects	Number of Units (Total/Affordable)
Occupied	9	558/281
In Construction	5	558/194
In Approvals	11	1,589/610+
Future	2	1,250+/300–600
Total	27	3,933/1,253
BRIDGE investment		$ 925,142
Public/private investment		12,562,400
Project value		287,806,000

Source: Project Summary Sheet, May 1986.

An example of a recent development that BRIDGE assisted by creating additional project value through increased density is as follows:

BRIDGE optioned 10 acres of land, zoned for eight units per acre, for $800,000, and then applied for rezoning to double the density, allowing 167 units instead of 80. The additional density doubled the value of the land, from $800,000 to approximately $1,670,000. BRIDGE held 10 percent of its equity in the project, and sold the remainder to a private developer for market value, with an agreement that BRIDGE would return a portion of its proceeds to the developer, to assist in providing affordable housing.

BRIDGE converted its return from the increased value of the land into an annuity to be used to provide below-market rents for low-income tenants. (HDR, February 24, 1986, p. 785) BRIDGE was then able to earmark 40 percent of the units in the bond-financed project for low-income tenants, instead of the 20 percent required by law. Those units were then made available at Section 8's existing-housing, rather than new-construction, rents. Thus, the units could be leased by tenants with Section 8 certificates.

Enterprise Foundation

Helen Szablya
Director, Public Affairs
505 American City Boulevard
Columbia, MD 21044
(301) 964-1230

The Enterprise Foundation is a nonprofit, publicly supported charitable foundation launched in 1982. Its objective is to help the very poor help themselves to decent, livable housing, and out of poverty and dependence into self-sufficiency. (1985 Annual Report) By building a national network of nonprofit neighborhood groups, the foundation works to help these groups "enlarge their capacity to reduce housing costs, to obtain low-rate financing, to find local business support, to establish job placement agencies, and to provide other social services."

The foundation has raised over $20 million from corporations, foundations, and individuals. These monies are used to provide neighborhood groups with "linchpin" money—small seed-money grants and low-interest loans—with which to tie together local funds into workable financing packages for housing rehabilitation and sometimes for new construction.

The foundation owns the Enterprise Development Company, a for-profit, taxpaying commercial real estate developer, and uses its earnings to support the charitable activities of the foundation.

As of June 1986, the foundation's total commitment of grants, loans, and other program-related investments was $8,781,627. As to the number of housing units that have been built, these comprise, in commitments to date, 2,367 new units, and, in construction starts, 1,094 rehabilitated units.

Although the foundation was established in 1982, the staff was limited to one field officer and one director for two years. In 1984, a full field staff was hired; this early lack of staffing has been the explanation given for the low housing production achieved so far. The foundation's network, however, has expanded to 63 neighborhood and community groups in 25 cities.

The foundation defines the poor as "[families] of four with an income of $9,000 or less. Most units developed by the groups have monthly rents of about $250." *(Engineering News-Record,* February 14, 1985)

The Enterprise rehabilitation work group develops new design and construction techniques, to cut the cost of housing rehabilitation by 20 to 40 percent. The work group provides on-site training and a newsletter describing cost-efficient construction methods.

The Enterprise Social Investment Corporation, "a subsidiary of the foundation, has helped neighborhood groups by structuring seven syndications that will raise $2.4 million. Corporations and individuals both invest in these projects."

Also, the ESIC is now establishing the Enterprise Loan Fund (Baltimore), the better to raise money at rates as low as 3 percent to finance housing for poor families. The fund offers benevolent investors the opportunity to place monies in insured accounts, the proceeds of which are dedicated to the development of low-income housing. (1985 Annual Report)

Inner City Ventures Fund

Jennifer Blake
Program Officer
National Trust for Historic Preservation
1785 Massachusetts Avenue, N.W.
Washington, DC 20036
(202) 673-4054

To date, the ICVF has funded 38 projects in 26 cities, and is in the process of making six more awards. All of the projects are serving low- and moderate-income people (earning 80 percent of the median or less); all are in historic structures.

The fund was established in 1981, with a $400,000 grant from the U.S. Department of the Interior (U.S. Park Service), and a $100,000 grant from the National Trust, which were subsequently matched by key grants from the Pew Memorial Trust, Atlantic Richfield Foundation, Grace Foundation, Inc., and Chase Manhattan Bank. The Ford Foundation also provided an important program-related investment loan of $500,000. Over 35 major corporations and foundations now support the ICVF's development of model rehabilitation projects to be administered by nonprofit, community-based organizations. Recent commitments by the Ford Foundation ($1 million loan), Standard Oil Company of Ohio ($200,000 challenge grant), and the Pew Memorial Trust ($4.15 million challenge grant) have brought the fund's four-year fundraising total to more than $4.7 million.

The Inner City Ventures Fund provides grants, low-interest loans, and technical assistance to neighborhood-based nonprofit organizations implementing housing, commercial, and industrial development projects involving the rehabilitation of historic properties for the benefit of low-income persons. Funding rounds are competitive. In addition, the fund organizes conferences and workshops in which it can disseminate learning experiences and information to its nonprofits, which do not receive monetary awards.

Funds can be used for acquisition, rehabilitation, and, to a limited degree, architectural costs. They may not be used for administrative costs. The use of these funds carries both a matching and a leveraging requirement:

- *Matching.* Recipients must have a direct cash investment in the project equal to at least 50 percent of the ICVF award. The sources of this match can be:
  –Foundation, corporate, or government grants;
  –Recipient's own funds; or the
  –Value of the organization's equity in the project at the beginning of the project.
  Ineligible sources are:
  –Funds used to plan or operate a project; and
  –Private or public loans.
- *Leveraging.* Recipients should multiply ICVF assistance at least five times with loans and grants from foundations, corporations, conventional lenders, governments, or other sources. This requirement may be waived under special circumstances.

Use of the ICVF award as an aid in fundraising is encouraged. The review cycle of the selection process takes from 10 to 12 weeks and has two stages. The first stage has prospective ICVF recipients submitting brief preliminary applications. The second stage involves detailed final applications, and site visits by ICVF staff to those projects that were selected in the first round.

Awards are generally given in amounts between $40,000 and $100,000; half of each award is a loan, the other half, a grant. The loan is generally used for construction financing or for a "bridge" loan. The maximum term of the loan is five years, during which time all units must remain low- and moderate-income units. Loans are currently made at an 8 percent fixed rate; the standard loan carries an interest rate of one-half of the prevailing prime rate (minimum, 5 percent). Payments must be made quarterly, with principal repayments usually commencing 15 months after the disbursement of the loan. The loan must be secured with real estate, with a certificate of deposit, or with other security acceptable to the trust. The recipient must produce evidence of adequate security before the loan can be closed. ICVF grants cannot be the first monies used in any project.

An eligible organization must:
1) Be community-based;
2) Demonstrate significant neighborhood involvement;
3) Be an incorporated nonprofit organization; and
4) Demonstrate the capacity to manage, staff, and finance the proposed project.

A project eligible for ICV funding must have all of the following attributes:

1) Be rehabilitation for continued or adaptive use of an old building, consistent with the sixth and final requirement in this list;
2) Have a neighborhood revitalization focus directly benefiting minority low- and moderate-income households;

3) Have the capacity to increase the sponsoring organization's financial and staff capabilities, with which it will undertake future real estate development;
4) Have the prospect of realization of the project within a reasonable length of time;
5) Have a location in a neighborhood threatened by or undergoing displacement of low- and moderate-income residents; and
6) Have a location in a historic district that is either 1) listed in the National Register, or 2) designated as a historic district by an appropriate local or state government body authorized by the U.S. Park Service to make such designations. The project buildings should at least contribute to the importance of the district.

Normally, ICVF awards are combined with city grants, foundation grants, bank loans, applicant contributions, syndication funds, state grants, corporate grants, Section 8 funding, and other mechanisms, to create a viable project. Some nonprofits have linked up with for-profit developers to take advantage of investment tax credits.

The fund works to ensure that a development will be maintained in long-term community control.

The production accomplished by the ICVF to date has provided the rehabilitation of 1,100 housing units, of 50 commercial locations, and of 210,000 square feet of industrial space; the creation of 800 + jobs; and a stimulus for the investment of $47.3 million in housing and economic development. The program-related investment portion of the ICVF portfolio includes 331 units (completed or under construction); one-third net additions to the housing stock; two-thirds rehabilitation of occupied units; two commercial properties; and a proportion of 88 percent of the units benefiting low- and moderate-income residents.

Nehemiah Plan Homes

I.D. Robbins
General Manager
c/o Our Lady of Mercy Church
680 Mother Gaston Boulevard
Brooklyn, NY 11212
(718) 346-2929

The Nehemiah Plan began in 1982 as a church-sponsored effort to develop low- and moderate-income housing on a large scale, in order to reconstruct and revitalize a deteriorating community. The program will ultimately build 5,000 single-family rowhouses for owner/occupancy in East Brooklyn. A coalition of 46 local congregations, known as East Brooklyn Churches, Inc., with the assistance of the Industrial Areas Foundation, a national organization specializing in community organizing, initiated the project to re-use the large tracts of vacant land created by extensive housing abandonment, disinvestment, or unrealized urban renewal plans.

Three key factors are responsible for the success of this program. First, the Nehemiah Trust, a revolving loan fund of $6 million, provides no-interest construction financing and saves 6 to 7 percent on the cost of each home. This fund was established by significant no-interest loans from major denominations and religious orders. As homes are completed, the funds are returned to the trust and made available to be loaned again. Construction costs are further reduced because of the existence of extensive infrastructure.

Second, the city of New York agreed to provide the vacant land for the project, and to defer property taxes for 10 years. After 10 years, the tax assessment will increase 10 percent per year, so that full taxes are due in 20 years. In addition, for each of the 5,000 proposed homes, the city is providing a $10,000 no-interest loan to the buyer. The city will keep a lien on its loan that must be returned when the house is sold. If the buyer does not sell, the loan is considered a grant.

Third, the New York State Mortgage Agency provides first-mortgage assistance at below-market rates, with minimal financing fees. The combined effect of these subsidies reduces the cost to the buyer to $43,500, so that a family with an income of $20,000 can afford a Nehemiah Plan home with a downpayment of $5,000.

The program requires that all homes be presold. To date, 906 homes have been built. The homes are single-family attached dwellings with two or three bedrooms and unfinished basements. These types of housing units can be built for almost 50 percent less than can equal-sized high-rise units. Furthermore, this program is considered to encourage safer and more stable neighborhoods. Most of the homes have been purchased by first-time homebuyers. Technical assistance to these buyers is provided by a homeowners' association.

Northwest Bronx Community and Clergy Coalition

Al Drummond, Executive Director
(212) 584-0515
Jim Buckley, Housing/Reinvestment
(212) 933-3101
Webster Avenue
Bronx, NY 10458

The Northwest Bronx Community and Clergy Coalition is a private, nonprofit community-based organization involved in a wide range of issues of importance to low-income renters, to merchants, and to owners in 10 Northwest Bronx neighborhoods. Established in 1975, the NWBCCC grew out of the arson, the investment exodus, the city-services decline, and the devastation that plagued the South Bronx in the late 1960s and 1970s. The coalition's main task involves organizing tenants and merchants to act to improve living conditions, as well as to acquire reinvestment funding for affordable rehabilitation and construction.

The NWBCCC has used both private and public money in packaging low-interest rehabilitation loans, so as to reduce debt-service and rent-increase pressures. The *Aetna Life & Casualty Project* is one example. The NWBCCC led a nationwide campaign to persuade insurance companies to invest more housing money in "member" communities. Aetna Insurance, after many discussions with NWBCCC leaders, created a revolving reserve for moderate and "gut" rehabilitation projects in the 10 neighborhoods. Since 1981, the NWBCCC has used approximately $12 million of Aetna money, combining these funds with other available funds at the city level (PLP, 8a) to bring down the cost of substantial rehabilitation and construction. There is no set cap on the reserve.

Chase Manhattan Commitment. In 1984, NWBCCC efforts convinced the Chase Manhattan Bank to commit $10 million to a loan pool for low-income weatherization system improvements. The Chase lump-sum deposit program is unique, for the city of New York pledged $3 million to Chase to act as collateral or guarantee for the Chase funds. Specifically, New York City's Article 8a loan program has committed the deposit with Chase, in exchange for Chase Manhattan's making competitive market-rate loans for up to three times the deposit amount. The city deposit earns interest, which is used to subsidize Chase's interest rate. The coalition has used this pool of money to attract other sources of rehabilitation financing.

The NWBCCC has two projects planned to address low-income housing needs: St. Edmunds Court, a New York City RFP submitted early in 1985; and "Project Reclaim," a gut rehabilitation project slated to create 1,500 low-income units.

St. Edmunds Court. In early 1985, the NWBCCC answered a New York City RFP for the construction of low- and moderate-income housing. St. Edmunds Court is slated to provide 120 units. The city's income guidelines for the project are low-income (below $25,000) and moderate-income, (below $48,000). The NWBCCC is negotiating to lower the guidelines to below $17,000 for low-income, and below $30,000 for moderate. The project financing would consist of $7 million from MAC surplus (RFP element), and approximately $2.5 million from Aetna (from above-stated relationship). Aetna is in fact shifting its focus a little, to consider new construction in addition to rehabilitation work. In the St. Edmunds Court development, a developer would hold the title. Tenants would lease with an option to buy after 10 years through a leaseback arrangement.

"Project Reclaim." This activity would provide approximately 1,500 units of low-income housing. The type of development involved is gut rehabilitation. The NWBCCC anticipates that the costs will run to approximately $82 million, of which close to 25 percent would be private. The NWBCCC is working with local banks (Dollar Dry Dock is close to committing approximately $20 million at prime rate), as well as with

LISC (first 100 units). In addition, The NWBCCC is developing an equity fund to enable private investors to get involved in the project for tax advantages. Income criteria are based on Section 8 guidelines (e.g., a family of four at or below $25,000). The NWBCCC will package, develop, and seek owners and managers for the project.

Broad Concerns. The NWBCCC is actively involved in organizing, largely that of housing. Neighborhood leaders and organizers, however, also focus on antidrug strategies, senior citizen issues, job training and job creation, parks and recreation issues, youth development opportunities and programs, and code enforcement and rehabilitation matters—to name only a few concerns.

Urban Edge Housing Corporation

Marie McLaughlin
620 Centre Street
Jamaica Plain, MA 02130
(617) 522-5515

Urban Edge, a private nonprofit housing development and housing services corporation, has been in existence since 1974. Its primary goal is to stimulate neighborhood revitalization in Jamaica Plain, which is located outside downtown Boston, and to develop housing opportunities for low- and moderate-income residents there.

At present, two corporate entities exist: the Urban Edge Housing Corporation, which oversees all of the organization's development activities; and Urban Edge Real Estate of Greater Boston, which oversees the brokerage and property management functions.

Urban Edge is an excellent example of a community housing developer's gaining access to operating and developing monies. Its extensive list of funding sources includes: the Boston Housing Partnership; the Boston Neighborhood Development and Employment Program; the Massachusetts Housing Finance Agency; the Boston Homesteading Program; the Boston Foundation; and a number of major banks and foundations in the greater Boston area.